"Lois Buntz understands that the key to activating the power of women as donors lies in respecting them as people who are eager for the joy and well-being that giving creates. Weaving diversity and inclusion throughout the text, she truly centers the unique experiences of women philanthropists as she shows a way to engage them fruitfully."

—Julie Castro Abrams, *Founder and CEO, How Women Lead*

"An informative and insightful philanthropic resource for those dedicated to empowerment of women and girls through gender-focused philanthropy. *Generosity and Gender* is a must-read guide to engaging women in fundraising. Research and stories from numerous women philanthropists from the frontlines will empower, inspire, and grow your current programs.

Bravo Lois Buntz!"

—Dawn Oliver Wiand, *President and CEO, Iowa Women's Foundation*

"The Women's Funding Network had a tagline for decades: 'Changing the Face of Philanthropy.' Alongside fundraising from women, grant-making decisions made by women, and investing in women, that face clearly and permanently changed. Lois's book clearly lays out the overlapping factors that influenced this trajectory; why women give; and most importantly, how to best engage with this powerful and growing force."

—Cynthia Nimmo, *Former President, Women's Funding Network and Gender Equity Advisor*

"Women's power to move money differently in the world is profound, and Lois Buntz's *Gender and Generosity* checks all the boxes about how this gender difference is manifesting in philanthropy. Readers of her book will become deeply familiar with the names and faces that power women's giving, as well as techniques for successfully working with women donors and their allies in carrying out bold strategies for a better world."

—Kiersten Marek, *Founder, Philanthropy Women*

"*Generosity and Gender* explores the evolution of women's philanthropy and captures the experiences of women donors who birthed and others that contributed to its expanded development. As a founder of this movement, I am grateful to Lois Buntz for writing this book, that many can now read and share as a resource and guide for fundraisers and women donors. Blending the best practices in fundraising with research of how women give, this book offers professionals and organizations an opportunity to create new and exciting partnerships with women. Now is the time for fundraisers to cultivate the ever-growing philanthropic capacity of women, support their passions, and help align their investments with causes. Thank you, Lois, for this inspiring contribution to the field of women's philanthropy."

—Helen LaKelly Hunt, *Author, Co-Founder of Women Moving Millions*

"Lois Buntz has created an insightful, comprehensive guide on how to partner with women philanthropists to advance causes important to them. Fund development professionals across many disciplines will benefit from her review of relevant research, along with valuable real-world scenarios."

—Kathleen R. Krusie, *SVP Community Physician Network Chief Administrative Officer*

"Lois Buntz in *Generosity and Gender* has dug into a story about the unfolding of new norms and stories and the significance of women donors using their resources for communities and for change rather than for the traditional rewards of recognition. Understanding women's giving better is a key to pursuing more ambitious and progressive impact in the future which makes this book a must have!"

—Stephanie Clohesy, *Consultant on Philanthropy Strategies, Design and Impact*

"This book is a great tool to engage our peers in philanthropy. We need more analysis that can lift up and recognize the impact of women in the philanthropic sector, and especially women of color, who are projected to be the majority of all women in the U.S. in the next few decades. I appreciate the expertise that Lois brings to the table, as philanthropy has a lot of learning to do."

—Amalia Brindis Delgado, *Associate VP, Strategy, Hispanics in Philanthropy*

"*Generosity and Gender* addresses the fundamental issues of how and why women give. The history, philosophy, economics, and sociology of this phenomenon are woven throughout the many stories that Lois Buntz has included in this text, and her story telling is compelling. The relevance of these stories is dramatically illustrated as we witness new ways of giving and more history being made by women like MacKenzie Scott. As women continue to dominate the philanthropic landscape, more of these stories will need to be told."

—Sally Mason, Ph.D., *President Emerita of the University of Iowa*

"As a director of a non-profit that supports women in arts and culture, fundraising is always on my mind. It is so refreshing to see positive data about the capacity of women to give back. This is a wonderful resource for learning to engage women donors in ways that will enhance donor loyalty and involvement. Giving to an organization is so much more than a financial gift, and this book provides tools for making an ask based on quality relationships and timing."

—Jordan Young, *Executive Director, Women's International Study Center*

Lois A. Buntz

Generosity and Gender

Philanthropic Models for Women Donors and the Fund Development Professionals Who Support Them

To Donna;
your leadership has inspired
women to be brave, bold,
and philanthropic.
Lois.

palgrave
macmillan

Lois A. Buntz
Lois Buntz Consulting LLC
Cedar Rapids, IA, USA

ISBN 978-3-030-90379-4   ISBN 978-3-030-90380-0   (eBook)
https://doi.org/10.1007/978-3-030-90380-0

This Palgrave Macmillan imprint is published by the registered company Springer Nature Switzerland AG
The registered company address is: Gewerbestrasse 11, 6330 Cham, Switzerland

To my mother, LaVern M. Faas, who gave selflessly to others.

Preface

What motivates people to give their time, talents, and treasures to benefit others? Why are some individuals abundantly generous and others can barely lend a dime to a worthy cause or help a person in need? How do life experiences, education, age, gender, or ethnicity impact an individual's decision to practice generosity and act philanthropically? These questions combined with an ever-present curiosity about the changing role of women in our society prompted my exploration of women's philanthropy and the writing of this book.

Today, women have the philanthropic power to change the world. They are becoming more educated, advancing to leadership positions in all economic, political, and social sectors, acquiring an unprecedented level of wealth, and demonstrating their desire and ability to have a seat at the table of change.

The recent news of MacKenzie Scott's $8.5 billion one-time donations to hundreds of charities has shaken up the philanthropy world in a good way. Although Scott is not the first woman to give a large gift, it is by all counts the *largest* demonstration of philanthropy by a woman. She has stepped into a sacred space—giving publicly, big and boldly, carefully researching her choices, selecting traditional and nontraditional nonprofits, universities and grassroots organizations, and giving the recipients maximum flexibility to do good. She trusted the experts who do the work to know how to use her gift in the most effective manner. And Scott says she is not done.

I began to explore the concept of *women's philanthropy* after a forty-year career working in nonprofits, education, and fundraising. My early years were spent in direct service work as a clinical social worker helping children and families in need. I transitioned from direct services to teaching social work at a small private college and a Big Ten university, integrating textbook theories with my practice experience. After several years, I returned to work at a social service agency, transitioned into administration, and eventually became a CEO at several nonprofits including a mid-sized United Way. It was United Way's *Women United* initiative (women's giving program) that sparked my interest in women as donors and I became a charter member of our local *Women United* program.

During my career I have met hundreds of women, some of them talented influential leaders, others who were quiet workers, committed volunteers, or energetic community advocates. No matter what their status, vocation or interests, the common thread in all of their lives was their desire to give back. Women are generous givers and they have demonstrated this for centuries.

Today, I consult with a wide range of nonprofits, advising leaders and fund development professionals about major gifts and endowment programs, while also providing seminars on women's philanthropy strategies at local and national conferences, including the Association of Fundraising Professionals and United Ways.

The topic of women's philanthropy is filled with a rich history, inspiring stories, and solid research that acknowledges what many women and fund development professionals knew, but were unable to document—women practice philanthropy differently than men. They give more, have different motivations, and desired outcomes. As I began to collect stories from women philanthropists, delved into the research provided by the Women's Philanthropy Institute at Indiana University, and reflected on my own work in the nonprofit sector, I realized that many fund development professionals are not aware of the potential of women donors. They continue to use traditional fundraising strategies that don't actively engage women and rarely apply a diversity, inclusion, and equity lens.

Other business and social sectors are acknowledging the wealth capacity of women as customers, consumers, and clients. Recognizing that women are major decision-makers in many aspects of daily life, they are using women as spokespersons, featuring them in marketing campaigns, and tailoring their social media strategies to specifically attract women. The philanthropy community needs to hold up a mirror and ask, what we are doing to partner with women and invite them in?

Women's philanthropy has moved through a series of historical movements or waves, the first beginning with the suffragists, a second wave between 1960 and 1990 when the women's movement and other social changes prompted the creation of new organizations including the Women's Funding Network, Women's Philanthropy Institute, and Giving Circles. A third wave developed when more women began to give bigger gifts through Women Moving Millions, major university foundations, United Ways, nonprofits, and women's foundations. Now, we are embarking on the fourth wave of women's philanthropy.

This phase will include a long predicted intergenerational wealth transfer, an exploding generation of entrepreneurs, a younger and more diverse donor base, new institutional models that are not third sector nonprofits, a societal reset based on global disasters including COVID-19, escalating social movements, and technological advances that will astound and challenge us. Nearly half of the world's population is women; a large percentage of fundraising professionals are women; and the number of women donors is growing daily. It is time to acknowledge that women will have a major influence on the future of philanthropy and begin by learning more about how women give, how to engage as many women as possible, and how to ask women to *step into* philanthropy and *step up*.

Cedar Rapids, Iowa, USA   Lois A. Buntz

The original version of the book was revised: Corrections suggested by the author have been incorporated. The correction to the book is available at https://doi.org/10.1007/978-3-030-90380-0_16

Acknowledgments

Writing is a solitary process; creating a book is a collaborative endeavor. It includes significant supporters, advocates, other authors, content experts, researchers, colleagues, and friends. It begins with an idea—a concept that blossoms over time into a multiyear project sustained by patience, pride, and tenacity. There are countless people to thank for their input, contributions, and assistance in the creation of *Generosity and Gender*.

More than seventy women shared stories, information, insights, laughs and tears as they bravely gave me permission to listen and record their experiences. Beginning with several local women philanthropists who agreed to meet with me when this book was purely a dream, they encouraged me to keep going. My sincere thanks to Dee Ann McIntyre, Kate Minette, Nancy Evans, Kathy Eno, Terri Christoffersen, Cheryle Mitvalsky, Suzy DeWolf, Mary Westbrook, Kathy Good, Mary Klinger, Johanna Abernathy, Lura McBride, Lila Igram, Sally Mason, Lynette Marshall, Diane Ramsey, Tiffany O'Donnell, Salma Igram, Lijun Chadima, and Julianne Smith.

So many professional colleagues from my career as well as esteemed women who had extensive knowledge and experience stepped up and offered their advice, counsel, ideas, editing, and support. Many of these women work at women's foundations or within women's networks. Others have been founders and early pioneers in the field of women's philanthropy. Dawn Oliver Wiand, Executive Director, Iowa Women's Foundation; Roslyn Dawson Thompson, former CEO, Texas Women's Foundation; Sunny Fischer and K. Sujata, former CEOs, Chicago Foundation for Women;

Lee Roper-Batker, former CEO of the Minnesota Women's Foundation; Lauren Casteel, CEO the Women's Foundation of Colorado; Ana Oliveira, CEO, New York Women's Foundation; Jacki Zehner; Christine Grumm; Tracy Gary; Cynthia Nimmo, former CEO, Women's Funding Network; Sarah Haacke Byrd, CEO, Women Moving Millions; Jeannie Infante Sager, CEO, Women Philanthropy Institute; Andrea Pactor, former interim director Women's Philanthropy Institute; Yolanda F. Johnson, founder, Women of Color in Fundraising and Philanthropy; Kiersten Marek, founder, Philanthropy Women; Jordan Young, Executive Director, Women's International Study Center; Stephanie Clohesy, consultant; Amalia Brindis Delgado, Associate VP, Strategy, Hispanics in Philanthropy; Melanie R. Brown, Gates Foundation; Gretchen Buhlig, CEO, Arizona State University Foundation; Kathy Krusie, SVP, Community Physician Network; Linda DeWolf, founder, GoPhilanthropic Foundation; Shannon Duval, Senior Vice President of Philanthropy and Deputy Chief Philanthropy Officer at CommonSpirit Health; Carla Harris, VP, Morgan Stanley; Laura Kohler, Senior Vice President, Human Resources, Stewardship and Sustainability, Kohler Company; Karen Herman; Nancy Hayes; Mary Lynn Myers; Julie Castro Abrams, CEO, How Women Lead; Michelle Branch, former Volunteer Chair of *Women United* Global Leadership Council; Hong Hoang, founder of CHANGE; and a very special thanks to Diane Ballweg, Abigail Disney and especially Helen LaKelly Hunt.

A huge and special thanks to two women who have paved the road in women's philanthropy and still support any new recruit. Martha Taylor and Sondra Shaw Hardy have been supporters and advocates from the early days, reading chapters, suggesting contacts, and just being there. Thank you both from the bottom of my heart.

My editors Suzanne Kelsey and Hope Burwell. Suzanne graciously accepted this task as my first editor and coach. When she could no longer continue to work on the project, the hand-off to Hope Burwell was seamless. In the world of technology, editing can happen anywhere and anytime. Hope and I took that concept to heart. We exchanged hundreds of pages as she edited from her home in The Netherlands, answered countless questions, offered suggestions, and made the narrative better. Charles Crawley, thanks for your help with technical editing of the citations. Tom Anderson, thanks for putting me in touch with the publishing world.

Tula Weis, Supraja Ganesh and John Justin Thomyyar, my editors at Palgrave Macmillan, you have been extremely helpful and took a chance on this endeavor. Thank you for answering all of my questions and supporting my work.

All of my colleagues at United Way, Association of Fundraising Professionals, fellow board members, and women within my professional networks, thank you for your support. My dearest women friends, including my two book groups, you asked regularly about the progress of this book and kept my spirits alive with your interest.

My family is filled with wonderful inspirational women, from my 93-year-old mother to my one-year-old granddaughter and all the women in between. We are fortunate to be supported by wonderful men who encourage us to be our best. Thank you all! Finally, and most importantly, a very special thank you to my husband Bob, who constantly supported and encouraged me, and was so patient and understanding as I spent countless hours in my home office. You are my soulmate in this journey of life and have my unending love and gratitude.

Contents

About the Author

Lois A. Buntz is a Certified Fund Raising Executive (CFRE) and fund development consultant. As the former CEO of United Way of East Central Iowa Buntz raised more than $125 million dollars throughout her career. She has held faculty positions at the University of Iowa Graduate School of Social Work and Clarke College. She consults on the topics of strategic planning, fund development and women's philanthropy.

Abbreviations

4W	Women, Well-Being in Wisconsin and the World
AAPI	Asian American Pacific Islander
AFP	Association of Fundraising Professionals
AHA	American Heart Association
AKA	Alpha Kappa Alpha
ARC	American Red Cross
ASU	Arizona State University
AWGC	Asian Women's Giving Circle
CAMH	Centre for Addiction and Mental Health
CAPS	Centre for Asian Philosophy and Society
CASE	Council for the Advancement and Support of Education
CFW	Chicago Foundation for Women
CTI	Center of Talent Innovations
ERA	Equal Rights Amendment
GC	Giving Circles
GIIN	Global Impact Investing Network
GLI	Gender Lens Investing
HIP	Hispanics in Philanthropy
HNW	High Net Worth
IFC-We-Fi	World Bank's Women Entrepreneurs Finance Initiative
IWEC	International Women's Entrepreneurial Challenge
IWF	Iowa Women's Foundation
LAI	Linkage, Ability and Interest Inventory
LCF	Latino Community Foundation
LLC	Limited Liability Company

Millennials	Generation Y
NAACP	National Association for the Advancement of Colored People
NGO	Nongovernmental Organization
NOW	National Organization for Women
NYWF	New York Women's Foundation
ROE	Return on Equity
ROI	Return on Investment
STEM	Science, Technology, Engineering, and Math
UI	University of Iowa
UWGLA	United Way of Greater Los Angeles
UWW	United Way Worldwide
WELRP	White Earth Land Recovery Project
WFCO	Women's Foundation of Colorado
WFM	Women's Foundation of Minnesota
WFN	Women's Funding Network
WMM	Women Moving Millions
WPI	Women's Philanthropy Institute

List of Figures

1

Introduction

This is not intended to be a "how to" instruction manual for fundraisers, but a guide to help professionals *think* and *learn* about women's philanthropy. Every fund development professional has acquired knowledge, theories, and methods that are the foundation of their unique style. Think of this text as another set of tools. These are not just new approaches, but new insights and ways of visualizing your women donors and prospects. The lists, suggestions, and questions contained in these chapters are intended to encourage a dialogue among organizational leaders, staff, fund development professionals, colleagues, and donors. While acknowledging that every organization and fundraiser is different, I know that there is one important message within women's philanthropy: gender matters.

The book is built around a six-step model that I have used in my fund development work. The steps: Awareness, Assessment, Alignment, Action, Acknowledgment, Achievement are familiar components of fundraising in philanthropy circles. What is unique, is how these traditional methods impact the broad range of women donors and how they can be adapted to address the differences among genders.

Fundraising is challenging in the best of times. The past two years have presented a new set of circumstances that required everyone in the philanthropic sector to be flexible and learn new ways to connect with donors. I have incorporated a few examples of how COVID impacted fundraising, organizations, and women.

As a former CEO I have biases for stable and effective organizations, structured programs, strategy, and a Systems Approach as important elements that support good fund development work. Women give to organizations that are well-managed and to people they trust. Integrating a women's philanthropy initiative into an organization will create change. The chapters about organizations are intended to be a guide to assess interest, readiness, and capacity.

Finally, for women donors, my intention is not to tell you *what* to give to or *how* to give. The stories and examples are here to help you understand your strengths, skills, capacity, and motivations so you can effectively and strategically make informed philanthropic decisions.

Definitions: Generosity and Philanthropy

I specifically selected generosity as part of the title of this book to emphasize the expansiveness and variety of giving. Herzog (2020, p. 22) describes generosity as "a broad term that encompasses orientations and actions that are intended to benefit the well-being of others beyond the self." Most often we think of generosity as giving time, money, sharing talents, or helping formally or informally. It's a relational act, an interchange that occurs between individuals or groups, within or outside of organizations. One of the most important distinctions is that generosity is about others—it is directed outward, although the giver may certainly benefit from the experience. Generosity occurs through everyday encounters, random acts of kindness, or ways that people enact their beliefs and values in social interactions (Herzog, 2020, p. 24). Anyone can be generous, it does not require wealth or status. Generosity is related to philanthropy, but it is also different.

Philanthropy is a defined and purposeful activity. Definitions of philanthropy abound, but one of the simplest is "private giving for public purposes" (Barnum, 2017, p. 222). Most often it is the practice of giving money and time to help make life better for other people (Merriam-Webster 2021). It usually takes place within the context of what is frequently called the third sector. The third sector can be referred to as nonprofits, the independent sector, social sector, voluntary sector, or nongovernmental sector (LeRoux & Feeney, 2014). Philanthropy has an end goal—to help a needy person, support an organization, influence system change, build facilities, fund research, or to volunteer. It has structure. Women's philanthropy can be thought of as purposeful generosity within the context of formal and informal networks.

Gender

I selected gender as the other key word in the title to remind fundraisers to broaden their conversations and practice inclusion, diversity, and equity in all their work. Gender refers to socially constructed roles, behaviors, and expressions that exist within a cultural context. Usually there are social expectations about how people behave and interact based on society's definition of their gender. Sex is a biological term referring to the chromosomes you have at birth, either male or female.

All the references to women within this book refer to both individuals who identify their gender as female and are biologically female.

Women's Philanthropy

Some scholars and fundraisers define women's philanthropy as women donors who invest in causes that impact women and girls. The history of women's philanthropy outlines clearly that many of the women's foundations and funds were developed for that primary purpose. But the world of women donors is expansive and diverse and not all women donors want to invest exclusively in women and girls' projects. *Women's philanthropy in this text will be defined as any and all women who give to any charitable cause.*

Initiatives versus Programs

Throughout the book I refer to women's philanthropy initiatives, not programs. I specifically use this term to emphasize the wide range of work within the women's philanthropy field. Initiatives imply a strategy to improve something, create, or innovate using a new approach. Some initiatives may be short-term projects, informal networks, or experiential. Others may be well-established programs within fund development departments, or completely independent third sector organizations.

Chapter Summaries

Chapter 2: **Awareness: The New Faces of Philanthropy**. Fundraisers have an image and belief about who is a philanthropist, but the picture is rapidly changing. The face of a philanthropist is no longer only white, male and aged.

Today, the faces are women, young and old, married, single, Caucasian, Black, Latinx, Asian, and countless others from diverse communities with varying capacities to give.

Chapter 3: **Awareness Built Social Movements: The Three Waves of Women's Philanthropy**. How did women's philanthropy develop? Three distinct historical waves or phases are outlined setting in motion the continued evolution of women's philanthropy, each building on the previous era's progress. Professionals and women philanthropists who played a role in these phases share their insights through stories.

Chapter 4: **Awareness: How Women Give**. Previous research on how women give has suggested that women have unique patterns of how they practice philanthropy. This chapter builds on that concept exploring how women connect to others and how fundraisers can connect with women donors. Women learn about philanthropy and develop an awareness about how it can be used through role models and mentors. Their yearning to tell stories, clarify their values, create change, and influence the next generation of donors are all characteristics of how women practice philanthropy. Several donors share their stories about learning philanthropic practices. Awareness is created in two dimensions: the *fundraisers'* awareness of women's patterns of giving and how women *donors* begin to identify their interest and awareness of philanthropy.

Chapter 5: **Assessing Your Donors**. Assessment is a two-lane road that merges into one as fundraisers collect information through subjective, personal encounters and an objective analysis of a donor's wealth capacity. How does the source of someone's wealth impact a donor's ideas about philanthropy? This is an area of donor research that has not been explored in much detail and a contributing factor to how women view their philanthropic choices. As women assess how they acquired their wealth it helps them evaluate how they feel about it and what they want to accomplish with it. Stories from women who have inherited, married, or earned their wealth illustrate their perceptions about their giving. Single, married, and widowed women are featured. This foundation of information helps fundraisers assess which donors may be prospects for philanthropy and helps women donors assess if and how they want to give.

Chapter 6: **Assessment: Is Your Organization is Ready for a Women's Philanthropy Initiative?** Capacity is a donor issue and an organizational issue. This chapter is designed to help fund development professionals and third sector leaders assess an organization's capacity, readiness, and ability to establish a women's philanthropy initiative. Hidden biases, assumptions about women's wealth and financial knowledge, staff skills and traditions frequently hinder an organization's ability to engage women. Key questions and evaluation instruments are included to help the organization's leadership and fundraisers evaluate the potential to grow their connections with women donors.

Chapter 7: **Alignment: Helping Donors Find Their Passion**. Research has proven that giving is an experience that increases an individual's life satisfaction and well-being. Offering women an opportunity to experience this sense of joy and have an impact on a cause they care about is magical. Two factors of alignment are featured: values clarification and wealth capacity. As women assess their values and match their interests with financial capacity, they can determine the type and significance of a gift, including those that are transactional, transitional, and transformational. A fundraiser's task is to help the donor discover her true passion. Donor stories illustrate the power of this alignment.

Chapter 8: **Action: Making It Happen**. How does an organization create and implement a women's philanthropy initiative? After the structure and developmental stages of an organization are reviewed, three examples of women's philanthropy initiatives at different stages of development are featured. Suggestions for the development of an initiative are included.

Chapter 9: **Action: Making the ASK**. If organizations are ready, donors have been engaged and assessed, interests and wealth aligned, the next step is to forge forward with an ask. Creating memorable experiences for women donors and executing successful asks is an art and a skill. Steps to prepare and implement an ask are outlined.

Chapter 10: **Acknowledgment: Myths, Mystery and Magic**. Thanking donors is one of the most important aspects of women's philanthropy and probably the area that gets the least amount of attention. How do we thank women donors for their belief in our work, our cause, and our organizations? Do they like a different type of acknowledgment than men? The bond of trust is sacred and essential in our work as fundraisers. Making thanks more than a perfunctory task, takes time, planning, and skill.

Chapter 11: **Achievements: Healthcare, Higher Education, Environment**. Three sectors that have had success developing women's philanthropy initiatives are healthcare, education, and environment. Higher education and healthcare have long histories of working with women donors and the environmental sector is rapidly acquiring new philanthropists, especially with younger donors. What has worked and why? Examples of programs that have been successful and lessons learned help guide fundraisers who work in these sectors.

Chapter 12: **Achievements: Women Investing in Business and Leadership**. Women's philanthropy can take many forms. Women donors help other women by investing in women-owned businesses and mentoring entrepreneurs, helping women get a seat on corporate boards, and offering training and development for career advancement. Donor stories and established programs highlight the success and achievement of women's philanthropy in the business and economic sector.

Chapter 13: **New Trends in Women's Philanthropy**. Impact and Gender Lens investing are two areas of women's philanthropy that are gaining momentum and spurring interests from women donors. These investment options are being integrated into women's foundations, global programs, and considered by a wide range of endowment managers. Other nontraditional philanthropy models led by women are described, including the Maverick and Emerson Collective, Blue Meridian, and the Audacious Project.

Chapter 14: **Diversity and Philanthropy: Engaging Women of Color and the Next Generation of Donors**. Women leaders from key organizations share their experiences and thoughts about how to engage and work with women of color. As fundraisers become more aware of how intersectionality is a constant and ever-changing dynamic in working with women donors it is essential that our learning continues. Melanie Brown, Gates Foundation; Yolanda F. Johnson, Founder of Women of Color in Fundraising and Philanthropy; Amalia Delgado, Associate VP Strategy, Hispanics in Philanthropy; and Hong Hoang, founder of the Vietnamese nonprofit CHANGE are featured.

The next generation of women donors are the future of women's philanthropy. Giving patterns of Generations, X, Y, and Z are explored and compared with the patterns of the Baby Boomers. Kiersten Marek, founder of Philanthropy Women, an online communication portal focused on feminist causes and donors discusses how the new generation of donors think about philanthropy.

Chapter 15: **A Call to Action**. As women's philanthropy continues to grow, now is the time to shine a light on the vast array of opportunities that await women who want to give and fundraisers who want to make it happen.

Bibliography

Barnum, E. (2017). The social biases of philanthropy. *Annual Review of Sociology,* *43*(1), 222.
Herzog, P. S. (2020). *The science of generosity*. Palgrave Macmillan, Springer Nature.

LaRoux, K., & Feeney, M. K. (2014). *Nonprofit organizations and the civil society in the United States*. Routledge.

Merriam-Webster. (2021). Retrieved December 27, 2021, from https://www.merriam-webster.com/dictionary/philanthropy

2

Awareness: The New Faces of Philanthropy

Philanthropy is a big word, an old word that usually brings to mind images of an older white male, a family inheritance, or a young tech millionaire in jeans and a hoodie. Does your vision ever include a woman? Melinda Gates, Oprah Winfrey, MacKenize Scott, and Abigail Disney are all women acting philanthropically whom many of us know. Other examples include:

Laurene Powell Jobs, widow of Apple founder Steve Jobs, who in 2015 gave $50 million through her organization XQ: The Super School Project (Di Mento, 2016). Diane Hendricks, owner and chairperson of ABC Supply, one of the richest women in the U.S. *Forbes* magazine listed her as the #1 most successful woman entrepreneur at a net worth of $4.9 billion. She has invested millions in economic development in Beloit, Wisconsin over the past 25 years (Stevenson, 2017). Sheryl Sandberg, the Chief Operating Officer of Facebook, #19 among the 50 top donors in 2018 contributed $100.7 million to LeanIn.org, a group promoting female leadership, and Opt ionB.org, an online website for grief support (Di Mento & Gose, 2019). And Mellody Hobson, co-CEO of Ariel Investments, who with her husband George Lucas recently received the Carnegie Medal of Philanthropy for their contributions to education and after-school programs for inner-city teens in Chicago. Mellody authors a column for the *Black Enterprise* magazine and is the first African-American woman to chair the Economic Club of Chicago (Carnegie Medal of Philanthropy, 2019). These are just a few of the new faces of philanthropy, women who have earned their wealth, married wealth, or inherited wealth. The current and future wealth capacity of women is a

© The Author(s), under exclusive license to Springer Nature Switzerland AG 2022, corrected publication 2022
L. A. Buntz, *Generosity and Gender*,
https://doi.org/10.1007/978-3-030-90380-0_2

major factor that will enable more women to give. It's a phenomenon that many philanthropic professionals should be watching closely.

In 2014, Women Moving Millions (WMM) a philanthropic group comprised of more than 300 women, each of whom gives at least one million dollars to charitable causes in their lifetime, commissioned a study, *All in for Her: A Call to Action*. Their findings estimated that U.S. women have the capacity to give $230 billion annually (Nelson, 2014). By 2023, women are expected to control between $81 and $93 trillion, 32% of all global wealth (Zakrzewski et al., 2020). The Rockefeller Foundation predicts that many women will experience a dual wealth inheritance in their lifetime: once from their parents and secondly from a spouse (Rockefeller Philanthropy Advisors). These predictions set the stage for more women of wealth to become philanthropists. But women who are philanthropists come with varying capacities and not all of them are high net worth (HNW) individuals.

People's perceptions about who can be philanthropic are as important as the reality. Billie Jean King, the American professional tennis player and founder of the Women's Tennis Association, shared this comment with Lee Roper-Batker, the former CEO of the Women's Foundation of Minnesota (WFM), "I believe that anyone who moves is an athlete." Roper-Batker adopted that philosophy as she grew the foundation believing that anyone who gives is a philanthropist. "I think people have a hard time with the term, so it's important for women to take up some of the space and see their power as philanthropists," Roper-Batker commented. Fortunately, WFM had a woman philanthropist Mary Lee Dayton who gave the first $1 million gift to launch the foundation in the early 1980s. Dayton defied the myth that women had minimal resources or were unwilling to make significant contributions. Another philanthropist Roper-Batker mentioned was a woman named Audrey who lived on social security and every month would send the WFM between $1.00 and $4.00 in cash. When Roper-Batker called to thank her and asked why she sent the donation, Audrey said she lived in subsidized housing and after she paid her bills and bought food, she gave money to four to five charitable organizations so that women could have more opportunities than she did (Roper-Batker, personal communication, May 12, 2021).

Asking women philanthropists to define the word philanthropy yielded some interesting responses. Ana Oliveira, CEO of the New York Women's Foundation said, "It's the love of humanity, an act of creating a world that is bigger than yourself, an expansion of yourself" (Oliveira, personal communication, November 22, 2017). Many other women mention volunteering, giving time, sharing skills, and money. None of the women I interviewed responded with any version of "it's only a financial transaction." They all talked about philanthropy as something broader: time, talent, treasure, testimony (telling their story), and ties (connections).

Some women interviewed disliked the word, proclaiming it outdated. Others proposed the creation of a new word for the new world of philanthropy, especially women's philanthropy. Approximately ten years ago, Katherine Swank, a fundraising consultant for Target Analytics, coined the term *femo-anthropy* in an article she wrote about women's philanthropic giving (Swank, 2010). The term never caught on as an alternative to philanthropy and no one since then has proposed any other option. K. Sujata, the former Executive Director of the Chicago Foundation for Women says, "It's a hefty word; use it, be proud of it, don't shy away from its power." A big word, for big ideas and big needs (K. Sujata, personal communication, April 18, 2019).

Has the image of a philanthropist changed? Will it continue to change? As women's philanthropy grows in scale and scope, women *will* be part of the picture and perhaps they can coin a new word to describe "women who give and practice generosity."

Bibliography

Carnegie Medal of Philanthropy. (2019, April 10). Retrieved June 10, 2020, from https://www.medalofphilanthropy.org/mellody-hobson-and-george-lucas

Di Mento, M. (2016, June). Women to watch. *Chronicle of Philanthropy*.

Di Mento, M., & Gose, B. (2019, February). Betting on tomorrow. *Chronicle of Philanthropy*.

Nelson, G. (2014, October 17). The powerful philanthropic intention behind women moving millions. *Nonprofit Quarterly*. Retrieved March 25, 2019, from https://nonprofitquarterly.org/the-powerful-philanthropic-intention-behind-women-moving-millions

Rockefeller Philanthropy Advisors. *Women and giving* (pamphlet, n.d.).

Swank, K. (2010, March/April). Femo-anthropy: Women's philanthropic giving patterns and objectives. *Advancing Philanthropy*.

Stevenson, A. (2017, August 5). A billionaire-fueled revival. *New York Times*. Retrieved April 11, 2019, from https://www.nytimes.com/2017/08/05/business/dealbook/beloit-wisconsin-revival-diane-hendricks.html

Zakrzewski, A., Reeves, N. A., Kahlich, M., Klein, M., Mattar, R. A., & Knobel, S. (2020). *Managing the next decade of women's wealth*. Boston Consulting Group. Retrieved February 14, 2021, from https://www.bcg.com/publications/2020/managing-next-decade-women-wealth

3

Awareness Built Social Movements: The Three Waves of Women's Philanthropy

The First Wave

It is easy to forget that there was a time in America when women were not allowed to speak in public, to attend school, or to control their own money. For more than 100 years after the Revolutionary War, women had limited access to financial resources. If their fathers established accounts for their inheritance, and they married, their husbands became owners of all of their property. One of the reasons some daughters of wealthy men never married was so they could control their own fortunes. And yet, even in these restrictive and oppressive conditions women became donors to important social changes.

The history of American women's role in philanthropy has been documented by numerous historians. Kathryn McCarthy, a professor of history and director of the Center for the Study of Philanthropy at the City University of New York edited a series of essays more than thirty years ago tracing the early years of philanthropic development and citing the caricature of Lady Bountiful as a popular reference to women donors (McCarthy, 1990).

The first recorded gift of women's philanthropy came from the English-woman Ann Radcliffe Moulson in 1643 when she endowed the first scholarship fund at Harvard—which then didn't admit women, though nearly two hundred years later when the women's annex to the university became a college it was given her maiden name, Radcliffe.

In 1806, Mrs. Isabelle Graham and Eliza Hamilton (wife of Alexander Hamilton) founded the first American orphanage, which is still in existence

© The Author(s), under exclusive license to Springer Nature Switzerland AG 2022, corrected publication 2022
L. A. Buntz, *Generosity and Gender*,
https://doi.org/10.1007/978-3-030-90380-0_3

under the name Graham Windham (Graham, 2021). In the early half of the 1800s women like the Grimke sisters risked their reputations by giving their time and voices to the movement to abolish slavery. And, by 1848 women were funding the first women's rights conference in the world, held in Seneca Falls, New York.

Mary Garrett, who inherited $6 million (equivalent to almost $154 million in 2019) from her father, John W. Garrett, President of the B & O Railroad and her friend, M. Cary Thomas, whose family would not permit her to get a college education or to enter the family business, established Bryn Mawr School, a girls' preparatory school in Baltimore in 1894. Garrett's influence extended even further. She forced Johns Hopkins Medical School to admit women by tying a large donation to the requirement that it admit women. When asked by Susan B. Anthony to join the suffrage movement, Garrett and Thomas agreed to help raise $60,000. By hosting suffragists at her home in Baltimore, Garret legitimized the movement in the eyes of her peers (Johnson, 2017).

Mrs. Frank Leslie, a very successful businesswoman who had assumed her husband's first name in order to position herself in a male-dominated world and to prevent her husband's sons from taking over the business, left her entire estate, estimated at $1 million, (equivalent to $25.6 million in 2019) to Carrie Chapman Catt, president of the National American Woman Suffrage Association and founder of the League of Women Voters and the International Alliance of Women (Johnson, 2017). These funds were dedicated to the suffrage movement.

Other women philanthropists helped fund colleges, nonprofits, and social service programs. By 1875, Sophia Smith had funded the opening of Smith College and established a school for the deaf. Clara Barton established the American Red Cross in 1882, and at the turn of the twentieth century, Elizabeth Milbank Anderson helped finance school nutrition programs and the Children Aid Society.

By the time American women won the right to vote in 1920, Jane Addams and her work at Hull House in Chicago was transforming the lives of women and immigrants. The success of Hull House was partly due to Addams' own philanthropy. Following her father's death in 1881, she inherited between $50,000 and $60,000 a substantial amount of money considering that at the time skilled artisans' yearly wages were only $1,000. Hull House survived for decades because Addams funded programs and supported the maintenance of multiple facilities by raising additional monies from Chicago's social elite, of which she was a member (Davis, 1973). Awarded the Nobel Peace Prize in

1931, her investment in social change was a personal commitment as well as a professional aspiration.

Early philanthropy by and for women marked a significant shift in society, a tide that had been building for hundreds of years and finally yielded many political and social changes, as money and activism were paired successfully in creating a new social order for women. Yet, while the suffrage movement was a great success, it was incomplete. The right to vote benefited predominantly white women. Women of color like Ida B. Wells, a journalist and civil rights activist, and Mary Church Terrell, one of the first African-American women to earn a college degree, are frequently missing from the recorded histories. Even after the passage of the 19th amendment, women of color in many southern states still could not vote.

The Second Wave

The 1963 publication of Betty Friedan's *The Feminine Mystique* was the beginning of an awakening, a match that lit the fire of a new women's movement. That same year, John F. Kennedy's Presidential Commission on the Status of Women criticized the inequalities facing American women. The report avoided the subject of a possible new Equal Rights Amendment (ERA) specifically for women, but Betty Freidan, Gloria Steinem and Bella Abzug formed a network to fight for its passage. While passing the ERA was the ultimate goal, secondary benefits of their struggle were consciousness raising, public attention, activism, and heightened awareness of women's social status. As women came together to discuss, protest, and explore social conditions, they were acutely aware that action on a political or social level would require money—and lots of it.

Stephanie Clohesy has worked with some of the most influential women philanthropists, the W.K. Kellogg Foundation, Ford Foundation and numerous women's foundations all over the world, including Helen LaKelly Hunt's foundation, The Sister's Fund. Her work has helped women's organizations with strategic visioning, knowledge acquisition, leadership development, research, and analysis.

After college graduation in the 1970s, Clohesy moved to New York and began working as an administrative director in a social policy research center and volunteering at a women's newspaper. "Moving to New York was an intentional decision for my husband and me," Clohesy said. "We wanted to be in the mix of all the social action, arts, and culture. We really had no idea what we would do. He was enrolled to begin his Ph.D. studies and I knew

I wanted to change the world" (Clohesy, personal communication, June 22, 2018).

Clohesy's young ambition and skill placed her at the heart of the action, a witness to the genesis of the second women's movement, including a ratification effort for the ERA and its connection to women's philanthropy. As they say, timing is everything. Within six years she had evolved from "no idea" to the Executive Director of the National Organization for Women's (NOW) Legal Defense and Education Fund. "There were two women's foundations developing during this time," Clohesy recalls, "The Ms. Foundation and the New York Women's Foundation. The NOW Legal Defense and Education Fund was an operating fund, not a grant making organization, while the Ms. Foundation made grants to women's and girls' programs. We were all part of an activist network" (Clohesy, personal communication, June 22, 2018).

She remembers one intense meeting with Betty Freidan and various attorneys trying to determine what legal options were available to address a legislative change that would extend the ratification process for the ERA to the Constitution. Attorneys are well-known for their conservative approach to change, and as Clohesy recalled, those present were coming up with all the reasons the proposed suggestions could not work. Finally, after a lengthy discussion, Friedan made a comment about getting the attorneys out of the room, and mixed with a little colorful language demanded—*find some people who can tell me what I can do, not what I can't.* She was articulating what all change agents know: focus on opportunities, not on barriers.

In October 1971, the Equal Rights Amendment won the requisite two-thirds vote in the U.S. House of Representatives and was sent to the Senate. In March 1972, the Senate overwhelmingly approved its passage and set a seven-year deadline for three-quarters of the states (38) to ratify it. That qualification proved to be an obstacle that has plagued the amendment for more than forty-eight years (National Organization for Women, 2021).

Yet, the women's movement continued to grow and expand, with Betty Friedan and Gloria Steinem as its recognized leaders. Friedan focused on the legislative aspects and publicity, while Steinem founded *Ms. Magazine* as a platform to spread the messages of women's empowerment. Originally funds raised through the magazine were directed to the national women's movement. But eventually the Ms. Foundation, an entity separate from the magazine, was founded by four visionary women; Gloria Steinem, Patricia Carbine, Letty Cottin Pogrebin, and Marlo Thomas, with a mission to deliver funding and other strategic resources to organizations elevating women's and girls' voices. (Recently, three more states, Nevada, Illinois and Virginia have ratified the ERA, but it remains in a state of limbo.)

Awareness Built Networks

While significant activism and community organizing focused on engaging women in funding political issues during the 1960s and 1970s, fundraisers recognized that nationally and regionally most private foundations were only minimally funding programs for women and girls. Two issues arose—how to increase the awareness of women donors of the need for their philanthropic engagement, and how to provide more funding for programs that impact women and girls.

The Council of Foundations (originally named the National Committee of Foundations and Trusts for Community Welfare) had been established in 1949 by Edward L. Ryerson, a steel executive in Chicago (Council on Foundations, 2020). A membership organization of community, family and corporate foundations, its representatives in the mid-1970s were predominantly white men from elite Eastern schools who were executives of those foundations. At the annual Council of Foundations Conference in 1975 Eleanor Peterson, Executive Director of the Chicago Women's Foundation, convened a *Women Only* meeting by posting a handwritten sign on a door at the hotel where the foundation's executives were meeting (Mollner & Wilson, 2005). Chaired by Congresswoman Martha Griffiths, who detailed how women and girls were being ignored and shortchanged in public and private funding, it resulted in a committee to develop the objectives and structure for Women and Foundations, Corporate Philanthropy, an affiliate of the Council of Foundations. Later renamed Women and Philanthropy, it became the first organization to begin to focus exclusively on this topic. The organization had two primary objectives: increase the level of philanthropic funding for women and girls, and enhance the status of women as decision-makers within private philanthropy (Lyman, 2005).

By the early 1970s, a small group of foundation program officers conducted a survey to determine the level of foundation giving for women and girls. The results documented that only 0.6% of foundation giving went to women (Mollner & Wilson, 2005, p. 17), even though there was a majority of female staff at the foundations. Shocked and amazed, the philanthropy sector suddenly realized that while the social and political arenas were bursting with messages about equality and opportunity, it too was plagued with sexist and discriminatory practices. The concept of a gender lens did not exist: donors, foundations, and funders didn't think about how their philanthropic investments impacted women.

Within two years a dozen women's funds had been formed including: Astraea, a National Lesbian Action Foundation, The Women's Sports Foundation (launched by Billie Jean King), and The San Francisco Women's Foundation. The three oldest women's foundations—The American Association of University Women Educational Foundation (1888); Zonta International Foundation (1919); and the Business and Professional Women's Foundation (1956) drew on their membership bases to raise money for scholarships, research and grants for women and girls (Mollner & Wilson, 2005).

By 1985, approximately thirty-five women's funds were in some stage of development. Tracy Gary, an activist and philanthropist, worked with other women philanthropists to help establish the National Network of Women's Funds, an organization representing women funds and foundations. As this network grew larger it became evident that it was time to bring the multiple women's foundations and organizations together to determine how to become more structured and effective. That year more than seventy women from twenty established funds, including representatives from the Netherlands and France, met outside of Washington, DC to discuss values, goals, and concerns regarding the establishment of a new organization. As a result of the meeting The National Network of Women's Funds became the Women's Funding Network (WFN), a membership-based organization that could act as a network for the women's foundations and women's funds. The keynote address by Dana Alston, the first woman president of the Black United Fund, declared it "a truly historic event" (Mollner & Wilson, 2005).

Following this meeting, women's funds began to develop at an accelerated rate. By the second half of the 1980s, twenty-five more funds had developed. Women's foundations and funds within community foundations grew and four women from California who believed that women's rights were essential to social, economic, and political change around the world created the Global Fund for Women.

In 1995, the Fourth United Nations Women's Conference was held in Beijing and concurrently, the International Nongovernmental Forum on Women helped develop a platform for action, linking women on a worldwide basis. Public dollars increased, and foundation funding and new models of philanthropy were explored. Women were funding women and a democratization of philanthropy was birthed (Grumm et al., 2005).

The WFN supported the concepts of empowerment and inclusiveness, leadership by diverse women, connections and collaborations, and a vision for justice and social change. However, by 2000, the WFN needed a new direction and more structure. Like any new organization, it needed vision—but also a clear path to success.

Christine Grumm had served as the president of Chicago Foundation for Women and deputy general secretary of the Lutheran World Federation in Geneva, Switzerland. Present at the 1985 meeting and an ardent supporter of women's philanthropy, Grumm was an ideal candidate to lead WFN into a new era. Under her leadership, the organization grew from a network of 75 funds and organizations to more than 160 with assets of more than $535 million. Collective grant making grew to more than $70 million.

Grumm, said of those days, women had to be challenged to "give more and give bigger." "WFN had to expand its reach and encourage all kinds of gifts and really examine what social change versus systemic change meant." The success of the Women's Funding Network established it as a model for women's philanthropy. By combining some of the goals of the women's movement with women philanthropists, the possibilities were endless (Grumm, personal communication March 21, 2018).

Articulating a vision and engaging donors in the cause required definition. Members of the women's funding movement were guided by four primary principles:

- Democratize: Share problems and solutions, with everyone finding a seat at the table.
- Decentralize: Distribute decision-making to multiple locations at the most impacted local level.
- Diversify: Listen to critical and too often silenced voices in every discussion.
- Demystify: Make fundraising and grant making open and transparent (Grumm et al., 2005).

The Third Wave

As the women's funds and foundations grew, focusing their efforts on funding programs for women and girls, another wave of women's philanthropy developed at institutions of higher education. In the late 1980s, Martha Taylor, Vice President at the University of Wisconsin Foundation and Sondra Shaw Hardy, an attorney and lead development officer at the Wisconsin State Historical Society, had been exploring women's giving patterns. Taylor knew that women donors were not being asked to give or being credited for the gifts they gave with their husbands. Nor were they involved in campaigns or volunteer leadership roles on boards. With the support of six women philanthropists from the university, Taylor and her group began to discuss how to encourage more philanthropic giving from women, especially major gifts during their lifetimes. In the next several months the group organized and became the Council on Women's Giving, later renamed the Women's Philanthropy Council, founded as part of the School of Human Ecology. Encouraged by the Council to explore women's giving patterns, Taylor and Shaw Hardy began collecting data and stories, Andrea Kaminski became the first director, and the Council's work grew. Taylor was asked to join The Council for the Advancement and Support of Education (CASE) and to provide a program on women and philanthropy, one of the first presentations on this topic at a national conference.

By 1988, the Council on Women's Giving was fully established at the University of Wisconsin and education for women donors and fundraising staff began to develop and grow. In 1991, Taylor and Shaw Hardy were asked to author an article about career women and giving for the National Society of Fundraising Executives Journal. The interest in women's philanthropy as a model within higher education had piqued the curiosity of professional fundraisers, although many were still skeptical.

Taylor and Shaw Hardy began holding focus groups to gain more insights. The themes of these discussions lead them to identify the six C's of women's giving: create, change, connect, commit, collaborate and celebrate (Shaw Hardy & Taylor, 2010). These characteristics have been substantiated in additional research, including my own. Taylor and Shaw Hardy defined these and added three additional C's: *control, confidence and courage.*

Another characteristic that has evolved as women's philanthropy has grown is *counsel*. Women donors interviewed for this book shared the experience of having a mentor—a counselor who influenced her philanthropic giving through volunteering and/or financial contributions. These counselors were family, friends, and colleagues. When women become donors, they also want to offer counsel and carry on this tradition of mentoring others. *Counsel* could be the tenth "C" that characterizes women's philanthropy.

Fortunately, as Taylor and Shaw Hardy forged ahead, several women advocated for this small band of women philanthropy leaders: including Kathleen McCarthy; Joan Fisher, Director of the Women's Fund in Washington D.C.; and Gerda Lerner, a University of Wisconsin (at Madison) historian, who offered encouragement and inspiration. In 1991, Anne Mathews, a University of Wisconsin graduate and writer published the article "Alma Maters Court Their Daughters" in the *New York Times* magazine after interviewing Taylor and Shaw Hardy. This article prompted national attention spreading the word about the unique qualities of women's philanthropy (Taylor, personal communication, April 3, 2018).

Overwhelmed with the subsequent number of calls and inquiries they started to receive, Taylor and Shaw Hardy developed a newsletter about women's philanthropy, distributing it to an initial mailing list of 300 and went on the road offering seminars and presentations. The newsletter helped establish a new organization, the National Network on Women Philanthropists. Recognizing that the WFN and women's foundations were focusing their efforts on recruiting donors to fund programs and services for women and girls, the National Network on Women Philanthropists (eventually renamed as the National Network of Women as Philanthropists) focused on "the empowerment of women as philanthropists, including educating volunteers and professionals about how to work with women donors and developing program models that involve women and donors at universities, women's groups and other organizations" (Shaw Hardy, 1997). This broader approach to women's philanthropy would engage donors who had interests in many different areas: cultural, arts, education, healthcare, and environment to name a few.

As interest grew at other colleges and universities, Taylor and Shaw Hardy struggled with managing their new endeavor and working their regular jobs. The need for funds to hire support staff became apparent and they approached Maddie Levitt, a fundraiser at Drake University in Des Moines, Iowa, hoping to engage her support and a financial investment. Levitt knew the importance of women's philanthropy and was inspired by Taylor and Shaw Hardy's vision. After a weekend of discussion and exploration, Levitt contributed $100,000 to hire staff and help spread the word.

By 1992, the audience for women's philanthropy had grown significantly and the need for a conference specifically dedicated to this topic seemed both essential and timely. The Johnson Foundation's Wingspread Conference was held in Racine Wisconsin and included nationally known speakers, women philanthropists, advocates, and professional fundraisers. It fueled the interest and passions of women and men who knew that women could give more.

Heeding the advice of her mother, who encouraged Taylor to write all of this down, she and Shaw Hardy began writing a book in 1993 and *Reinventing Fundraising—Realizing the Potential of Women's Philanthropy* was published in 1995. In 1997, the National Network of Women as Philanthropists was renamed The Women's Philanthropy Institute (WPI), National conferences, workshops, and articles in philanthropy journals began to emerge on a regular basis. But like many nonprofits, the funding necessary to sustain the work became a struggle. Another pressing issue was a need to verify the qualitative findings of Taylor and Shaw Hardy. WPI needed a strong partner and an academic connection would be ideal; having a stable, well-established administrative home was the goal. In 2003, Cheryle Altinkemer from Purdue University was President of WPI's Board of Directors and Eugene Temple was Director of the Center of Philanthropy at Indiana University. They began to talk about a home for WPI and forged a connection that resulted in Indiana's Center of Philanthropy becoming a permanent base for WPI. In 2008, Dr. Debra Mesch became the Director of WPI and in the past twelve years, the Center has produced more than twenty reports about research studies, received $5 million from the Gates Foundation, and held six national symposia. In 2013, the Center was renamed the Lilly Family School of Philanthropy. In 2019, Jeannie Infante Sager was hired as the new Director of WPI.

Helen LaKelly Hunt

Helen Hunt's story of discovering her wealth and developing her philanthropic interests is chronicled with humor, candor, and historical research in her book, *And The Spirit Moved Them: The Lost Radical History of America's First Feminists*. She writes that while discovering the sisterhood that was a part of the abolitionist movement, "I was struck how these women spoke to my journey—how I learned as they had, that power was not given, but stepped into and that its full expression occurred in the arenas of voice, money, empowerment, solidarity and faith" (Hunt, 2017, p. 8).

Hunt had grown up in a 1950s traditional, patriarchal chauvinistic home, where money was never discussed with the women in the household. Assuming typical gender roles, her brothers became involved in the family business, while she and her sisters followed their mother's lead and learned to be good southern belles, even learning how to curtsy.

An early epiphany occurred one summer when she chose to work as a church camp counselor and was surprised to find the camp filled with a wide diversity of people. Her own Baptist church had emphasized concern for the poor, but also had segregated services—one for whites and one for people of color. At camp she met people who were not rich and not white. They came from varied backgrounds, yet shared Hunt's faith and compassion for others. The experience opened her eyes to the harmony and joy that could come from sharing her personal gifts, not her possessions or wealth. The experience also sparked her smoldering feelings of rebellion.

Hunt had struggled with her family's defined parameters for women and always felt strangely uncomfortable and frustrated, especially when she was relegated to the parlor while her father and husband discussed business in her father's office. She felt there was something inherently wrong about not being included in the family business discussions, but had no avenues of entry into the world of money.

Hunt pursued a teaching degree and eventually landed a job in an inner-city high school in Dallas, much to her husband's dismay. There she saw first-hand the inequities that existed outside of her comfortable home and neighborhood. How could she have so many resources and others have so little? Her concern for the people in those neighborhoods did not resonate with her husband. His purpose and goal in life seemed to center around acquiring wealth—the more, the better. Finally, Hunt and her husband agreed to divorce and in 1979 she moved to New York with her two small children and began to craft a new life.

Yet, her real awakening came one day when her sister Swanee called and asked if she had a current copy of *Forbes* handy. There in black and white was their financial worth, listing them as some of the wealthiest individuals in the world. Stunned and surprised, the sisters also felt a bit foolish. After exploring the structure of her family trust and assessing the monthly allowance given to her, Helen decided to "exit the parlor and enter the counting house" (Hunt, 2017, p. 8).

With newfound access to money, Hunt increased her attendance at philanthropy forums and began to learn about the needs of women and girls. Why were so few funds being directed to programs for them? Why didn't more women philanthropists support this? With her network of relationships in Dallas, she began to explore the possibility of building a Dallas Women's Foundation, calling on her friend and colleague Tracy Gary to share the model used by the San Francisco Women's Foundation.

Hunt recalls those early 1980s conversations with possible supporters. Many wealthy women with whom she interacted did not support women and girls' causes or write big checks. She was discouraged by the scores of people who told her, "You need to know—in Texas, we don't use the words *women* and *money* in the same sentence. And you definitely, definitely, definitely don't use the words, women, money, *and power*. No one's going to fund you. The women will not fund you. Men will hate you" (Hunt, personal communication, December 21, 2017). Despite that rhetoric, the Dallas Women's Foundation became the fourteenth women's foundation to be established in the U.S.

Helen Hunt continued her pursuit of helping to establish women's foundations and with the consultation of Tracy Gary, helped cofound the New York Women's Foundation and was on the first board of the WFN. She continued to increase her participation in global women's philanthropy and grew more determined each day to change the status of women's philanthropy.

Women Moving Millions—Voice, Values, Vision

In 2005, Hunt had been documenting the history of visionary women donors who had pledged a million dollars or more to women and girls, when she was challenged by her sister Swanee to "raise the bar on women's giving" (Hunt, personal communication, December 21, 2017). Swanee had promised to pledge a portion of her inheritance to Helen if she would help develop a global collective of committed, purposeful women making unprecedented gifts of $1 million or more for the advancement of women and girls. She believed that her sister's interest in the status and well-being of women and gender-based philanthropy, as well as her capacity and drive for raising substantial funds made her a perfect spokesperson and advocate (Women Moving Millions, 2020).

Hunt and Stephanie Clohesy had been on the search committee that hired Chris Grumm many years earlier when WFN was getting established. As the CEO of the Women's Funding Network, Grumm had a successful track record as a fundraiser, executive, and manager. Recognizing that Grumm's organizational and fundraising skills would be a tremendous asset in the development of this new initiative, Hunt asked Grumm to co-chair the effort. The community of women donors who had given million-dollar gifts partnered with the Hunt sisters and Grumm to establish a giving campaign that would raise $150 million in two years and establish a giving campaign that would unleash the women's "voice, values and vision" into the world.

Hunt called her friend Kathryn McCarthy at the Center for the Study of Philanthropy at the City University of New York and asked if something like this had ever been done. McCarthy's research indicated that it had not, at least not at this level. Although women had donated million dollar gifts in the past and previous waves of women's philanthropy demonstrated that they could create change through advocacy and money, there had never been a campaign quite this large. The marketing brochure designed for the campaign proudly asked women to step up, with the tagline, "Welcome to your place in history. We're glad you're here" (Hunt, personal communication, December 21, 2017). Hunt remembers fondly how flattered and humbled women were to be asked to give a million dollars. "They were being asked to use *their money*, and they responded."

Hunt and her team compiled stories and quotes from more than seventy women donors and published *Trailblazers*, a book-length testimonial to the power of women's philanthropy. As women saw the stories and photos of other women giving, they often responded with awareness and awe. "Oh goodness, this is my tribe. I want to join; I want to be part of this group." History was made when the goal was exceeded: $181 million was pledged by 102 donors to 41 Women's Funding Network member funds.

The community of Women Moving Millions (WMM) was a turning point in the history of women's philanthropy. Universities, foundations, and other nonprofits had received million-dollar gifts from women, but this type of campaign was one of the most comprehensive efforts to secure major gifts from women and its success proved there was a large amount of untapped capacity. Following the campaign, the plan was to formalize and create a nonprofit-based organization. With financial support from donors and a $1.5 million grant from JP Morgan Chase, Women Moving Millions became an official organization with Hunt as the Founder and Swanee Hunt as the Catalyst (Women Moving Millions, 2020). The success of WMM inspired other women and organizations in their quest for more women donors. Today, WMM has raised more than $680 million. Sarah Haack Byrd, the current CEO, launched another significant campaign in 2019 with a $100 million goal and the theme *Give Bold, Get Equal*.

Hunt's story is just one example of a woman who through experiences, education, and a piqued interest developed an awareness of a cause that was important to her. She came to realize she had the capacity to create change, the financial means to inspire others to engage, and the capability to act as a role model for other women. Her investment has left an enduring legacy and helped launch a new phase of women's philanthropy—one that encourages women to give bigger and bolder.

Questions and Suggestions for Fundraisers

The historical development of women's philanthropy demonstrates how building awareness of women's needs, concerns, and challenges can engage women as supporters, advocates, prospects, and donors. Understanding this historical context can help fundraisers think about awareness-building on several different levels: individually, through groups or networks, or on a community level. As women become aware of community issues and causes, they will want to learn more. Here are some questions for fundraisers to consider.

1. Why did women create their own philanthropic funds or funding networks? How can you avoid repeating the same frustrations women experienced?
2. What issues in your community or organization are currently not being addressed or solved?
3. Could women help create solutions? How?
4. What causes do the women donors you work with care about? How can you align these causes with your organization's mission?

Expanding the number of women interested in your cause and enhancing the engagement of women already interested is your opportunity to ask women to step into learning. Awareness happens through a variety of communication methods: information and education, direct and indirect experiences, and role-modeling. Consider these suggestions to help raise the awareness of prospective donors (Fig. 3.1).

1. Where on this continuum of awareness would you place your current women prospects?
2. How can you connect with them and encourage their increased participation?
3. Think about all the women in your community and network as potential donors. This includes women of all ages, races, ethnicities, and economic classes. How many of them do you know? Do you know how to reach them through multiple channels of communication?
4. Many potential women donors are unaware of the needs in your community and your job is to inform, educate, engage, and inspire. Determine how to tell your story—this is usually called a *case for support*. It might be as formal as a brochure, video, Ted Talk, article in a publication, or a featured event. It should answer the following questions. What is the need or issue? Why is it important? How many people are impacted by it? How does it impact women? What will your organization do to address

Fig. 3.1 The continuum of awareness

the issue? Why do you need support/philanthropic investments? How will invested resources of time, talent, or treasure be used?

5. Pay attention to the language used in your informational materials. Will women respond positively to the words you have chosen? Ask women to review your materials.

6. Use your website for a "Did You Know" community update about your cause highlighting how women are impacted.

7. Women want to be engaged on many levels, usually first as observer or volunteer. Invite women in groups or pairs or as part of a family/couple to learn about your cause. Women like to be invited by other women.

8. If women are interested, they will want to learn more. Your task is to build curiosity: shock or surprise them with new information, engage their emotions and their business sense. Observe their responses. Check hits on social media. Anticipate the kinds of questions they may ask.

9. Take advantage of the power of role-modeling and ask a woman to be the spokesperson for your cause.

10. Begin building relationships with prospective women donors. Invite them to other related events or send them additional information. Encourage them to visit a facility or to see the cause as an actual observer or volunteer. Direct experiences are worth a million words.

11. Participate in community activities where women congregate. Establish connections through multiple sets of networks. Use these opportunities to "tell the story" of your work.

Bibliography

Council on Foundations. (2020). *History of the council on foundations*. Retrieved May 18, 2021, from https://www.cof.org/sites/default/files/documents/files/History-Council-on-Foundations.pdf

Davis, A. F. (1973). *American heroine: The life and legend of Jane Addams*. Oxford University Press.

Graham Windom. (2021). *About us: Graham caring for kids and families since 1806*. Retrieved May 18, 2021, from https://www.graham-windham.org/about-us/

Grumm, C. H., Putenney, D. L., & Kishawi, E. K. (2005). Women's biggest contribution: A view of social change. In E. Clift (Ed.), *Women, philanthropy, and social change: Visions for a just society* (1st ed., pp. 139–157). Tufts University Press.

Hunt L. H., (2017). *And the spirit moved them: The lost radical history of America's first feminists* (pp. 8–13). The Feminist Press.

Johnson, J. M. (2017). *Funding feminism: Monied women, philanthropy, and the women's movement, 1870–1967.* The University of North Carolina Press.

Lyman, J. (2005). Exposition to a conference: How did it all start? In E. Clift (Ed.), *Women, philanthropy, and social change: Visions for a just society* (1st ed., p. 17). Tufts University Press.

McCarthy, K. D. (Ed.). (1990). *Lady bountiful revisited: Women, philanthropy and power.* Rutgers University Press.

Mollner, C., & Wilson, M. C. (2005). History as prologue: The women's funding movement. In E. Clift (Ed.), *Women, philanthropy, and social change: Visions for a just society* (1st ed., pp. 13–28). Tufts University Press.

National Organization for Women. (2021). *Chronology of the equal rights amendment, 1923–1996.* Retrieved October 12, 2019, from https://now.org/resource/chronology-of-the-equal-rights-amendment-1923-1996/

Shaw Hardy, S. (1997). *The evolution of the Women's philanthropy institute: The early days 1987–1993.* White Paper.

Shaw Hardy, S., & Taylor, M. A. (2010). *Women and philanthropy: Boldly shaping a better world.* Jossey-Bass.

Women Moving Millions. (2020). *Our story.* Retrieved May 5, 2021, from http://womenmovingmillions.org/about/our-story/

4

Awareness: How Women Give

If developing awareness of the history of American women's philanthropic giving capacity is the first step in building a philanthropic community of women donors, the next task for fundraisers is to understand how women approach philanthropy and their giving patterns. Are women really more generous than men? Do they think differently about philanthropy? How do they want to be engaged?

According to the research conducted by the Women's Philanthropy Institute single women, are more likely to give to charity and give higher amounts than similarly-situated men (Mesch et al., 2015a). Women prefer to distribute their giving to multiple organizations or charities, while men tend to concentrate (Mesch et al., 2015a). When using technology and online giving platforms, women give smaller gifts than men, and give to smaller charitable organizations (Mesch et al., 2020). This last trend may discourage fundraisers looking for donors who give major gifts, but it is important to recognize that gift size does not necessarily equate with a donor's capacity.

As women's incomes rise, they become more likely to give to charity than their male counterparts (Mesch et al., 2015b). In a restricted sample of households in the top 25% of permanent income, Baby Boomers and older women give 156% more to charity than men (Mesch, 2012). And, the Women's Philanthropy Institute reports that 93% of high net worth women give to charity compared to 87% of high net worth men (The U.S. Trust Study of High Net Worth Philanthropy: Portraits of Generosity, 2018).

© The Author(s), under exclusive license to Springer Nature
Switzerland AG 2022, corrected publication 2022
L. A. Buntz, *Generosity and Gender*,
https://doi.org/10.1007/978-3-030-90380-0_4

Women are demonstrating they have capacity and are willing to be philanthropic. According to the Million Dollar List, individual women gave more than 1,686 gifts of $1 million or more between 2000 and 2016, about 31% of all gifts given by individuals (Faculty of the Lilly Family School of Philanthropy, 2019, p. 30).

All of these facts are good news for the hundreds of philanthropic programs working to engage women donors. The universe of women donors is broad and varied. The Women's Philanthropy Institute continues to research how race, sexual identity, income, age, geography, and marital status impact women's giving patterns. As more information is collected, fundraisers will be able to refine efforts to engage specific subsets of women donors.

The economic and philanthropic power women hold continues to increase. Women earned an estimated $24 trillion worldwide in 2020 and are expected to control $43 trillion of global consumer spending (Frost & Sullivan, 2020). Today, women comprise half of all workers on U.S. payrolls and mothers are the primary breadwinners or co-breadwinners of nearly two-thirds of American families (Faculty of the Lilly Family School of Philanthropy, 2019, p. 29). With an increase in American female labor force alone, research shows that acceleration to the American GDP could add $5.87 trillion to the global market capitalization over the next ten years (Peterson & Powers, 2021).

This economic power extends beyond women's earnings. In the U.S., women exercise primary or joint decision-making control over $11.2 trillion, or 39% of the $28.6 trillion national investable assets (Turner Moffitt, 2015). Decisions about how to use current and future wealth will continue to rest in the hands of more and more women. Finding new ways to work with women donors should be a goal of all fund development programs.

How women practice philanthropy is as important a consideration as how much they have to give. Making connections with others, telling their stories, working collaboratively, aligning their interests and values with causes they care about, creating change, using mentors, and influencing the next generation are all key elements of the ways women translate their thoughts and ideas into action. Let's examine these in more depth.

Connections

Relationships are built on connections. Women donors want to be connected in a variety of ways before considering the possibility of making a financial contribution. They want to know you—the fundraiser and your organization.

4 Awareness: How Women Give

They like philanthropic causes that help them network with others, meet new people, and allow them to work collaboratively.

More than fifty years ago, Harvard psychologist Carol Gilligan, Ph.D., described her research on women's moral development in her famous book *In a Different Voice*. She learned that women define who they are by describing their relationships, while men define themselves by separation and independence. Through the socialization process women learn to value relationships more than rules. Women are more likely to consider moral problems in terms of care and responsibility in relationships rather than a more typical masculine examination of rights and rules (Gilligan, 1982, pp. 12, 16).

Given these traits, it's not surprising that one of the most popular forms of women's philanthropy is one that builds on connections—Giving Circles (GC). Colleen Willoughby of the Washington Women's Foundation in Seattle is frequently credited as the catalyst for this form of nonhierarchical, inclusive, egalitarian approach to philanthropy (Shaw Hardy, 2009). GCs are a blend of networking, socialization, and collaboration. Each woman donates a set amount of money per year on a prearranged annual schedule in order to join. The funds are pooled. Proposals for philanthropic investments are presented to the membership and the women make a collective decision about which projects to fund. Usually, there are no restrictions about what type of nonprofit or cause to support. Asking each woman to give the same amount of money levels the playing field, avoiding competition which many women distain. Women have fun, learn about philanthropy and do it in relationship with others.

The popularity of giving circles grew significantly when an article about Willoughby's concept appeared in *People* magazine in 1998 (McManus, 2020). A year later, New Ventures in Philanthropy, a project of the Forum of Regional Associations of Grantmakers, provided $10 million in funding to engage more people in philanthropy, some of which was focused on starting, growing, and sustaining giving circles (Shaw Hardy, 2009). Patricia Lewis, President of the National Network of Women as Philanthropists coined the term *Women's Giving Circles* in 2000 (Shaw Hardy, 2009). Several books on the topic followed the explosion of this popular form of women's philanthropy. Sondra Shaw Hardy wrote one of them, a workbook for creating giving circles in 2000, and authored a second book, *Women's Giving Circles, Reflections from the Founders*, in 2009. By 2017, the Gates Foundation, the Women's Philanthropy Institute and the Charles Stewart Mott Foundation had funded new research on giving circles; *The State of Giving Circles Today: Overview of New Research Findings from a Three-Part Study* was released by the Collective Giving Research Group. The number of giving circles has tripled since 2007. Today, there are 1,087 independently run and currently active GC's along with 525 chapters. About half of all GC's operating started in 2010 or later (Bearman, 2017).

Sondra Shaw Hardy, called by some the "mother of women's giving circles," continues to be one of primary thought leaders on this form of women's philanthropy (wgci.online). In 2017, she traveled to London to share the story of GCs with Marliese Ammon, the wife of the German Ambassador to Great Britain, and other women from around the world. She said, "That visit opened my eyes to the interest in women's philanthropy and giving circles by so many women internationally. I found that women across the world are primed and ready to embrace the concept, and thus was born Women's Giving Circles International, whose mission is to grow, birth, and sustain women's collective giving around the world through education, empowerment, and engagement" (Shaw Hardy, personal communication, August 2, 2020).

The popularity of giving circles exemplifies how important connections are to women donors. In comparison to emphasizing giving levels, a method used to identify donors in most traditional fund development programs and focused on "status," giving circles build on connectivity.

In 2021, Philanthropy Together, a new nonprofit focused on growing the giving circle movement hosted *We Give* a four-week summit bringing together hundreds of fund development professionals, giving circle leaders, and philanthropy professionals from around the world to share innovative ideas about giving circles. They estimate that there are currently 2,000+ giving circles globally. Their goal is to scale and strengthen this movement to 3,000 circles, 350,000 members and give $1 billion by 2025 (https://phi lanthropytogether.org/directory/).

Using Your Story

One of the roles of a fundraiser is as a relationship manager, helping women build relationships with people within your organization and within a network of women donors. From the perspective of the field of sociology, there is a gender difference to charitable giving due to differences in social networks and societal norms between males and females. Women are more motivated than men by their "social capital," such as upbringing, community, and faith (Einoff, 2010). Telling stories and having our stories listened to are among the most profound ways of making connections—facts that fundraisers too often ignore or forget as they rush to secure a gift or contribution.

Women's stories reveal more than a list of chronological experiences. Rachael Freed, a Senior Fellow at the University of Minnesota's Center for Spirituality and Healing, encourages women to share the stories of their lives verbally or in writing. "We tell our stories to transform ourselves," she says. "We use our stories to make a difference in the world and broaden our perspective to see further than normal" (Freed, 2011). The power of storytelling has long been recognized as having substantial impacts on psychological and physical health. Some of the benefits of storytelling include:

(a) realizing your story can help others
(b) finding your voice, helping to structure your life events
(c) re-affirming your values
(d) finding peace and hope (Hamby, 2013).

While looking at data and analyzing the potential of donor prospects is very important, meeting with someone and asking her to share a bit about herself is a rich and enlightening experience. But it won't happen in one luncheon or meeting; it happens over time while relationships grow. Consider for example, Diane Ballweg's story.

Diane Ballweg

Ballweg has an impressive philanthropic resume. President of the Endres Manufacturing Family Foundation and a major shareholder in Endres Manufacturing, she serves on the Kennedy Center National Committee for the Performing Arts in Washington, DC, is president of the Dane County Community Foundation in Madison, Wisconsin, and has served on more than twenty other boards. But it certainly wasn't clear in her upbringing or early adulthood that she would come to hold these positions.

The granddaughter of Lawrence M. Endres, founder in 1926 of L. M. Endres Manufacturing in Waunakee, Wisconsin, and daughter of Larry Jr., she watched as her family grew the company into one of the most successful structural steel businesses in the country. Her father was the CEO and her mother, Leona, became the first full-time bookkeeper after giving up her nursing career following the birth of Diane's brother in 1957. Ballweg didn't really have a place in the company, a traditionally male-dominated business.

As she put it, "I have one brother and he wasn't interested in the company. In that day and age, if you wanted to pass on the family business - and it was steel construction - you sure weren't going to pass it on to your daughter" (Ballweg, personal communication, August 1, 2018). So, she pursued a music degree and taught special education and music.

In 1965 Ken Ballweg joined the company while attending the University of Wisconsin at Madison. After graduation he served a term in the Army Reserve and later returned to the company. While working there he met Diane and they married in 1974. "I always said, if you couldn't get your son to work in the business, the next best thing was a son-in-law. It was kind of an arrangement marriage," Ballweg chuckles. After Larry Endres's retirement in 1990, Ken was named CEO.

In the late 1990s Diane was looking for something more, something that was her own, and she found it through learning to fly. At age 45, she obtained her pilot license, a dream she had pursued secretly, hesitant to share her ambitions with her family. Her husband didn't find out about it until he read an article in the local newspaper about her as a pilot.

Just over 5% of all pilots are female. For the first time, Ballweg was entering a world dominated by men, and was intent on making her mark. "When I first started taking flying lessons, an instructor told me, 'If God had meant for women to fly, he would have made the sky pink. You can see that it's blue.'"

"He was a good instructor," she continued, "but an older, chauvinistic guy. So, I became known as the pink pilot. I decided to use the joking and demeaning comments and turn them into something positive." Pursuing her pilot's license taught Ballweg to be fierce and dedicated in her goals. "It helped me become visible to others, especially my family."

When her father died in 2006, he left his shares of the family business to her. Surprised that her brother or husband did not get a portion of the shares, she asked the family attorney, "Why?" Like a parent speaking to her from the grave, he said, "Your father saw the potential in you. He trusted you and wanted you to be part of the business. Your dad saw how you had grown and changed."

As much as I loved my dad, sometimes I feel like pounding on the table and saying, 'Why didn't you do this when you were alive?" Ballweg said.

Given what we know about women's needs for connectedness, it's not surprising that Ballweg went in search of other women in charge of fortunes. She recalls joining Women Moving Millions in the early years of its founding, "Through Women Moving Millions, women were taught to question their giving, get involved in the selection, and give where it makes the most difference to impact the world: health, education, peace, safety, environment, and a diverse array of women-led missions and businesses" (Ballweg, personal communication, August 1, 2018). The energy and momentum of WMM helped Ballweg to connect with other women of wealth and to encourage each other to be bolder about their giving.

After attending a 2010 retreat in New Mexico that Helen LaKelly Hunt hosted, and inspired by Hunt's goals for the WMM campaign, Ballweg created a list that was the culmination of her thoughts and priorities about how to help women and girls. The causes she selected included local programs in Wisconsin, scholarships for female student aviators, women's healthcare, nursing scholarships, and global educational programs for girls in Rwanda through World Vision.

So many insights about Ballweg's life and career path inform a professional fundraiser. The evolution of her philanthropic interests from passive donor with limited philanthropic power to leading her family's foundation provides many lines of inquiry a fundraiser could follow to help determine what a donor's priorities are now and may be in the future.

With Ballweg, for example, exploring how each of her major life interests (music, flying, owning a business) changed her perspective on philanthropy would fill many meetings. Asking what she learned from each of those experiences and how she would like to use those lessons to help others would begin to reveal her values and priorities. Her desire for recognition and achievement were motivational factors in her very successful career as a pilot. Asking her how she could help other women working in male-dominated professions could spark new philanthropy opportunities for her.

Ballweg found a network through WMM. Her introduction into the world of women's philanthropy was an opportunity to learn from other women, to understand how she would influence the lives of other girls and women, to be braver about her philanthropy and strategic in her giving. Making a list of causes that she would like to fund was the first step in developing her priorities for giving. Reviewing this list annually helps her plan and predict what she wants to accomplish. A fundraiser could begin to present opportunities to her that align with her interests and values, ask her to engage her friends and dream big. Never underestimate the power of a story.

Identifying Interests and Values

Our values are an expression of our lives. When women donors begin to learn about philanthropy and to practice it, they develop a greater awareness of their interests and values. These insights are critically important as they become more engaged in philanthropic investments. In future chapters, suggestions for helping women align their values with philanthropy and to become more strategic in their choices will be provided.

Studies indicate that becoming invested in a cause and giving to it actually increases life satisfaction for single women, single men, and married couples (Mesch et al., 2017). Yet, single men see the greatest increase in life satisfaction when they become donors, while single and married women experience increased satisfaction when they increase their giving (Mesch et al., 2017). Initially women give to those causes that pique their interests and the reasons can be as varied as being asked by a friend or colleague to participate in a school fundraiser to making a contribution to a cause that has personally touched her life. When women's interests and values are not defined, they experiment and respond with a contribution when asked, but with little emotional or personal investment. Neither women nor fundraisers view this as "women's philanthropy."

Initially, women may not link their interests with their values. As they seek to learn more about causes presented to them and to investigate issues in more depth, the connection between their interests as an expression of their values begins to resonate with the realization that their investments will have an impact. They may start asking themselves, "Why is this important to me?" or, "What could I do about that?" Choices become more deliberate and distinct. Understanding the relationship between women's philanthropy and cause is important for fundraisers because it can help them structure conversations and interactions with women prospects. The following two stories are examples of women, who through life experiences and self-exploration, began to identify their interests and values, influencing their philanthropic decisions.

Dee Ann McIntyre

Dee Ann McIntyre came into the world of philanthropy late in life. Her family was never in a position to be philanthropic, so learning how to give money didn't occur until after she married Scotty McIntyre. They met when she worked as a regional manager for a national insurance trade association in Chicago and called on Scotty to persuade him that his company should join the association. He was the CEO of a second-generation, family-owned insurance business that had developed and thrived in the Midwest. Born with cerebral palsy, Scotty was an intellectual with an uncanny business sense, a biting sense of humor, and a generous spirit. He had a history of philanthropy, having donated to many capital campaigns and nonprofits, and he approached philanthropy from a business sense, according to Dee Ann. He wanted to know that the organizations he donated to were well run. Having made a lot of money, he felt it was his responsibility to give back, especially to the community that had supported his business.

Dee Ann and Scotty married in Santa Fe, a favorite spot for Dee Ann, an artist, art collector, world traveler, and photographer. For fifteen years she observed her husband's philanthropy. He created a foundation that gave philanthropic contributions in addition to his personal gifts and his company gifts. He had favorite charities and special relationships built on trust. After their move to Santa Fe, Dee Ann watched and listened as Scotty practiced philanthropy in his new community.

After his death in 2009, McIntyre inherited significant resources. For the first time in her life, she had the ability to make philanthropic investments and influence the philanthropic decisions at the McIntyre Foundation where she holds a seat as a board member. She was approached by many nonprofits asking her to consider charitable causes Scotty had supported in the past. Having not been raised in his community, her first job was to learn about the nonprofit organizations he favored and to seek guidance from some of his closest friends. The foundation he established was a good bridge for contributions while Dee Ann learned and began to make her own decisions on investments. For the first several years, there was very little change. Her philanthropy was reactive in response to requests, but also targeted at children's issues and cultural arts. She knew over time she would have to develop a unique sense of philanthropy and determine the causes she wanted to support.

Slowly she began adding her own connections and interests to the mix. Having confidence in the leadership of an organization was an important part of her decision-making process, as was building connections to the people and the causes. Numerous fundraisers spent time with Dee Ann getting to know her and her interests so they could begin to understand her values and philosophy about philanthropy.

Several causes are near and dear to McIntyre, including child-focused projects, the arts, the environment, and the Cerebral Palsy Research Foundation, obviously sparked through her personal experience with Scotty. Her passion for art, fueled by connections to a wide variety of artists, a second residence in Santa Fe, and her grandson, Chris, a young photographer looking for opportunities to grow, learn, and exhibit his work, resulted in increasing her support for many art-related causes, particularly helping new artists get recognized and new grassroots organizations launched. One of her most important community investments is the New Mexico School for the Arts where she is a board member (McIntyre, personal communication, August 30, 2017).

More recently she has invested time and money in global philanthropy for women through the GoPhilanthropic Foundation, a nonprofit based in Santa Fe. Through the Santa Fe Women's International Study Center, she is helping launch new women artists, filmmakers, and writers. She sponsored an Iowa Writers' Workshop Scholar to come to Santa Fe for a month to teach creative writing, and supported children's programs in Nicaragua and Guatemala. These organizations and projects are personal to Dee Ann. She has the ability to do so much for many nonprofits, but the investments that make her feel intensely happy are those that help artists develop their creativity, help children succeed, and help the environment and women thrive.

Tracy Gary

Another woman who traveled the values clarification path is Tracy, a legend in the women's philanthropy world. Author of *Inspired Philanthropy* and founder of twenty-three nonprofits, Gary embodies the evolution of strategic giving. Born into wealth, her socialite mother was a scion of the Pillsbury family and her grandfather held the patent for the dial telephone. As a teenager in the 1960s she was told she would inherit millions of dollars. For some that would be like winning the lottery, for Gary it was scary.

There was an imbalance between how much money she observed her parents making each week and what the staff at their family home was paid. This inequality gnawed at Gary until she decided to do something about it. As Gary witnessed the needs in communities, nonprofit organizations, and vulnerable populations, she made it her mission to become a broker, to match wealthy donors with needs. She resolved to give away a significant portion of her inheritance by her 35th birthday.

Gary visited hundreds of organizations and became familiar with the work of many social service agencies. She protested the Vietnam War and sought to turn around the attitudes of mega-rich matriarchs such as those of the Levi Strauss and Hewlett Packard fortunes who gave exclusively to museums, art galleries and private colleges.

Gary had a focused mission and purpose. Her enthusiasm, energy and passion are evident in her stories and work with donors. She truly believes that investing in people and nonprofits-in-need has brought her much more joy than just buying more things. Her values have aligned with and influenced her philanthropy. For the last 40 years, Gary has significantly influenced women's philanthropy: she has raised more than $750 million, leveraged billions for social justice change, and donated the majority of her wealth to nonprofit causes with an emphasis on supporting women and girls. Another mission of Gary's was to help wealthy families learn how to use their resources. Her book *Inspired Philanthropy* is a step-by-step guide used by many fund development professionals and donors.

Every fundraiser would like to meet a Dee Ann McIntyre or Tracy Gary, but you will only know you're meeting one of them by listening carefully to their stories, and perhaps by helping them explore their interests and values. Here are questions that will help:

1. What are three concerns you have about your community, country, the world?
2. Identify your top three interests in life.
3. Identify your top three values.
4. Name three issues or topics that excite you and that you would like to learn more about.
5. How do you like to learn about topics that interest you?
6. Name three ways that you would like to get involved with these interests and causes.

Writing down one's interests and values makes them explicit, helping prospective donors think about how they might be actualized through philanthropic investments. For some women, answering the questions above in writing before they talk with a fundraiser will be helpful. For others, following up the conversation with the request that she think about it and answer the questions in writing will provide the space and time she needs to take an inventory of her priorities in a thoughtful, private space.

Create Change

When men have money and think about philanthropy, they often use it to advance themselves with a name on a building or donating to a college or hospital. They're not shy about promoting what they have done. According to Debra Mesch, the former Director of the Women's Philanthropy Program at Indiana University, "Women are not socialized to brag or have their names on things" (Chira, 2018). A recent *Harvard Business Review* study found that women in emerging markets reinvest 90% of every dollar earned into human resources, their families, education, health, and nutrition, compared to only 30–40% of every dollar earned by men (VanderBrug, 2013). Women differ from men in how they perceive wealth. While they see wealth as providing financial security and independence, just as men do, once these priorities are met, women look to wealth to provide a larger basket of goods, not just for themselves and their families, but also for society. Fully 90% of women in the global sample conducted by the Center for Talent Innovation say making a positive impact on society is important. Women much more than men, at least in the developed world, want to invest according to their values (Turner Moffitt, 2015).

This impact can happen in many different forms: a long-term investment, a sizeable financial contribution, or the creation of a new and different approach to philanthropy as Lila Igram did.

Lila Igram

As a young Muslim woman and entrepreneur, Igram knew she wanted to help women on a global level but didn't have the resources to work with the thousands of causes and organizations that existed, so she built a virtual organization. ConnectHER is a crowdfunding and communications platform matching donors to causes. It creates and supports on-the-ground projects in developing communities in the Middle East, Africa, Southeast Asia, and South America. It also creates awareness of social and economic issues affecting women globally through the ConnectHER Film Festival in partnership with the Harvard Social Innovation Collaborative.

The festival encourages high school and undergraduate students to submit short films that address women's global issues and are judged by a panel of stellar supporters including Elizabeth Avellan, Hollywood producer of the Spy Kids series, and Sharmeen Obaid Chinoy, an Oscar-winning documentary filmmaker. Over $75,000 in scholarships have been awarded to the winners.

ConnectHER awarded a grant to Leymah Gbowee for her peace work in Liberia, and in 2016 helped host fifty film screenings all over the world for International Women's Day. ConnectHER funds a women's development center in Pakistan, financial self-sufficiency programs in Zimbabwe, and education programs for girls in Afghanistan. Igram and her team have garnered support from Eloise De Joira, an actress and entertainer based in Austin, TX, the Ian Somerhalder Foundation, and the Stahl Foundation.

Igram has created change through women, causes, and connections (Igram, personal communication, July 19, 2019).

Fundraisers can use creativity as one of the most exciting and useful aspects of a women's philanthropy initiative. Creating solutions in collaboration with others is a bonding experience, one that honors and respects the donor's ideas and interests while fundraisers softly mold the range of options. Offer some initial ideas to start the conversation, then ask a woman donor how to solve a problem and you will be amazed at the ideas that emerge. Some of them will be useful and practical, depending on the time and resources available, and others may be pipe dreams. The most important aspect of this interchange is to ask and then use some of the ideas to create a path to philanthropy. When women's foundations developed in the 1970s, one of the guiding principles was to engage recipients of services to help create solutions. Creating solutions can be a rich mix of conversations among donors, recipients and professionals. Use your women donors as your dream team. They will have ideas, time and treasure. Their input establishes a personal investment in the cause and solutions; they have their footprint on it, will want to see it succeed, and the likelihood of a financial contribution will increase.

Influencing the Next Generation

Surveys with women donors document that women talk more openly about money than do men, talk to their children about inheritance and estate plans more often than do men, and believe it's important to leave a legacy to the next generation (Damen & McCuistion, 2010). Family is important to women and investments in their communities or causes that impact families are usually high on the list of their priorities. Women want to learn about philanthropy themselves, but they also want to share what they know and pass on their knowledge and practices to their children.

But women can be uncomfortable with wealth. "Girls, as they are growing up, are not socialized to feel that it's okay for them to have ambition about creating wealth, not the way it is for little boys," says Mariko Chang, author of *Shortchanged*, a study of the wealth gap between men and women (Chira, 2018). Sex differences begin in the ways daughters are treated by their parents, particularly their fathers, suggests Cynthia Ryan of the Schooner Foundation. Men feel entitled to money and are more comfortable with it, while women rarely take money for granted (Ryan, 2005, p. 185).

More recently, researchers are beginning to examine how philanthropy can be taught, asking if it is a learned behavior. Parents have asked how to best transmit "the generosity gene" to succeeding generations. A recent study suggested that "If only 5% of the assets projected to pass from Americans' estates over the next decade were captured for philanthropy, it could create the equivalent of 10 Gates Foundations" (Joselyn, 2018). This predicted intergenerational transfer of wealth opens up substantial possibilities. An understanding of how parents transmit the behavior and beliefs of charitable giving to their children is critical. The Women's Philanthropy Institute Faculty summarized the most recent research on this subject.

- Adult children, both sons and daughters, whose parents give to charity are more likely to give to charity.
- The relationship between parents' giving and adult daughters' giving is stronger than the relationship between that of parents and adult sons.
- Parental frequency of giving matters more for adult daughters than for adult sons.
- The sex differences in how parents' giving relates to their adult daughters' and sons' giving is influenced more by parents who have higher incomes and assets.
- For parents who have wealth over $100,000, a daughter's likelihood of giving is 27% higher if her parents give (Mesch et al., 2018).

Women can influence the philanthropic behavior of their children, specifically daughters, through their behavior, giving patterns, and conversation.

Karen Herman

One family taking seriously the job of teaching philanthropy to the next generation is the Hermans of Kansas City, Kansas. In 1985, while their children were young, Karen and Mike Herman were one of the first families to establish a fund at the local Kansas City Community Foundation. Karen recalls their twelve-year-old son reading about his father's salary in the paper and commenting on their family wealth, so introducing the concept of philanthropy was a natural evolution. Karen says, "We wanted to teach our children that with wealth comes responsibility."

Their partnership with the Kansas City Community Foundation where the Herman Family Fund is held is just one example of how they invest in their community. Family funds generate interest and every year a percentage of the funds can be used for charitable contributions; the family decides where these donations will be made. When their fund was established, the Hermans told their children that everyone gets a vote when it comes to making philanthropic decisions, although Karen admits that the first time her daughter disagreed with her, she was a bit shocked. "They take their role as decision makers very seriously," she said.

While Mike has served as the President of the Ewing Marion Kauffman Foundation, Karen has served as President of the Kansas City Women's Foundation. Each year the Women's Foundation presents an award named after her. "The Karen Herman Advocate for Women and Girls" award is given to a philanthropist who exemplifies leadership, mentorship and acts as a change agent for the Women's Foundation. Today, Karen and her daughter talk frequently about what causes should be supported and why. The generosity gene is definitely at work in the Herman household (Herman, personal communication, September 5, 2018).

As demonstrated by the rise in donor-advised funds at community foundations and other wealth management firms, multigenerational giving is becoming very popular. Family foundations established by Baby Boomer parents will continue the legacy of family wealth while encouraging the next generation to continue to give. Fundraisers need to think about women donors in terms of grandmothers, mothers, daughters, and granddaughters. Acts of volunteering, giving and the frequency of both are factors influencing children and encouraging them to be philanthropic. Fundraisers can share this information with women donors, teaching them how to help build the next generation of givers. Consider developing a multigenerational giving program, encouraging parents to match gifts given by their children.

Giving Counsel: Mentoring

Ask a woman donor how she learned about philanthropy and most will mention someone who influenced them. It may be a parent, teacher, family member, neighbor, colleague or boss. A woman donor has usually observed the actions of others, listened to their stories, and come away with ideas about philanthropy. The ideas may be fuzzy and unformed, but they lie within their psyche waiting to emerge at the right moment and time. Other women have been specifically instructed how to be involved in philanthropic endeavors, usually through professional colleagues; it may be part of their career advancement path or an expectation within their workplace. Research on the impact of mentors in the field of women's philanthropy is very limited and mostly anecdotal, but that doesn't diminish its importance.

The stories of how women learned to be fruitfully philanthropic are as varied as their philanthropy, but it always comes back to a relationship with someone important and influential in their lives. Mentors who have influenced others are genuine about their choices and actions. They walk the talk, living their philanthropy as well as talking about it. Just as women want to influence the next generation and their own families, they also have the opportunity to influence other women in their professional and social networks, acting as a mentor.

Carla Harris

Carla Harris had a mentor and is a mentor to thousands of women today. Currently Vice Chairman and Managing Director at Morgan Stanley, a performer at Carnegie Hall, an advocate for working women, conference presenter, Harvard graduate, and author of two books, Harris is a force of nature. Tall, beautiful, Black, she influences young women everywhere when she talks about business, her career path, and how to build confidence.

Harris was born in Port Arthur, Texas, and raised in Jacksonville, Florida. As a teenager, she sang in the Catholic and Baptist church choirs and has always had a passion for music as well as finance. Inspired by her mother and grandmother, Harris never settled for A; it was always, go for the A+. After graduating from Harvard with undergraduate and graduate degrees, she accepted a job at Morgan Stanley. Being a woman of color had barriers, although as Harris noted in an interview for *ForbesWomen* in 2016, her plumbing was more of a problem than her color (Marcus, 2016).

Her entrance into philanthropy began with volunteering and going to nursing homes as part of the Anchor Club in high school. When her career brought her to New York City, she met Austin Fitts, one of the most senior women on Wall Street. Fitts introduced her to the New York City Food Bank and encouraged her to get involved. "I couldn't get my mind around the fact that in a city as rich as New York City there were people literally making the decision every day whether to have a roof over their heads or eat… The board thought they were going to work themselves out of job. They convinced me that in five years there would be no need for the food bank."

Well, that didn't happen. But Harris's introduction to philanthropy was ignited and she continued to be involved as a donor and advisor. "I started my philanthropy as a first-year associate and never looked back." She has served on eight nonprofit boards and continues to advise other nonprofit directors and to serve as a connector to other philanthropists in the city.

Harris remembers watching numerous colleagues at Morgan Stanley act very philanthropically and is grateful to have had those mentors, both male and female. Now, she prioritizes education, hunger, healthcare and the arts as her philanthropic priorities. She continues to present at conferences, inspiring others to step up and be bold. As she says, "Girl, own your power. Take risks. Don't be afraid. Be yourself, be authentic, and don't give your power away" (Harris, personal communication, October 18, 2017).

Fundraisers can use mentoring as a strategy to connect women who want to learn about philanthropy with seasoned donors. Younger or inexperienced donors want to create relationships with women they respect and admire and they want access to them. Being a conduit between the seasoned and the new is an easy way to build awareness about causes and to teach the young how to practice philanthropy. Consider inviting successful women donors to present a panel discussion on how they learned about philanthropy and invite younger or less experienced donors. Match a current donor with a new woman prospect, developing a mentoring relationship. Ask a seasoned donor to challenge a new woman donor to begin giving by offering to match her gift to a specific cause. Share stories from current donors about a mentor who influenced their philanthropic practice and publish it to build awareness.

Universities, United Ways, and other nonprofits have developed mentoring programs and opportunities as part of their women's philanthropy initiatives, recognizing the power of women connecting to other women.

Bibliography

Bearman, J., Carboni, J., Eikenberry, A., & Franklin, J. (2017). *The state of giving circles today: Overview of new research findings from a three-part study*. Collective Giving Research Group.

Chira, S. (2018, March 10). Money is power: And women need more of both. *The New York Times*. Retrieved May 24, 2019, from https://www.nytimes.cop/2018/sunday-review/women-money-politics-power.html

Damen, M. M., & McCuistion, N. N. (2010). *Women, wealth and giving: The virtuous cycle of the boom generation*. Wiley.

Faculty of the Lilly Family School of Philanthropy. (2019). Eight myths of U.S. philanthropy. *Stanford Social Innovation Review, 17*(4), 29, 30.

Freed, R. (2011, November 15). The importance of telling our stories. *Huffington Post*. Retrieved June 29, 2018, from https://www.huffpost.com/entry/legacy-telling-our-story_b_776195

Frost & Sullivan. (2020). Retrieved March 3, 2021, from https://ww2.frost.com/news/press-release/global-female-income-to-reach-24-trillion-in-2020-says-frost-sullivan/

Gilligan, C. (1982). *In a different voice: Psychological theory and women's development.* Harvard University Press.

Hamby, S. (2013, September 3). The four benefits of sharing your story. *Psychology Today.* Retrieved January 3, 2019, from https://www.psychologytoday.com/us/blog/the-web-violence/201309/resilience-and-4-benefits-sharing-your-story

Joselyn, H. (2018). $9 Trillion will transfer from Americans' estates, new analysis says. *Chronicle of Philanthropy.* Retrieved November 2, 2019, from https://www.philanthropy.com/article/9-trillion-will-transfer-from-americans-estates-new-analysis-says/

Marcus, B. (2016, March). Carla Harris was raised to be a winner. Retrieved January 7, 2019, from *ForbesWomen.* https://www.forbes.com/sites/bonniemarcus/2016/03/16/Carla-harris-was-born-to-be-a-winner/?sh=1d9cc5157f4

McManus, D. (2020, September 30). *Giving circles: A womanly approach to philanthropy.* Retrieved January 20, 2021, from, https://www.lustre.net/home/2020/9/25/ddssalzlm1zw2et5kfh73tpj3pna

Mesch, D. (2012). *Women give 2012: New research about women and giving.* Women's Philanthropy Institute.

Mesch, D., O'Gara Lamb, E., Osili, U., Pactor, A., Ackerman, J., Dale, E., Bergdoll, J., Kalugyer, A. D., Scholl, J., Ware, A., & Hyatte, C. (2015a). *How and why women give: Future directions for research on women's philanthropy.* Women's Philanthropy Institute.

Mesch, D., Osili, U., Pactor, A., Ackerman, J., Bergdoll, J., Kalugyer, A. D., Scholl, J., Ware A., Hyatte, C., Dale, E., Hawash, R., & Yang, Y. (2015b). *Do women give more? Findings on three unique data sets on charitable giving.* Women's Philanthropy Institute.

Mesch, D., Osili, U., Okten, C., Han, X., Pactor, A., & Ackerman, J. (2017). *Women give 17: Charitable giving and life satisfaction: Does gender matter?* Women's Philanthropy Institute.

Mesch, D., Osili, U., Ackerman, J., Bergdoll, J., Skidmore, T., Pactor A., & Sager J. (2020). *Women give 2020: New forms of giving in a digital age: Powered by technology, creating community.* Women's Philanthropy Institute.

Mesch, D., Ottoni-Wilhelm, M., Osili, U., Bergdoll, J., Han, X., Pactor, A., & Ackerman, J. (2018). *womengive18, Transmitting Generosity to Daughters and Sons.* Women's Philanthropy Institute.

Peterson, D. L., & Powers, T. (2021). *Women as the drivers of economic growth.* S&P Global. Retrieved February 10, 2021, from https://www.spglobal.com/en/research-insights/featured/women-as-drivers-of-economic-growth

Retrieved December 27, 2021, https://philanthropytogether.org/directory

Ryan, C. (2005). From cradle to grave: Challenges and opportunities of inherited wealth. In E. Clift (Ed.), *Women, philanthropy, and social change: Visions for a just society* (1st ed., pp. 182). Tufts University Press.

Shaw Hardy, S. (1997). *The evolution of The Women's Philanthropy Institute: The early days, 1987–1993* (White Paper).

Shaw Hardy, S. (2009). *Women's giving circles: Reflections from the founders.* Women's Philanthropy Institute.

Turner Moffitt, A. (2015). *Harnessing the power of the purse: Winning women investors.* Rare Bird Books.

The U.S. Trust Study of High Net Worth Philanthropy: Portraits of Generosity. (2018). U.S. Trust, Bank of America and IUPUI, Lilly Family School of Philanthropy. p. 11.

VanderBrug, J. (2013, September 13). The global rise of female entrepreneurs. *Harvard Business Review.* Retrieved December 5, 2019, from https://hbr.org/2013/09/global-rise-of-female-entrepreneurs

Women's Giving Circles International. Retrieved May 21, 2021, from https://www.wgci.online/our-story

5

Assessing Your Donors

Wealth Acquisition and Giving History

The three primary avenues for wealth acquisition are inheritance, marriage, and earned income. Inherited wealth occurs most often through familial relationships when parents pass on assets to their children. Marital wealth is the combined assets of a couple acquired through work or inheritance. Earned wealth is the accumulation of assets achieved through career, business or professional employment. We find women philanthropists in all three categories and many have developed their asset base through a combination of them.

The Rockefeller Foundation describes a phenomenon called "dual wealth transfer" that will significantly impact these women. Baby Boomers (1946–1964) make up 23% of the U.S. population and many are entering or already in retirement. Often their parents, the Depression Era saving generation, have now died and passed on their life savings to children, many of whom are married. According to a Global Wealth Study, 56% of Baby Boomer women accumulated their wealth through inheritance, the first wealth transfer identified by the Rockefeller Foundation (RBC, 2018). The second occurs when a spouse dies. Considering that the life expectancy of American women is nearly seven years longer than men, the likelihood of women being the recipients of their parents' *and* their spouse's wealth is fairly high, creating a tremendous wealth opportunity for women as they age.

Intergenerational transfers of wealth account for at least 50%, and perhaps as much as 80%, of the net worth of American families (Hirsch, 2011).

© The Author(s), under exclusive license to Springer Nature
Switzerland AG 2022, corrected publication 2022
L. A. Buntz, *Generosity and Gender*,
https://doi.org/10.1007/978-3-030-90380-0_5

Children of wealthy families often end up controlling the family fortune. Consider these examples of women inheriting family wealth, controlling some of the largest family foundations in the U.S., and influencing what investments their families will make in communities, countries and causes.

- Warren Buffet's daughter, Susie, manages the Buffett Foundation.
- Michael Bloomberg's daughter, Emma, sits on the board of The Bloomberg Philanthropies.
- Linda Johnson Rice is the former CEO of Johnson Publishing and daughter of John H. Johnson, founder of Johnson Publishing. Her mother, Eunice Johnson, was producer and director of *Ebony Magazine*.
- Carrie Walton-Penner, a third generation of the Walmart Waltons, is the board chair of the Walton Family Foundation.
- Laura Kohler, great-granddaughter of Kohler Co. founder John Michael Kohler, manages the company's corporate social responsibility strategies.

Numerous philanthropists have commented on family wealth and inheritance. The most notable have been Bill and Melinda Gates and Warren Buffet, who together designed The Giving Pledge in 2009. This effort targeted the ultra-wealthy (billionaires) asking people to pledge or donate at least half of their wealth to philanthropy. It was hailed as the biggest fundraising drive in history (Gunter, 2019). More than 210 people signed on; 10 are single women, 155 are from the U.S., 111 are married couples; 2 couples who originally signed on have divorced. The wives of the divorced couples have continued their commitment to The Giving Pledge. Most notable is MacKenzie Scott, former wife of Jeff Bezos. Her recent gifts totaling more than $8 billion distributed among more than 200 organizations demonstrates how seriously she takes her commitment to philanthropic investments.

Inheriting vast sums of money may seem like winning the lottery, but Gates and Buffet have noted that there is a corrosive nature to inherited wealth. "Leave enough money to your children so they feel they could do anything, but not so much that they could do nothing," Buffet has said. Bill and Melinda Gates agreed. "We are strong believers that dynastic wealth is both bad for society and the children involved. We want our children to make their own way in the world. They will have all sorts of advantages, but it will be up to them to create their lives and careers" (Callahan, 2017, p. 43).

Barbara Blouin uses a term coined by Joanie Bronfman author of *The Experience of Inherited Wealth: A Social-Psychological Perspective* in discussing the challenges and opportunities of being an heir. "One of the phenomena that wealthy people experience is what some social psychologists term wealthism" (Blouin, 1987) she says in *For Love and/or Money: The Impact of Inherited Wealth on Relationships*. Wealthism, a set of attitudes or actions that dehumanize or objectify wealthy people, including resentment, envy and awe, differs from other "isms" in that racism and sexism are perpetrated *by* those who have power whereas wealthism is directed *at* those who have power (Blouin, 1987).

One of the most difficult things for anyone who is financially secure, whether their wealth is inherited or earned, is to answer the question, "What can I do to make a difference?" For anyone taking his or her wealth seriously, it is a very big question. Many women heirs struggle with their identity, their purpose in life, and their unearned bank account. Donna Hall of the Women Donor Network has concluded that, at least anecdotally, older women are more apologetic about their inheritance, even ashamed at times. Women under thirty-five seem more comfortable with money and social power (Ryan, 2005). No matter their ages, one of the biggest challenges women who have inherited great wealth face is determining what to do with their fortunes; consider for example Abigail Disney.

Inherited Wealth—Abigail Disney

The granddaughter of Roy O. Disney, co-founder, with his brother Walt, of The Walt Disney Company, she grew up in southern California. After high school she left the west coast to attend Yale. As a member of the Disney family, she had automatically been given a seat on the family foundation board at age eighteen, although she didn't really know what serving on the board meant. She didn't have any preparation regarding her role and though there was money to give, the board had established neither a process for grant distribution nor priorities for their funding. Decisions were made without a lot of strategic thought or education.

After moving to the east coast and working on her bachelor's and master's degrees in literature, Disney began to yearn for more purpose in her life. She had purposely avoided working in the film industry, trying to steer clear of any connection to the Disney dynasty; an advanced degree in the fine arts seemed like a good alternative. As she was struggling to complete the last phase of her education, a Ph.D. from Columbia University, she stumbled into philanthropy through friends and travel abroad.

Volunteering had not been part of her life, because as she said, coming from a famous family, her inclination was to be rather reserved with other people. However, volunteering became a solution to feelings of emptiness. She got connected to the Robin Hood Foundation in New York, an aspiring young nonprofit organization. Founded in 1988 by hedge fund manager Paul Tudor Jones, its mission is to alleviate problems caused by poverty in New York City. There she learned about grant making, nonprofits, and community building. As she said, "Once you open the door, especially if you have money, all these other doors go flying open." She joined the New York Women's Foundation and eleven other boards. While starting her family and becoming a mother, she was falling in love with philanthropy. She admits to being a maximalist. "I have a hard time saying no to anything and frankly when you perceive yourself to have so much more than everyone else, it's hard to say no to anything because it's really hard to know when you're doing enough. So, I got swallowed up in it pretty quickly" (Disney, personal communication, December 15, 2017). In 1991, she and her husband, Pierre Hauser, created The Daphne Foundation which distributes grants to organizations that empower residents directly affected by poverty, violence, and discrimination in five boroughs in New York City.

After her last child started school, Disney finally felt she had some freedom to travel and explore, so when Swanee Hunt asked her to go to Liberia with a delegation of women, she accepted. "Swanee had been an ambassador and had gotten very interested in international relations, especially the role women play in conflict resolution and peacebuilding," said Disney. Although she didn't believe that she had anything to offer, she was interested in learning. What she found was that women in Liberia had played an essential role in peace building during the country's second civil war. "I came home realizing there was an important story to tell. You know, I had avoided filmmaking like the plague, but a film was the right thing to do with this information and I just couldn't come home and pretend I didn't know it. So, in 2006, I got a director and funded the film myself. It definitely did better than I ever, ever, ever in my wildest dreams thought it would and it opened the door to a whole bunch more filmmaking" (Disney, personal communication, December 15, 2017).

The film, *Pray the Devil Back to Hell*, is about Liberian women praying for peace to protect their children and their community. The protagonist, Leymah Gbowee, helped to organize and lead the Liberian Mass Action for Peace, which brought together Christian and Muslim women in a nonviolent movement engaging in public protest, confronting Liberia's ruthless president, and even holding a sex strike. The movement brought the second Liberian Civil War to an end in 2003. Eight years later, Gbowee shared the Nobel Peace Prize with fellow Liberian Ellen Johnson Sirleaf and Yemen-native Tawakkol Karman for this work.

"I approached filmmaking as a political act," Disney said. Her films explore difficult social justice issues. In addition to The Daphne Foundation, she personally gives money to many causes. "I like the freedom of being able to just write a check and I don't have to be accountable to anyone. I can be flexible and quick." She estimates that she gives away between $2 and 3 million annually. "Generosity has never been the wrong choice for me. Money is only an instrument. Philanthropy has to be rooted in love."

Disney learned a lot about philanthropy from Helen LaKelly Hunt and the New York Women's Foundation. They taught her how to give, how to understand women's issues, and how to be strategic. Over time her philanthropy has evolved. After years of making grants through the Daphne Foundation, she finally wrote a mission statement. "I decided to retroactively understand what I had been doing, so the unifying word as I understand it now is *peace*. I am interested in women, because I am interested in peace. I'm interested in governance. I'm interested in fairness. I'm interested in human rights. I believe we haven't built a culture of peace in the world" (Disney, personal communication, December 15, 2017).

Assessing the Origin of Wealth

When fundraisers work with women who have inherited their wealth, it's important to realize that family legacy will influence their beliefs about what wealth means and how it is to be used. The stories of a family's acquisition of wealth are multilayered, changing with each generation, and interpreted differently by each individual. It is important to assess how an individual woman's views of her wealth are similar to or different from her parents' and if there were formal or informal instructions about how to use inherited assets.

Ask open-ended questions about the family history of giving. How did they make their wealth? How do they make decisions about philanthropy? What did they invest in? Why did they make those choices? What was their level of philanthropy? How much did they give? What practices of the family philanthropy will she continue or change? How does she feel about her inherited wealth? What does she want to accomplish with her wealth? These questions help a fundraiser build an assessment, a history, and an inventory of the family wealth as well as helping the donor begin to identify the links between her patterns of giving and her family's philanthropy.

For Better or Worse, for Richer or Poorer—Married Wealth

Women may acquire their wealth through marriage in two different life phases, once during the marriage and a second time as a surviving spouse. Married couples are wealthier than people in all other family structures (Aloni, 2018). The top 10% of wealth holders are, in great proportion, married. Even among the wealthiest households, married couples hold significantly more wealth than others (Aloni, 2018). Of the top 50 philanthropists listed in the 2020 *Chronicle of Philanthropy*, thirty-five are married couples (Rendon & Di Mento, 2020).

For a number of reasons, the wealth of married couples is often significantly greater than just double that of two individuals. In consolidating their assets, married couples enjoy economies of scale; they share the cost of housing, food, and educating their children. Marriage also contributes to the concentration of wealth because marriage patterns are increasingly assortative: wealth tends to marry wealth. Individuals in different social economic classes sometimes "marry up" to a higher socioeconomic class, but most of us associate with people similar in social class, income level, and interests. Thus, it is logical that we tend to select spouses of similar education and social status. This concentrates levels of wealth among wealth.

Women acquire wealth through marriage due to a variety of different factors that favor the husband's wealth accumulation: the gender-pay gap, the age differential in spouse selection, and the fact that women more frequently than men interrupt their careers or work history to assume childcare responsibilities. A recent Merrill Lynch study found that an average woman spends 44% of her adult life out of the workforce, compared to 28% for men (Merrill-Lynch, 2019). This means that women have fewer years to accrue assets including social security, investments, and savings. In 2020 a full-time female worker had a median weekly income of $891 compared to males at $1082 (U.S. Bureau of Labor Statistics, 2021). If women marry someone close to their own age, men have usually accumulated more assets prior to a marriage, due to higher wages. In addition, if a woman marries a partner older than she, he has had more time to accrue wealth.

The recent COVID pandemic has disproportionately impacted women and their work lives. In the spring of 2020, 5.1 million American mothers of young children stopped working for pay. Fifteen months later, as the country was increasingly vaccinated, 1.3 million women were still out of work (Miller, 2021). Childcare responsibilities traditionally have been assumed by women and when daycare and schools were not available, many had to make tough choices about giving up their careers, jobs, and livelihood to care for their young children. It will take years for women to regain what they have lost in their careers, wages, and advancement options.

The gender wage gap, less full-time work, and careers interrupted by child-care responsibilities have tended to leave the impression with fundraisers that women have less access to philanthropic power than men. We forget at our peril that later in life women tend to be the wealthy holder of the family's assets.

Philanthropic Decision-Making Between Couples

Assessing how couples make philanthropic decisions is important information for fund development professionals considering that at least 70% of all charitable giving comes from individuals or couples (Giving USA, 2020). A common assumption is that a couple's assets are shared equally, but research does not support that assumption. Formal ownership of, or legal right to, is not the same as control of wealth. Control involves making decisions regarding how to spend it, save it, or give it away. Couples may engage in "voluntary specialization," where financial resources are viewed as collective, though one person has the primary responsibility for making the types of investment decisions most directly linked to the acquisition and control over wealth (Chang, 2010, p. 102). Each couple determines who will have primary responsibility over financial matters. The degree of education of each partner is sometimes a factor and appears to be closely coupled with financial proficiency, contradicting traditional gender norms in which men have historically assumed the role (Chang, 2010, p. 105). Nearly 75% of girls versus 66% of boys graduate from high school and women are 1.5 times more likely than men to graduate from college, thus increasing the number of women who may have more education than their spouses.

When women have their own earnings or wealth, they may exert more power over the financial decisions. Women who earn more than their husbands are more likely to influence philanthropic decisions. Paula Wasley, in a *Chronicle of Philanthropy* article, reported that in a survey of 1000 adults who give $1000 or more to charity, 80% were married and the majority of male respondents reported that their spouse was the primary influencer in charitable giving decisions. Women, on the other hand, reported that many people influenced their decisions about philanthropy (Wasley, 2009). Professor Eleanor Brown, Pomona College, has identified three types of philanthropic decision-making among couples.

1. A cooperative unitary agreement when one partner decides.
2. A joint decision that involves bargaining.
3. A separate decision made by each individual (Brown, 2005).

A recent WPI study found that more than six out of ten couples make charitable decisions jointly (61.5%) and that around three-fourths of the 1,000 couples surveyed agree about the amount and recipients of their giving (75.6 and 77.5% respectively) (Mesch et al., 2021).

A Fidelity Charitable study of 694 couples supports the WPI study, finding that eight out of ten married-couple donors make decisions together and they overwhelmingly agree on those decisions (Fidelity Charitable, 2016). Many of the women interviewed for this book were married and most reported making philanthropic decisions jointly with their spouse. Couples who share the same values and belief systems use these as guidance when they make philanthropic decisions. But deciding what *resources* to use in their charitable giving is sometimes a matter of perception. While women believe that they share equally in this decision, the Fidelity survey found that men think they take the lead (Fidelity Charitable, 2016).

Working with Married Couples

One of the most significant errors fundraisers make when working with married couples is excluding the wife in the philanthropic conversation. Other examples of implicit bias are: not including her name on invitations or letters, directing verbal questions primarily to the husband, acknowledging gifts only in the husband's name, or meeting with the husband alone to discuss philanthropy. Unfortunately, many database systems used by fundraisers are not designed to effectively address and acknowledge *a couple* for contributions. This results in a woman feeling ignored and unacknowledged for her philanthropy. For example, consider a couple who were generous and dedicated donors to United Way. Each had a successful career and contributed financially. The wife was a fundraiser at a nonprofit and her husband gave through his place of employment. The United Way database frequently pulled only the husband's name as a donor because his gift was matched by his employer. When the publication of donors was sent out listing only the husband's name, the wife called United Way and voiced her concerns. The situation was remedied, but this oversight can occur if databases are not designed to recognize the entire family unit.

If fundraisers want to engage women donors, they must understand the dynamics of the married couple's philanthropic relationship and value the woman's input, perspective, knowledge, and role in decision-making. Asking couples how they make decisions about philanthropy will provide insights. Ask each member of the couple to list the causes they care about and discuss how they would like to support these causes. Forming a close relationship with each spouse will ensure that connections and contributions continue even if one of the spouses passes away. Make sure every acknowledgment includes both spouses, and honor each equally for their philanthropy.

One other aspect to working with couples is recognizing that 45–62% of women aged 25–54 have been married a second time (Livingston, 2013). Exploring with each person their previous history of giving, their plans for philanthropy as a couple, and how legacy will be handled are all aspects of ongoing challenging conversations. Recognize that previous patterns of giving may change with subsequent marriages. Most importantly stay connected to all of the individuals.

Working with Single Women: Widowed, Never Married, Divorced

Almost seventy percent of women age 75 or older are widowed, divorced, or never married (Houser, 2007). Women outnumber men 2:1 in age group 90-94 years and a ratio of 4:1 for centenarians (Statistics Times, 2020). The likelihood of an elderly widow being a donor in your women's philanthropy initiative is very high.

Married couples usually own most, if not all, of their valuable property and assets jointly. Generally, when a spouse passes away the survivor inherits a substantial portion of the couple's combined assets. Yet, having a will, understanding state and federal laws and inheritance taxes, and having a plan for asset distribution developed prior to death are all factors that influence if and how the woman inherits wealth from a marriage. Some women are very knowledgeable about the couple's wealth portfolio and others are confused and anxious about handling the financial affairs after the passing of a spouse. As women age, many do not make significant changes to wills or estates developed when they were married.

Working with women who are widowed is a delicate and sensitive endeavor. Factors that may influence changes in estate plans include the age of the woman at the time she is widowed, whether she remarries, and her own personal philanthropic interests. One of the first factors to determine is whether the donor wants to continue the couple's giving pattern, or has her own philanthropic interests to pursue. Is she interested in making small or large changes to her giving plan? If there is a strong and trusting relationship between the fundraiser and woman, discussions about legacy or endowment gifts may be explored, as the survivor adapts to her new status as a single person.

A Survivor's Story

Terri and Art Christoffersen had been philanthropic donors, well-known volunteers, and community leaders in Cedar Rapids, Iowa for many years. Art had joined the team of a very profitable telecommunications company in the 1980–1990s. His expertise as an accountant and his creative skills quickly propelled him to the executive team and when stocks for the company soared, the couple reaped the benefits accruing substantial resources.

Both had come from modest backgrounds. Terri grew up in a rural community. Her original high school class had eleven students. After a two-school consolidation, she graduated with a class of twenty-four. Her parents farmed with other family members and volunteered in the community. She learned a lot about giving by observing them.

They met in high school. After graduation Art worked in a factory until he was drafted into the U.S. army in 1966. After nineteen months in Berlin, he returned home and enrolled in a community college. Meanwhile, Terri had been pursuing her Bachelor of Science degree in nursing at a local college. They married after her graduation and Art continued his education while working several jobs and benefitting from Terri's support and encouragement.

Growing up in the Christoffersen family had been challenging for Art. With an absent father, three younger brothers and a sister, he took on a significant role in raising his younger siblings. His understanding of philanthropy came from the personal experience of being part of a family in need. Early in his career at Life Investors, he chaired an annual United Way company campaign, frequently telling his personal story to his employees and others, encouraging them to give to charitable causes. "Many of the nonprofits I support were ones that my family could have used during my childhood," he often said. His story and his unlikely rise to success always inspired Terri.

Terri's experience as a leader and philanthropist began when she volunteered in numerous community organizations while raising her children. Over a period of years she began to take on bigger roles, serving on boards and committees, and learning from other women philanthropists and fundraisers.

Her organizational and leadership skills began to emerge. When the local women's homeless resource center needed to launch a major capital campaign to build a shelter, Terri led the charge. After that she became known as one of the best fundraisers in the community. She continued on this path, serving as a United Way campaign chair and a member of numerous boards of directors, usually in a leadership position. She and Art gave generously to local universities, healthcare, and nonprofits.

Unfortunately, in early 2005 at the age of fifty-eight Art was diagnosed with cancer. He passed away within six months, cutting the couple's life dreams short.

Eventually, Terri had to decide how to practice her own form of philanthropy. Faith played a significant role in this transformation. She had learned from Art that helping others is a privilege, one not everyone can do. Together, they had developed and embraced a philosophy of "giving without judgment;" one never knows someone else's story of need, what happened, how they got into their current situation, or why they need help, so give without judgment.

Terri is a smart, organized, and thoughtful woman who wanted to carry out the philanthropic priorities she and Art had established together. She also wanted to be strategic in her future choices. Since Art's passing she has carried on a tradition of volunteering, chairing numerous nonprofit boards, and the hospital foundation. Healthcare is a major priority, partly because of her career as a nurse, but also because of Art's health crisis. As she uses her wealth to generously influence many causes, she teaches her children and granddaughters about philanthropy.

When asked if her philanthropic priorities had changed after Art's death, she said, "I have to believe that the age of the surviving spouse at the death of her husband impacts this decision. However, the passion and basic philosophy that has driven our previous philanthropic decisions will not change" (Christoffersen, personal communication, August 31, 2017). At fifty-seven, she had a lot of life ahead of her. While she supports many of the same causes, she admits that she is constantly exposed to new projects and her community is changing. There may be more and different needs that result in making different plans regarding her estate. Terri has regularly engaged her two children and their families in making philanthropic decisions and she knows that they will carry on the legacy established by herself and Art. Being a survivor is not easy. Making decisions that honor your spouse's legacy while carving out your unique interests takes time and patience. Terri has accomplished both.

Divorced and Single Women

Melinda Gates may be getting lots of attention these days as the most recent high net worth woman who will be getting a divorce, but thousands of others have been in similar situations with far less resources. Data highlighted in Chapter 4 documented that single women may be more likely to give and give higher amounts than their male counterparts (Mesch et al., 2015).

Divorce is a tipping point for many women in their relationship with money and philanthropy. It may be the first time she is a financial entity unto herself, a state that could be empowering or frightening. She alone can make choices about how to use her resources. Establishing relationships with women after a separation or divorce provides support for her, and offers her an opportunity to build new networks or connections with other women.

The following story is an example of faulty assumptions, a set of negative and positive experiences, and some valuable feedback for fundraisers.

Lori, is an advocate, donor, and volunteer at a women's foundation. During her marriage, nonprofits and fundraisers frequently asked her and her husband to donate to many causes and events. Her husband had a substantial income from his executive job; fundraisers considered them a HNW couple. What many fundraisers did not realize is that Lori initiated 90% of the philanthropic decisions. It had never been part of the conversations that occurred during solicitations. After their divorce, Lori was surprised that very few of the previous fundraisers or organizations reached out to her. In fact, she was shocked and a bit dismayed. "They assumed I no longer had access to any wealth and never bothered to establish a relationship with me. I felt that my influence on where our contributions had been directed had been significantly overlooked" (Lane, personal communication, February 19, 2020).

Several months after her divorce a friend invited Lori to attend a luncheon at the women's foundation. Following her attendance, the women's foundation staff reached out to her, met with her, and encouraged her to join their board. After learning about the programs funded by the foundation, she increased her participation, continued to be an annual donor, and eventually was inspired to give a legacy gift. The staff listened to her and valued her time, talent, and treasure.

Single, unmarried, or never married women are always prospects for women's philanthropy initiatives. Many have substantial resources and are accustomed to making independent choices about their philanthropy. Connecting these women with others who have similar interests and helping them build a network can be a mutually beneficial endeavor. Women like to help other women and many are strong supporters of programs for women and girls. Remember to tailor organizational materials to all audiences, not just couples. Make a special effort to invite these donors as a group or connect them with a mentor, colleague, or other donor. These donors are also ideal prospects for legacy gifts.

Earned Wealth—Jacki Zehner

A 2018 cover of *Forbes* featured young entrepreneur Kylie Jenner with the headline: "America's Women Billionaires." The article listed 60 women as America's most successful entrepreneurs. Twenty-four were billionaires—up from the 18 listed a year earlier. All told, these women held $712 billion in wealth (Robehmed, 2018).

The number of women who fall into this huge wealth category is small, but as women become more educated, enter a fuller range of professions, and have better career opportunities, the numbers earning their own wealth will only grow. Earned wealth empowers women and enables them to manage their philanthropy differently than when it is a resource acquired through marriage or inheritance. Consider, for example, Jackie Zehner.

Well known in women's philanthropy circles as the former Chief Engagement Officer and cofounder of Women Moving Millions, Zehner has been very public and outspoken about the need for more women to get engaged in philanthropy. Today, she is president of the Jacquelyn and Gregory Zehner Foundation based in Park City, Utah.

Zehner's path to philanthropy began with her extraordinary and extremely successful career in the finance industry. In 1996, she was the youngest woman and first female trader to be invited into the partnership at Goldman Sachs. Recognized as a trailblazer and next-generation role model for women, she has transitioned from a wealth manager to full-time advocate and philanthropist.

As a young girl growing up in Kelowna, British Columbia, Canada, she watched her family help others, not with money but with time and talent. Working as a cashier at her father's grocery store taught her the basics of money management and a degree from the University of British Columbia in finance set her on a path for career success. Over the course of fourteen years, she advanced among the ranks at Goldman Sachs to become one of the few senior women traders on Wall Street.

In 2002, she left Goldman Sachs to devote her energy and skills full time to the development of women's philanthropy. Digging in and doing her own research she said, "a relatively small percentage of overall philanthropic capital actually went specifically to focus on women and girls … despite the fact that we are half of the population and arguably because of gender and equality. That really catalyzed my deep, deep passion to not only activate my own capital, but really get the message out there" (Zehner, personal communication, November 17, 2017).

Zehner's experiences with WMM, the Women's Funding Network, and the Women Philanthropy Institute have given her wide perspective on the topic of women's philanthropy. She believes that there are more similarities than differences between general philanthropy and gender-based philanthropy, but recognizes that women want to bring their whole selves to the table, not just write a check. They want to bring their voice, and influence, and networks to bear as well as their skills and talents.

As a woman who has earned her own money, Zehner finally had the means to be philanthropically focused. She formed a family foundation, supports and publicizes research about women's philanthropy on her website, has served on boards of organizations that support women, and acted as a spokesperson for women's philanthropy. In addition to supporting nonprofits that she cares about, she believes she can be a catalyst for other women to get involved.

She has had many choices about what to support with her wealth. Her experiences as a minority in her profession and acknowledgment of the gender imbalance in the workplace and in philanthropy all prompted her to become a vocal advocate for women's philanthropy. She asks others constantly, "Why aren't more women engaged? Why don't more women care? Why aren't more men engaged and caring about human rights, women's rights? Last time I checked all men had mothers, grandmothers, perhaps daughters." Since her retirement from WMM in 2018 Zehner has become very focused on gender-impact investing and likes to borrow this quote from her friend Ruth Harnish, "Finance is the new frontier of feminism" (Zehner, personal communication, November 17, 2017). The best place to start is to earn your own money, learn about your finances, and help support other women who starting businesses.

Assessing Women as Prospects

Prospecting is a standard practice in fund development programs and usually includes collecting several types of information in three primary categories:

wealth capacity, giving history, and connection to or interest in an organization or cause. Usually, prospecting is done with the goal of finding new donors or enhancing the probability of major gifts.

Discovering wealth capacity and history of giving is like going on a scavenger hunt. If the woman is a current donor, your organizational database is the logical place to begin. Documenting her pattern of giving includes amounts given and the causes she supports, her lifetime giving, and the types of gifts she prefers: annual, projects, or legacy. If she is not a current donor here are a few examples of resources a fundraiser can use to collect relevant information on donor prospects:

1. Review donor lists from other nonprofit organizations.
2. Read annual reports or publications from capital campaigns, nonprofits or foundations, seeking who the donors are and at what level they are giving.
3. Attend social functions to see the attendees—are your current donors or prospects there?
4. Watch the live auctions at fundraisers, noting the sponsoring organizations, families, companies, and who is bidding.
5. Read the lists of boards of directors of nonprofit and for-profit organizations.
6. Find out where your donor lives and if she is engaged with local schools or civic organizations.
7. Ask colleagues of the potential donor to share any insights into her wealth capacity or interests.
8. Research real estate transfers, news articles, business briefs, and the obituaries.
9. Google political donations, stock sales, and news stories about the prospect.
10. Use your board of directors, trustees or other committee members to help you brainstorm potential women prospects.
11. Review the list of members of civic organizations or neighborhood associations.
12. Research a prospect's connection to companies.
13. Purchase a wealth scan or data mining package to assess your current donors and prospects.
14. Explore the woman donor's history and life circumstances with her colleagues or acquaintances.

These sources, combined with conversations with your prospect about how she acquired her wealth and how she uses it, begin to create a pattern and picture of her philanthropy. When donors have capacity, the next critical question is does she have a connection and interest?

Interest is demonstrated by involvement with an organization or cause. The type of involvement and frequency may vary over a period of time from a long-time engagement to none at all. Discovering connection to or interest in an organization or cause can be assessed by finding the answers to these questions:

1. Is a donor serving on boards or volunteering at events?
2. How often and in what capacity?
3. Is she active or passive, a leader or an attendee?
4. Is she interested in one cause or many?
5. Why is she interested? What is her connection to the cause?
6. Does she steadily increase her involvement?
7. Is it consistent or sporadic?
8. Does she have friends within the organization or as other volunteers?
9. Does she have a relationship with any of the staff?
10. Has she visited your website, how often?
11. Is she connected on LinkedIn, Facebook, Instagram, or other social media?
12. Has she signed up for your newsletter?
13. Has she requested information about your organization?

Leslie Crutchfield, John Kania, and Mark Kramer in their well-known book, *Do More Than Give* discuss the two premises of catalytic philanthropy. The first and the one most relevant to donor assessment is, "Donors have something valuable to contribute beyond their money" (Crutchfield et al., 2011, p. 4). They go on to discuss how donors can use social position, influence, and power to create change and solve problems. In addition to serving on boards and committees, they act as catalysts for social change by leveraging the power of the private, nonprofit, and public sectors. This is not new information for a fundraiser, but often professionals don't spend enough time developing a plan for how to increase the engagement of donors on all levels.

Encouraging prospective women donors to give advice, offer suggestions, serve on a committee, or help staff build a network with other donors or organizations are all ways of leveraging a donor's capacity without ever mentioning money. Women have unique skills they bring to an organization. They are great networkers and relationship experts, they focus on collaboration and consensus building, and are usually better than men at coaching, mentoring, and teamwork. Asking them to use these skills as a volunteer fosters and deepens engagement.

Women traditionally have donated more of their time than men to community service and single women volunteer almost twice as many hours as men (Mesch et al., 2006). This means that women donors more often than men may have had the opportunity to serve on a committee, work on project, attend an event, or be a board member. Unfortunately, many nonprofits seek board members and volunteers who hold influential positions in the community. Given there are fewer women than men in these positions it is essential that a fundraiser look for women in nontraditional roles and spaces and ask them to serve and promote them into leadership roles.

A fundraiser would rarely ask a woman to donate to a cause without any previous connection to her or without having invited her to learn about the organization's mission. Rating the level of donor interest is based on frequency and type of engagement. A popular alignment tool is called the LAI, the Linkage, Ability, and Interest Inventory (Cannon, 2017). Based on similar data points as listed previously, the fundraising team researches how the prospect is *Linked* to your organization through friends or colleagues, as a former donor or committee member. *Ability* relates to the capacity to give a gift or what resources the donor has available for giving. *Interest* rates an individual's involvement in community issues, her passions, or connections to nonprofits. Donors are assigned points in each of these areas, the higher number indicating a greater level or frequency of linkage, higher capacity to give, etc.

Matrices may also be developed that assess additional criteria including job title, community networks, or connections to a specific industry. Jennifer Filla, President of Aspire Research Group, suggests that fundraisers try to limit the number of criteria to five or fewer (Filla, 2020). The higher rating you give each of these factors, the higher the probability that the donor prospect will be a good candidate for a philanthropic gift. As prospects are identified, fundraising staff can prioritize their work and contacts, focusing on the best prospects first. Here is an example (Table 5.1).

Finally, remember every fundraising tool is only as good as the people who use it. Donors are not widgets or tools, they are unique people. Employ some judgment, think about how intimately you know this donor, and ultimately what kind of connection and gift she might be interested in. Use your mind to gather the data and your heart to guide your approach.

Table 5.1 Rubric for Linkage, Ability and Interest

	Poor prospect 0	Marginal prospect 1	Fair/Average prospect 2	Good prospect 3	Ideal prospect 4	Score
Linkage						
Service	No history of volunteering or serving	Volunteers sporadically	Volunteers consistently	Desires to serve on a board or committee	Steadily increasing her involvement. Serves on board, committees	
Connections to cause or organization	Knows no one affiliated with cause or within the organization	Is friends with a volunteer and familiar with organization	Is active through social media with the cause and knows staff, volunteers	Is connected to someone within the organization and understands the cause	Is closely connected to staff, volunteers; requests and reads information	
Ability						
Time	Unable to give time due to other commitments	Expresses interest in giving time, but rarely follows through	Volunteers for the organization and causes occasionally	Offers time to a cause or org, committed to serving. Brings a skill set	Offers suggestions for ways to be involved. Gives time frequently	
Money	Has limited resources and is not a donor	Gives small amounts when asked	Donates regularly in small/moderate amounts to causes/org. Has modest resources	Gives generously to related causes/orgs. Has substantial resources	HNW, looking for useful ways to use it. Gives at a major gift/legacy level	

	Poor prospect	Marginal prospect	Fair/Average prospect	Good prospect	Ideal prospect
Interest					
Commitment	Neither donates nor attends events	Writes checks but rarely attends events	Regularly attends events, but is not actively involved	Regularly attends events and engages, participates	Leads events and plays an active role in engaging others to attend
Connection to cause/issue	Has no connection(s)	Is theoretically interested but not personally connected	Knows someone affected by the cause or issue	Has been directly affected by the cause or issue	Has a passion and personal interest in the causes/org

Total:

Bibliography

Aloni, E. (2018). The martial wealth gap. *Washington Law Review, 93*(1), 16–26.

Blouin, B. (1987). *For love and/or money: The impact of inherited wealth on relationships.* University Microfilms.

Brown, E. (2005). Married couples' charitable giving: Who and why. *New Directions for Philanthropic Fundraising, 50*, 69–80.

Callahan, D. (2017). *The givers.* Alfred Knopf.

Cannon, J. (2017, October 20). *Determining linkage, ability and interest (LAI) via CPD.* Retrieved January 26, 2020, from http://medium.com/@MaxMedia Group/determining-linkage-ability-and-interest-lai-via-cpd-34599257d5c2

Chang, M. L. (2010). *Shortchanged.* Oxford University Press.

Crutchfield, L., Kania, J., & Kramer, M. (2011). *Do more than give.* Jossey-Bass.

Filla, J. (2020, June 25). Why and how to cultivate women donors. *Chronicle of Philanthropy,* Webinar.

Fidelity Charitable. (2016). *How couples give: Fidelity charitable survey shows giving brings couples together, highlights importance of discussing values.* Boston, MA.

Giving USA Foundation. (2020). *Giving USA: 2020—The annual report on philanthropy for the year 2019.*

Gunter, M. (2019). Good intentions. *The Chronicle of Philanthropy.* Retrieved June 21, 2020, updated information from http://givingpledge.org

Hirsch, A. (2011). *Freedom of Testation/Freedom of Contract,* 95 MINN. L. REV. 2180, 2182 n.7 ("Economic studies have found that a large fraction [possibly in the range of eighty percent] of household wealth in the United States traces to gifts and inheritances, as opposed to participation in the labor economy").

Houser, A. N. (2007). Women and long-term care. Retrieved December 26, 2021, from https://www.aarp.org/home-garden/livable-communities/info-2007/fs77r_ltc.html

Livingston, G. (2013). *Chapter 2: The demographics of remarriage.* Pew Research Center. Retrieved May 3, 2019, from https://www.pewresearch.org/social-trends/2014/11/14/chapter-2-the-demographics-of-remarriage

Merrill-Lynch. (2019). *Women and financial wellness: Beyond the bottom line. A Merrill Lynch study conducted in partnership with Age Wave.* Bank of America Corporation.

Mesch, D., Osili, U., Pactor, A., Ackerman, J., Bergdoll, J., Kalugyer, A. D., Scholl, J., Ware, A., Hyatte, C., Dale, E., Hawash, R., & Yang, Y. (2015). *Do women give more? Findings on three unique data sets on charitable giving.* Women's Philanthropy Institute.

Mesch, D. J., Rooney, P. M., Steinberg, K. S., & Denton, B. (2006). The effects of race, gender and marital status on giving and volunteering in Indiana. *Nonprofit and Voluntary Sector Quarterly, 35*(4), 565–587.

Mesch, D., Osili, U., Ackerman, J., Bergdoll, J., Skidmore, T., & Sager, J. (2021). *Women give 2021: How households make giving decisions*. Women's Philanthropy Institute.

Miller, C. C. (2021, May 23). What women lost. *The New York Times*. Retrieved April 22, 2019, from https://www.nytimes.com/interactive/2021/05/17/upshot/women-workforce-employment-covid.html

Rendon, J., & Di Mento, M. (2020, February). *Billion-Dollar giving streak*. Chronicle of Philanthropy.

Robehmed, N. (2018, August 31). Money for nothing …and the clicks for free. *Forbes, 201*(6), 67–72.

Ryan, C. (2005). From cradle to grave: Challenges and opportunities of inherited wealth. In E. Clift (Ed.), *Women, philanthropy, and social change: Visions for a just society* (1st ed., pp. 183–200). Tufts University Press.

Statistics Times. (2020). Retrieved December 23, 2021, from https://statisticstimes.com/demographics/country/us-sex-ratio.php

RBC Wealth Management. (2018). *The new face of wealth and legacy: How women are redefining wealth, giving, and legacy planning*. Retrieved February 14, 2020, from https://www.rbcwealthmanagement.com/en-us/insights/the-new-face-of-wealth-and-legacy-how-women-are-redefining-wealth-giving-and-legacy-planning

U.S. Bureau of Labor Statistics. (2021). *Table 39: Median weekly earnings of full-time wage and salary workers by detailed occupations and sex* (Data Set). Labor Force Statistics from the Current Population Survey.

Wasley, P. (2009, May 19). Women take the lead in couples' charitable giving decisions. *Chronicle of Philanthropy*.

6

Assessment: Is Your Organization Ready for a Women's Philanthropy Initiative?

United Way Worldwide is the largest privately funded nonprofit organization, consisting of nearly 1,800 autonomous charities spanning forty countries on six continents and serving 48 million people annually. Founded by a woman, Frances Wisebart Jacobs, a priest, two ministers, and a rabbi in 1887 in Denver, Colorado, the vision for the organization was to collect funds for local charities, coordinate relief services, distribute grants, promote collaboration, and respond to changing community needs in the areas of health, education, human services, and economic stability (United Way, 2021). The *federated charity model* has members or chapters that operate as individual nonprofits—the local United Way organization in your community. The model allows 7.7 million donors to give a charitable contribution through a payroll deduction or directly to any United Way. These donations are combined with contributions from 45,000 corporate partners and distributed to multiple nonprofits. Through coordinated fundraising the organization has been able to distribute billions of dollars to local communities.

Listed as America's #1 Favorite Charity in the 2019 *Chronicle of Philanthropy* list (Stiffman & Haynes, 2019), this 133-year-old fundraising giant continually reinvents itself to address the changing tides of donors' interests, new technologies, and competition from more than 1.5 million other nonprofits in the U.S. One of these reinventions occurred twenty years ago when organizational leadership recognized how many women were in their donor base and developed an *affinity group model* originally called the Women's Leadership Council. Affinity groups are subsets of donors aligned

© The Author(s), under exclusive license to Springer Nature Switzerland AG 2022, corrected publication 2022
L. A. Buntz, *Generosity and Gender*,
https://doi.org/10.1007/978-3-030-90380-0_6

by demographic factor, contribution level, or professional affiliation. Many United Way chapters developed women's affinity groups during this time, but did not truly recognize their potential.

In 2014, the United Way of Greater Los Angeles (UWGLA) found a startling statistic in data from United Way Worldwide. Compared to the prior decade, fundraising across the federated charity was mostly flat, but donations via women's affinity groups had increased more than 170% (O'Neil, 2016). A staff was assigned to develop a five-year plan for the Women's Leadership Council. Within two years, the UWGLA held an event for 1,000 Women's Leadership Council attendees and raised $600,000.

Today, the Women's Leadership Councils within United Way World-wide have rebranded as *Women United*. These affinity groups have more than 70,000 members in 165 communities across six countries. Since 2002, *Women United* has raised $2 billion. It remains one of the most successful fundraising sectors within the United Way system.

Integrating a women's philanthropy initiative into the existing network of annual campaigns required commitment to empowering women, and a concentrated effort on the part of leadership. Women were connected to each other through professional and social groups. They selected causes they wanted to support, and worked in collaboration with United Way staff to determine how much each woman would contribute. Although *Women United* operates slightly differently in each United Way chapter, the cumulative success of the initiative is stunning. It has added new donors, revenue and volunteers, and helped to create solutions to many community-based problems including reducing teen pregnancy in Milwaukee, Wisconsin, increasing women's economic stability in San Francisco, California, and improving children's early literacy rates in Ft. Lauderdale, Florida. *Women United* affinity groups have grown more in membership and contributions than any other affinity group within the United Way system.

Michelle Branch, an attorney in San Francisco and current volunteer chair of *Women United* Global Leadership Council, shared these thoughts about its success.

The *Women United* brand brought many diverse women together under one umbrella. It has been successful because women want to be part of something bigger. There is an advantage to being part of a large network. You can share knowledge, expertise, and use data to make informed decisions. United Way has moved to an impact model, one that recognizes the power of women as community leaders who can create policy change. I'm proud of my work with United Way Worldwide to develop and highlight pathways that women can use to advocate to their local, state, and federal elected officials. At my local United

Way Bay Area, I've been focused on reducing income inequality, increasing the affordable housing supply, and providing healthcare for all (Branch, personal communication, March 5, 2020).

Several other national nonprofit organizations have launched successful women's philanthropy initiatives, including the American Cancer Society, American Heart Association, and the American Red Cross. Symbolism, color schemes, and effective media campaigns were key elements when the American Cancer Society and Susan B. Komen Foundation wanted to raise awareness about breast cancer in 1982. Charlotte Haley, a breast cancer survivor, originated the concept of a peach colored cancer awareness ribbon and started to raise funds through a grassroots campaign. In 1992, Alexandra Penny, editor in chief of *Self* magazine, wanted to collaborate with Haley to further promote the cause, but Haley rejected her offer as being too commercial (Fernandez, 1998). In an effort to put the Breast Cancer Awareness Month issue of the magazine over the top, Penny changed the color to pink and enlisted cosmetics companies to distribute them to New York City stores. The pink ribbon was born. Awareness about breast cancer grew and so did financial support for breast cancer research. Community walks and events annually educate thousands of women about the disease, encouraging them to take preventive action and seek treatment. The number of women donors has increased significantly.

In 2004, the American Heart Association (AHA) recognized that nearly half-a-million women suffered annually from cardiovascular disease and strokes. A special initiative was created to reach women donors with the dual goal of education and financial support for research. The *Go Red for Women* movement symbolized by a red dress became an instant hit. Luncheons and fundraising events educate women, connect members who have experienced heart disease, and build networks of supporters or family members of survivors. The American Heart Association (2021) added *Men Go Red* in the past several years to engage male donors. Today, *Go Red for Women* is active in most major American cities and in 50 countries. Macy's Department Store, the primary sponsor, has raised more than $69 million to fund research and build awareness.

The American Red Cross started its own women's giving efforts in 2006. The Tiffany Circle requires each woman to give an annual $10,000 donation to support Red Cross local priorities. The Circle is named after the Louis Comfort Tiffany stained-glass windows at the charity's national headquarters in Washington, DC. The windows were commissioned by women on both sides of the Mason-Dixon line as an act of reconciliation after the Civil

War. By 2016, Tiffany Circle membership had climbed to 800 with donations totaling $7.7 million (O'Neill, 2016).

These are a few examples of how large-scale national nonprofits have integrated specific women's philanthropy initiatives into their pre-existing fundraising models. The secret to these successes is understanding how women practice philanthropy, dedicating time and resources to the effort, and carving out specific strategies and programs that engage, excite, and inspire women donors. They treat women as unique and special donors by addressing their needs and interests.

Incorporating women's philanthropy into smaller nonprofits may be more challenging. With limited staff, communications, and technology resources, smaller nonprofits need to scale their programs to fit within their organizational structures. But, developing a program is not impossible. Any organization, regardless of size, can build a women's philanthropy initiative.

Women's Philanthropy—Unique and Integrated

Every organization that engages in fundraising currently works with women donors, even if they are not defined as a separate and unique subset of your philanthropic base. But, prior to the development of a women's philanthropy initiative, organizational staff need to think about women donors as both wholly integrated into organizational structures and systems *and* unique. It's a situation of and/both.

Using Systems Theory to understand and assess your organization's readiness to develop a women's initiative is a good place to start. Systems Theory, originally developed by biologist Ludwig von Bertalanffy in the 1940s has been used as a model to understand science, business, medicine, environments, and the sociological study of organizations. It proposes that rather than reducing an entity to its parts or elements, focus should be on the arrangement and relations between the parts (Heylighen & Josley, 1992). One easy way to understand Systems Theory is to think about your body as a system. None of the systems within your body (nervous, digestive, cognitive) can function independently; each part is connected in some way to the other systems. Just like our bodies, organizations are complex systems. What happens in one part of the system affects other parts. It is all interconnected and interacting constantly. Thus, in an organization, no basic function, department or program exists independently of any other (Heylighen & Josley, 1992).

When staff think about beginning a women's philanthropy initiative, remember that integrating a new program for women donors or modifying the operations within an existing fund development department to incorporate a women's initiative will impact the other parts of the organization in varying degrees. Consider the following example:

When Dr. Sally Mason was appointed President of the University of Iowa (UI) in 2007, she brought with her a history of engaging women in philanthropy. Prior to coming to UI, Mason had served as Provost at Purdue University and had a distinguished career as a scientist, educator, and administrator. During her tenure at Purdue, Mason realized that many of the women students and alumnae felt very isolated in the male-dominated professions of science and biology. She had experienced this herself. Knowing that there were great alumnae who had the potential to give, but weren't being asked, she partnered with the university foundation staff and helped Purdue complete a successful $1.7 billion campaign. Today at Purdue, there are special programs designed for women donors, including the Science for Women Purdue Giving Circle.

At the University of Iowa, Mason was delighted to find a seasoned fundraising professional leading the foundation, Lynette Marshall. In an effort to reach out to women donors, she suggested to Marshall that they invite 8–10 women donors to a weekend retreat. During the retreat the women discussed issues they cared about, their philanthropic journeys, and how they could become engaged both as volunteers and funders. Women were ready to talk and Marshall and Mason were ready to listen., "We talked about the responsibility of stepping up and being at the table as professionals" (Mason, personal communication, February 17, 2020). Mason recalls the friendly conversations leading to creative ideas about women funding scholarships or other special projects at the university. After President Mason left the university, the women's retreats were discontinued and Marshall pursued other strategies to engage women donors.

From a systems perspective, the UI and Purdue experiences reflect different strategies. At Purdue there wasn't a formal strategy of working with women donors and Mason capitalized on the opportunity to lead an initiative as an alumna, scientist, and administrator. She knew the women students and alumnae needed an advocate and convinced the foundation staff to integrate the women's philanthropy initiative into their existing systems. By targeting women in science, a specific subset of donors could be nurtured. She helped women align with a cause and she found an advocate within the foundation to lead the effort and support its continuance.

At UI there was a strong foundation of working with women donors prior to Mason's arrival. There was an existing advocate for women through Marshall's role as Foundation President and there was not a specific subset of women donors to align with a cause. Mason's interest in listening to women's stories prompted ideas and new partnerships, but not the need for a new initiative. Marshall's decision to strengthen the current system and work within it rather than to introduce another initiative that would need tending and leadership made the most strategic sense (Marshall, personal communication, February 14, 2018).

These experiences demonstrate how different approaches and thoughtful planning are all necessary as organizations consider creating women's philanthropy initiatives. In *Women's Philanthropy on Campus*, the Women's Philanthropy Institute found that separate niche programs designed specifically for women donors, but not integrated into the organizational fund development plan and organizational systems, fail for a variety of reasons:

- A mid-level manager (most often a woman) creates the initiative and the institution marginalizes it.
- When the mid-level manager leaves, the institutional knowledge about the program leaves with her.
- The institution fails to invest long-term in the human and financial capital needed to build the program.
- The program is maintained in isolation and not integrated into the total development strategy.
- Development staff see the women's philanthropy initiative as competition to ongoing efforts, such as annual fundraising or alumni giving (Mesch & Pactor, 2009).

So, how does an organization determine if a women's philanthropy initiative is the right fit for their organization? The first step is to conduct an organizational assessment. This process helps staff examine the resources and challenges that exist within their current system, learn about the issues that impact women's philanthropy, engage stakeholders, and outline possible program options.

The Elements of an Assessment

The following graphic illustrates the essential ingredients in an assessment: what needs to be assessed, by whom, your role as a fundraiser, and a reminder that women donors are at the center of the work (Fig. 6.1).

Assessments are instruments used to inform, educate, enlighten, challenge, and inspire organizational staff. Based on the information collected, decisions can be made based on facts and feedback; actions can be contemplated and implemented. Clearly identifying the purpose and goals of the assessment helps structure the work and determines the depth and breadth of the assessment process.

There are three primary elements to an assessment:

- What to Ask? What information is needed and why is it important?
- Who to Ask? Who should be involved in the process?
- How to Ask? How will information be obtained?

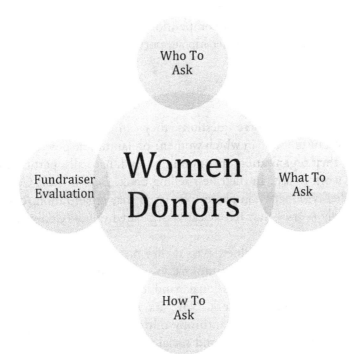

Fig. 6.1 The organizational assessment

What to Ask? Vision, Values, Mission, Culture

Start with the end in mind. Visions are aspirational; a future state built on the current successes and strengths of the organization. What does the organization envision as a result of a women's philanthropy initiative? Think about this difficult question throughout the assessment process, returning to it often as information is gathered, feedback provided, and the vision refined.

Vision: Here Is a List of Questions to Consider

1. What is the vision for your organization?
2. What is the vision for the women's philanthropy initiative?
3. Why, specifically does the organization wish to develop one?
4. Are there compelling reasons to do so; what are they?
5. Does the vision for a women's philanthropy initiative fit within the organizational vision?
6. Describe how they align with each other.
7. Would they be in conflict or competition with each other?
8. Does the organizational leadership support developing an initiative?

Values

As participants ponder these questions, they can dream, hope, be creative, and imagine a future state in which women's philanthropic power is fully realized within their organization or community. And, naturally, participants will want their work to last. In their best-selling book, *Built to Last*, Collins and Porras studied visionary companies observing that organizations/companies last specifically *because* they have clearly articulated values (Collins & Porras, 1994).

All organizations have values, even if they are not written or articulated. Ask a staff member for an organizational value and they will usually describe several found in most organizational handbooks: respect, honesty, innovation, excellence, and/or teamwork. Now, ask yourself, what values would be consistent with a women's philanthropy initiative? Gender equity, diversity, cultural awareness or sensitivity, and social impact are a few that may come to mind. Engage staff in a discussion about the interactions they have had with women donors, both positive and negative. What did they learn? What could be improved?

At times our personal and professional values are so embedded in our lives that it is difficult to verbally describe them, but behaviorally they are explicit; do staff treat women donors differently from men? If so, how?

Mission Statement

Among "What-to-ask" questions are those re-examining your organization's mission statement. A good mission statement describes both what your organization is here to do, and how it does its work. Most mission statements are vague; few truly articulate the true nature of the work of an organization. Write a mission statement for a women's philanthropy initiative. Then, ask, does it fit within the organization's mission? Why or why not? Here are a few good examples of mission statements from organizations that work with women donors.

> We connect with changemakers across sectors to spark powerful collaborations and build strong partnerships. We drive exponential change, not just incremental impact, to accelerate progress toward a gender equal world. (Women Moving Millions, 2021)
>
> The Women's Philanthropy Institute increases understanding of women's philanthropy through rigorous research and education-interpreting and sharing our insights broadly to improve philanthropy. (Women's Philanthropy Institute, 2021)

To encourage philanthropy, leadership and mentoring of the next generation, Women and Philanthropy at UCLA seeks to:

- Engage and educate women philanthropists through programmatic activities that highlight the diversity of achievement at UCLA.
- Broaden and deepen the base of financial support by women at UCLA.
- Cultivate and mentor women as philanthropists and leaders and provide them with a personal connection to the University and the tools to be successful.
- Identify and support programs at UCLA that reflect the varied interests of women.
- Advocate on behalf of women's leadership across the campus on boards, committees and the UCLA Foundation.
- Embrace a Culture of Diversity, Equity, Inclusion, and Access that encourages, supports and advocates for the diverse voices of our members and builds pathways to philanthropy for women from all backgrounds (UCLA, Women and Philanthropy, 2021).

Culture

Edgar Schein the author of *Organizational Culture and Leadership*, describes culture as "a pattern of basic assumptions, invented, discovered, or developed by a given group as it learns to cope with problems of external adaptation and internal integration." There are three different levels that can be examined in relation to organizational culture: level 1, artifacts; level 2, espoused values; level 3, underlying assumptions (Schein 2004). Level 3 is where the power of organizational culture can be found. What is your organization's culture? The best way to answer this question, is to ask what is the organization's personality? Is it structured or innovative, creative or rule bound, collaborative or independent?

Within organizations that have philanthropy as a key part of their mission, a culture of philanthropy should be embedded in the whole organization. However, fundraising is often viewed as the task that belongs only to the fundraising staff. Yet, when there is a culture of philanthropy within the organization, everyone in the organization thinks about philanthropy and how they can help engage donors in their mission.

Does your organization have a culture of embracing diversity or of gender sensitivity? Who is approached for contributions and why are these donors chosen? Is there a culture of including women in all aspects of the organization including serving on the board, committees, leading campaigns, being featured in publications or given awards?

A prominent woman philanthropist in the Midwest described her experiences with some fundraisers. "They don't seek *me* out. People go to my husband first, and if he says no, they come to me thinking, *she's an easy touch*. It's not true. I want to see the results of the money: how is it spent, how much goes to administration and how much to the participants?" This couple has significant resources and their wealth is the result of the husband's business. What fundraisers should know is that the wife is an equal partner in their philanthropic decision-making and she is led as much by her head as her heart. Naïve and inaccurate assessments of her role hindered some organizations' abilities to form a relationship and obtain a gift.

Think about how your staff talk about, think about, and recognize women donors. What assumptions underlie the practices that have been used previously to work with women donors? How does the staff determine which donors to lead the board, special projects, or programs? It's difficult to assess all the aspects of an organization's culture, but these are a few questions that can prompt robust discussion.

Finally, it is helpful to test your reality with objective outside observers. Ask donors and volunteers who are <u>not</u> in your organization for feedback about your work. Then, collect data that will help support or negate staff assumptions. These practices help bring a more realistic assessment to the philanthropic culture within the organization.

Martha Taylor, former Vice President at the University of Wisconsin Foundation, explains that when she was developing the foundation's fundraising program it was perceived that alumni would be the main contributors and a large percentage of the alumni body was women. But approaching women donors was not part of the Foundation's culture. "There were underlying assumptions that women would not give large gifts and deferred to their husbands in decisions" (Taylor, personal communication, March 24, 2020). Through her long-standing work with women donors she knew these assumptions were faulty. She embarked on a campaign to raise money to help fund the School of Human Ecology by asking women donors each to give a $100,000 contribution. One hundred women responded. Today, a beautiful stained-glass wall showcases those 100 women—a testament to the power of women and their giving. The School of Human Ecology is the first building on the campus named in honor of a woman philanthropist, Nancy Johnson Nicholas, a 1955 graduate of the school.

Who to Ask—Key Stakeholders

Stakeholders are those individuals and groups who have a vested interest in the organization, participate in its operations or will be impacted by it. Four core groups should be asked for feedback: organizational staff, volunteers, community partners, and donors.

1. Organizational staff includes key leadership, fundraising staff, support, and communications experts. Create integrated groups by mixing disciplines, genders, ages and ethnicities, if possible, allowing staff to hear the perceptions, visions, and concerns about developing a women's philanthropy initiative from others within the organization.
2. Board members and key volunteers need to provide input about their experiences and perceptions of the organization's current work with donors. These individuals can reflect on the organization's strengths, challenges, and proven or unproven capacity and ability to integrate new programs.

3. Community stakeholders or critical partners such as funding partners, foundations, and programs within the community that serve women provide perspectives from the outside looking in.
4. Most importantly, you need to hear from current women contributors to your organization or to other organizations within your community.

A designated leader within the organization can assemble these groups, but having an outside facilitator lead the process and structure the discussions can be very helpful in providing objective perceptions and analysis. Meeting with each of these groups separately allows the leader or facilitator to ask questions that are the most meaningful to the members.

How to Ask? Getting the Information You Need

Think about creating multiple ways for stakeholders to provide information about their experiences, visions, concerns, and support. The most successful options are focus groups, personal interviews, surveys, questionnaires, and social media campaigns. The choice of methods is determined by the amount of resources available. Focus groups and personal interviews will provide the most robust information, but take a considerable amount of time and can only reach a limited number of people. Questionnaires, surveys, or social media inquiries will reach a broader range of participants, but the data is limited to written responses. Consider engaging the services of an experienced researcher to assist in developing these instruments and evaluating the collected data.

Database and Technology Analysis

Subjective information gathered through verbal feedback, opinions, perceptions, and discussions is truly valuable in helping to develop awareness among staff about an organization's previous engagement and work with women as well as identifying whether there is genuine interest in pursuing a women's philanthropy initiative. The next step is to gather objective information through a data analysis that helps develop a baseline of the organization's work with donors, and assess its technological capacity. Here are some data points that are essential to gather.

1. How many women donors are in the pool of the organization's donors?
2. What is their history and level of contributions?

3. How many new women donors join your organization each year?
4. How are they recruited?
5. Do they give as an individual or a couple?
6. How do you recognize women in your data system?
7. If women donors have left your organization, do you know why?
8. What name and salutation are used for mailings? (Remember, some data bases used for fundraising do not recognize the spouse, or address the couple as the donor, rather than individuals).
9. What causes do women support?
10. How do they like to get information?
11. Do you have a wealth scan for women donors? What does it tell you?
12. How many contacts do you have with women donors? What type?
13. Who among the staff has the best connections to women donors or women's networks?
14. Does your database have the ability to integrate and track information for a women's initiative?

   Having database experts help in this part of the assessment process is critical. Once the information is collected, it should offer some insights into the organization's current and future pool of women donors. What does the information tell you about your work with women donors?

Communication Analysis

Another aspect of an organizational assessment is a communication and marketing analysis. This is the public face of the organization. It's how information is communicated to the general public as well as to donors, clients, and customers. What stories do your communication materials tell about the organization's work, especially with women? One method of accomplishing this is to have individuals from outside your organization look at your publication materials, website, social media, and any other form of public communication. Ask them to assess the visual materials answering the following questions:

1. How are women recognized in your communications materials?
2. Are they featured as donors? Volunteers? Committee members? Chairs or leaders of campaigns or community projects? Are they given awards?
3. Are they featured as part of a couple, or as individuals? Is the representation accurate?

4. What faces do you see when you look at the website, brochure(s), or social media?
5. Are women of diverse backgrounds featured?
6. Are women spokespeople for the organization as often as are men?
7. Are women encouraged to be donors? If so, how?

Actually counting the number of times women are recognized or featured compared to all donors or customers may provide a perspective of their importance in your organizational story. There is no standard benchmark to achieve, but the exercise itself may be enlightening as the staff review communication materials and begin to analyze how choices have been made in the past, and what could change in the future as they think about the universe of women donors.

Human Resources

Philanthropy is built on relationships. Building a women's philanthropy initiative will depend on several key human resources—organizational leadership and trained fundraising staff. It is critical that organizational leadership fully support and embrace these initiatives through verbal and financial commitments and delegated staff. Fundraisers have to be willing to engage in training and to re-educate themselves about working with women donors, adjusting their traditional strategies, listening to women donors, and adding new tools to their array of fundraising techniques. Other staff who will be interacting with women donors will need additional training about how to work with a diverse range of donors while being sensitive to their varying styles of practicing philanthropy. Who on your staff has the best relationship with women donors? Why does that person relate well to women? Do your organizational policies and practices reflect a diversity, inclusion, and equity lens?

Questions for Community Stakeholders

Assessing the organization's role in the philanthropic community helps to determine if the development of a women's philanthropy initiative is the right decision. After assembling community partners, begin by asking if other organizations have programs designed specifically for women donors. Providing some data on the potential of women's financial capacity and research that supports why this topic is important can be enlightening. How would community leaders or other organizations react if a women's philanthropy initiative were developed? Does the community environment support this type of work? Is there a primary funder/sponsor that would be interested in collaborating, or a foundation that could support your work with women? What organizations within your community are doing similar work? Is there an existing initiative that could be used as a model?

Gathering this information will help the organization determine if this is a niche that needs to be filled or is duplicative. Perhaps it would open the door for new partnerships. When United Ways embarked on developing *Women United*, some chapters partnered with local women's foundations or community foundations. Women's foundations had data about the needs of women in the community that could be used to encourage women donors to give to many different nonprofits. Smaller United Ways with limited administrative capacity used community foundations as the administrative agent for their *Women's United* programs. Although there is always an element of competition for donors, community conversations are usually enlightening, and open the door to new partnerships while relaying the importance of women's philanthropy.

Questions for Women Donors/Volunteers

Asking women to share their personal philanthropic experiences is essential and can be extremely insightful as women's philanthropic initiatives are developed. One of the questions used while interviewing women philanthropists for this book was, "Describe your best and worst philanthropic experience." Fortunately, the majority of donors had positive memorable experiences. Negative experiences focused on the donor's embarrassment when her contributions were made public without her consent, occasions when donors felt pressured to give, or were placed in competition with other women. How do you like to be recognized? What types of information about the organization or cause do you want to receive? Are you interested in developing or participating in a women's philanthropy initiative or project? What do you like about working with other women? What could the organization do to improve our connections with women?

Other useful points of inquiry for the woman donor are: Describe your interactions with staff. Share your perception of the organization's work with women and for women. Who do you identify as your key supporter within the organization? What would be your vision for a women's philanthropy initiative? Why would it work or not? What would the organization need to do differently if it incorporated a women's philanthropy initiative?

The Fundraiser's Role and Self-Evaluation

The fundraiser has three roles when working with women donors. The first is to learn about how women practice philanthropy in order to understand their capacity and to develop specific strategies that will engage and steward them. The second role is to educate others within the organization about women donors and how to work with them. Thirdly, fundraisers must assess how to integrate women's philanthropy into an organization or fundraising department. Simone Joyaux, an author and fund development expert says that fundraisers need to be organizational specialists, or people who "understand how and why an organization's infrastructure affects all of its activities, fund development included. The most effective fundraisers pay attention to corporate culture, respect systems, and learn about group behavior. These highly competent fundraisers are change agents. They assess fund development by looking at everything else in the organization—maybe even first" (Joyaux, 2011).

Assessing your organization's capacity to work with women donors can be a humbling process. Most nonprofits engage in fundraising techniques that were developed over time by philanthropy professionals and have become established as accepted "best practices." These practices do not have to be cast aside, but rather modified to meet the needs of women donors.

Good fundraisers come in all genders, ages, and ethnicities. Women want and like to work with a wide variety of fundraisers, but especially appreciate professionals who have an interest and desire to helping them learn about philanthropy and grow as a giver. What matters are an individual's perceptions about women, interactions with them, understanding of how they practice philanthropy, and most importantly, a desire to partner with them and help them find their philanthropic passions.

Good fundraisers know that relationships are at the core of their work. Dale Carnegie, the famous self-help guru, is reported to have said, "You'll have more fun and success when you stop trying to get what you want and start helping other people get what they want" (Joyaux, 2011). Put your donors first and listen to them. Here is a brief self-evaluation for fundraisers interested in this work.

1. What education, experiences or other characteristics make you a good candidate to work within a women's philanthropy program?
2. Think about an early childhood experience you had with a female relative, teacher, or friend that established some of your beliefs about women's philanthropy. What are those beliefs? Write them down.
3. What experiences have you had in your education or professional career that influenced your ideas about women and their philanthropy? Describe them and what you learned.
4. Think about your beliefs about how women learn about and understand financial matters. Is there any gender bias about women's knowledge base? What has informed your beliefs? What are your beliefs and attitudes about financial management and wealth accumulation?
5. Have you observed fundraisers treating men and women donors differently? If so, what was the situation and your interpretation of it?
6. Do you have different perceptions of women's philanthropy based on the woman's age, marital status, education, or experiences? Do you believe there are generational differences? If so, what might they be?
7. What would you uniquely bring to a women's philanthropy initiative that would make you a valuable fundraiser?
8. Why would you want to work within a women's philanthropy initiative?
9. Women's philanthropy is about leadership, investments, and advocacy. Which would you be the most interested in? Why?
10. What do you want to learn about women's philanthropy and why?
11. What is your vision for a women's philanthropy initiative?
12. How does your vision for an initiative align with your personal values and vision?

Finally, as organizational leaders think about the investment of building a women's philanthropy initiative remember this observation, "The work of nonprofit organizations has shifted in the past several decades from investing in program replication, to building organizational capacity, to serving as catalytic agents of change" (Crutchfield & Grant, 2008). The shift that Crutchfield and Grant mentions mirrors what women donors want—to make a difference in their community. Women have the power and resources to create change and make a difference, if they are organized and encouraged. Women's philanthropy initiatives are one avenue to achieve that goal.

Bibliography

American Heart Association. (2021). *Milestones*. Retrieved May 21, 2019, from https://www.Goredforwomen.org/en/about-go-red-for-women

Collins, J. C., & Porras, J. I. (1994). *Built to last*. Harper Business. Harper Collins Publishing.

Crutchfield, L. R., & Grant, H. M. (2008). *Forces of Good*. Jossey Bass.

Fernandez, S. (1998). History of the pink ribbon: Pretty in pink. *Think before you pick.org a project of the Breast Cancer Society*. Retrieved February 22, 2019, from http://thinkbeforeyoupink.org/resources/history-of-the-pink-ribbon

Filla, J. (2020, June 25). Why and how to cultivate women donors. *Chronicle of Philanthropy*. Webinar.

Heylighen, F., & Josley, C. (1992). *What is systems theory*, principia cybernetica web. Prepared for the Cambridge dictionary. Cambridge University Press.

Joyaux, S. (2011). *Strategic fund development*. Wiley.

Mesch, D., & Pactor, A., (2009). Women's philanthropy on campus. The women's philanthropy institute. Retrieved August 3, 2021, from http://hdl.handle.net/1805/6261.

O'Neil, M. (2016). Women primed to give big—If nonprofits are willing to change. *Chronicle of Philanthropy*. Washington, DC.

Schein, E. H. (2004). *Organizational culture and leadership* (3rd ed.). Jossey Bass.

Stiffman, E., & Haynes, E. (2019, November 8). Can the boom times last? America's favorite charities. *Chronicle of Philanthropy* (based on cash support). Washington, DC.

Teegarden, P. H., Hinden, D. R., & Sturm, P. (2011). *The nonprofit organizational culture guide*. Jossey-Bass.

United Way. (2021). Retrieved May 1, 2021, from https://www.unitedway.org/about/history

Women and Philanthropy at UCLA. (2021). Retrieved May 2, 2021, from https://women.support.ucla.ed/index/home/philanthropoy/mission/

Women Moving Millions. (2021). Retrieved May 24, 2021, from https://womenmovingmillions.org

Women's Philanthropy Institute. (2021). Retrieved March 10, 2021, from https://philanthropy.iupui.edu/institutes/womens-philanthropy-institute/index.html

7

Alignment: Helping Donors Find Their Passion

Aligning a donor's wealth with her charitable interests and values takes time, patience, and knowledge on the part of a fund development professional. It doesn't happen quickly or easily, but when it does, it's truly magic. Because there is a positive relationship between giving money, or volunteering time to others and the well-being of the giver, alignment is what makes philanthropy a joyful and memorable experience for both donor and fundraiser (Konrath, 2014/2016, pp. 287–426). Volunteering and giving to charitable organizations results in increased psychological well-being, enriched social relationships, and better physical health (Konrath & Brown, 2012). Only recently have researchers explored whether men and women experience the joy of giving differently, or if the impact of giving on overall happiness varies by gender. This chapter will help answer those questions and focus on two key strategies for alignment: identification of a donor's values and understanding her wealth capacity.

Charitable Giving and Life Satisfaction: Does Gender Matter?

The terms life satisfaction, happiness, and well-being are sometimes used interchangeably. The following research conducted by the Women's Philanthropy Institute focuses on life satisfaction using the definition "an overall assessment of feelings and attitudes about one's life at a particular point

© The Author(s), under exclusive license to Springer Nature
Switzerland AG 2022, corrected publication 2022
L. A. Buntz, *Generosity and Gender*,
https://doi.org/10.1007/978-3-030-90380-0_7

in time ranging from positive to negative" (Prasoon & Chaturvedi, 2016, pp. 25–32). Here are some of the findings.

- *Giving makes us happy.* Giving to charitable organizations is positively related to life satisfaction. The more a household gives as a percentage of income, the higher the household's life satisfaction (Mesch et al., 2017, pp. 5, 18).
- *Changes in giving habits affect men and women differently.* Single men see the biggest increase in satisfaction when they become donors. For single and married women, satisfaction increases most when they increase their giving (Mesch et al., 2017, p. 5).
- *When women drive charitable decisions, more giving means more satisfaction.* In households where either the woman makes charitable decisions or spouses make them jointly, life satisfaction increases with the percentage of household income given to charity (Mesch et al., 2017, p. 5).
- *This impact is greater in lower and middle-income households.* For households where charitable decisions are driven by women and more than 2% of their income is given to charity, households making less than $100,000 annually experience more boost in life satisfaction than those making $100,000 or more (Mesch et al., 2017, p. 5).

So, if giving makes us happy, increases our life satisfaction, and positively impacts the lives of women and their households, how can fundraisers help women align their values, interests, passions, and aspirations with their wealth capacities? The fundraiser's task is to learn as much as possible about these elements and to guide the donor, helping her discover how to strategically use her wealth to achieve her aspirations while fueling her passion for specific causes.

What Do Women Care About?

Jacki Zehner, the former Chief Engagement Officer for Women Moving Millions once said, "Women want money not so much for what it can buy, but rather for what it can do. They want to provide for their family, but also be in service to others" (Zehner, personal communication, November 17, 2017). Women care about their families, communities, and nonprofit causes. They care about other women. They know that investing in the future of families and the community will pay high dividends in the long term. The Center for Talent Innovations (CTI) surveyed nearly 6,000 investors in the

U.S. and five international locations and found that fully 90% of women in the global sample said making a positive impact on society is important (Hewlett et al., 2014). Seventy-nine percent of women versus 62% of men want to invest in organizations that invest in social good, and women are 48% more likely than men to want to invest in alleviating poverty (Turner Moffitt, 2015, p. 51). Women are 88% more likely to donate to education charities and 46% more likely than men to want to invest in initiatives that improve education or access to it (Turner Moffit, 2015, p. 51). The environment is another priority for women, and they are 25% more likely to invest in this agenda (Turner Moffit, 2015). Finally, women want to invest in the future of women. Overall, 77% of women in the CTI survey wanted to invest in companies or organizations with diversity in leadership (Hewlett et al., 2014).

As women continue to acquire financial resources, they begin to identify key areas of interests that align with their philanthropic choices. The Women's Philanthropy Institute surveyed a small sampling of HNW women who had made significant gifts to support women and girls and found that these women had similar philanthropy journeys: (1) they learned about philanthropy early in life, (2) they made small, but meaningful gifts as adults, (3) they acquired more wealth, (4) they educated themselves about giving and (5) they made multi-million-dollar commitments (Mesch et al., 2018, p. 13). Many of these women selected investments in women and girls because they had observed or experienced the injustices and inequities women face and identified with the challenges women encounter as they mature and enter the work force.

When women think about making philanthropic investments, they want to know that their gift makes a difference and has an impact. Some of their giving may be short term and transactional in nature, but over time and with greater awareness of their personal values, they can move into a deeper level of philanthropy, one that is truly transformational for themselves and others. One of the tasks of the fundraiser is to help women clarify and prioritize the values that drive their decision-making in all areas of life and will ultimately influence their philanthropy.

Exercise for Values Clarification and Decision-Making

In Chapter 4, we discussed the linkage between a woman's interests, values, and her giving. Now is the time to refine those so a donor can begin to become more strategic in her giving. Values are those characteristics that we hold in the highest esteem. They drive our behavior and choices, where and how we spend our time and money. When meeting with a donor, plan to spend some time exploring the development of *her* values. It is important to focus on *her* values versus a couple's values, because they may not be the same. Open-ended questions are best because they require more explanation and may lead to a productive conversation. Here are some possible questions for discussion:

1. Identify several people who have influenced your life. Explain why each was important to you.
2. What did each person teach you about life and philanthropy?
3. Name two or three experiences, positive or negative, that shaped your life.
4. List your top five values in order of priority, beginning with the most important. Explain why these are important and why they are rated in this sequence.
5. How would those values align with some philanthropic investments?
6. What are your biggest fears or concerns that might interfere with your philanthropy journey?
7. Name three things you would like to accomplish with your philanthropy.
8. Name three ways that you would like to give.
9. What would you like your legacy to be?

Though brief, these are tough, thought provoking questions not easily answered without some serious consideration. Questions can be asked in a group or in one-to-one meetings with a donor or couple. Keep in mind that each member of the couple may respond differently to the questions. The goal is to help a donor think about her philanthropy as an extension of her life and her legacy.

Author and philanthropist Tracy Gary suggests that donors write a mission statement after they have discussed and clarified their values. Answering question #7 above is the beginning of that mission statement. It can be a sentence or paragraph, visionary, or practical. It just has to be unique to the prospective donor. Gary recommends including personal interests, what a donor thinks she can improve or change about the issue(s) she cares about, and some specific action over a specific period of time (Gary, 2008, p. 64).

The next step is to align values and interests with a cause to support. This process helps the donor examine her range of philanthropic options. Have her list her top causes or concerns about the community, her region, or the world. Prioritizing the causes and concerns can be matched with values. Causes that are rated lower on the list may be identified as areas for smaller contributions, transactional gifts, or dropped off the list so that more important causes may be considered for more intense levels of involvement, including volunteering, transitional, or transformational gifts. Identifying the level of engagement that a donor wants will help align her philanthropy with the cause, creating a matrix of interests and gifts, so she transitions from giving reactively to being more proactive.

Journey from Transaction to Transformation

Most fund development professionals know the evolution of a donor's giving or potential giving. Donors begin with small transactions and minimal involvement in the cause, program, or service. Over time and through cultivation donors either increase their engagement and investment, decrease their giving, stop giving, or swerve to a different cause or organization. Transactional giving is an exchange where the focus is the gift, it meets a need, perhaps satisfies the fundraiser, but rarely does it build a relationship with the donor. Transactional philanthropy will always be a part of a donor's life cycle, but research shows that women want more. They want to understand, become engaged, and create change. Moving from a transaction to philanthropy that is deep and meaningful takes time. Rarely do donors jump from small transactions to large-scale gifts that challenge their capacity and touch their soul. The movement along this continuum usually includes a middle stage, frequently referred to as transitional giving (Fig. 7.1).

Transitional donors are individuals who have been giving to a cause or nonprofit consistently usually in a mid-level range (defined by the organization). These donors care about a cause that aligns with their values and interests, but they haven't made a distinct connection about how to deepen their engagement. They have capacity and may have steadily increased their giving, but they hover between becoming more engaged or staying comfortably distant (Qgive, 2021). New evidence suggests that by combining the elements of direct marketing and a major gifts strategy transitional donors may increase their contributions. Consider for example when the Kennedy

Fig. 7.1 Transactional to transformational gifts

Center in Washington, DC targeted this group of donors, developed a Circles Board (an advisory group of mid-level donors), and shifted their direct mail marketing to an outside firm to free up staff time. Twenty-five of their 45 Circle board members increased their giving by $2,400 (Wallace, 2018). Many women are giving in mid-level ranges (usually defined at $1,000–$10,000) and will be good prospects for increased philanthropy. However, be aware that sometimes women donors take longer to make decisions about increasing their level of giving. That is the time to provide more information, more connection, and to explore through conversations her interests, concerns, and goals.

Frequently, the goal of fundraisers is to move donors toward larger or more impactful gifts—a strategy referred to as *moves management*. It is a process of working with a donor to help identify causes and to align different types of gifts and amounts with the cause. Most often, the goal is an increase in the size of a contribution, but it might also include increased volunteer involvement, acting as a spokesperson for the project, or championing the cause to other donors. It is important to provide a wide range of options. Donors identified for moves management usually receive very strategic interactions from the fund development team. Donors who respond with interest in deeper levels of engagement may be identified as prospects for transformational gifts.

Transformational gifts are those opportunities for a donor to express her deep commitment to a cause with a very personal and impactful investment. They are built on trusting relationships and can create new partnerships, inspire others, prompt system changes, or significantly impact the future of a person, program, or organization. Transformational gifts are true alignments based on a woman's values, interests, passions, and deep commitment to change. These gifts don't happen every day, and not every donor will become a transformational giver, but when it happens, it may look something like this:

A Transformational Gift

Philanthropic giving has become a part of Suzy and Chris DeWolf's life. Known as generous and regular supporters of education, social services, arts, culture and healthcare, they have been influenced by their families, community, faith, and entrepreneurial spirit. As their wealth capacity has changed, they have stepped into philanthropy with larger and more impactful gifts.

Suzy grew up in the Midwest and during her childhood her parents were modest donors mostly focused on giving at their church. When her father decided to purchase a business called Lil' Drug Store Products in 1978, the family's ability to give through the company, as well as personally increased. In 1995 Suzy married Chris and they began their philanthropy on a small scale, participating in charity events, giving at their church, raising three children, and volunteering for causes. In 2005, after the death of Suzy's father, Dennis, Suzy and her husband purchased the business. The family's loss prompted Suzy and her mother to work with a local hospital to design and create a hospice house for families with loved ones in the final stages of life. The Dennis and Donna Oldorf Hospice House of Mercy was opened in 2007. Suzy was inspired by her mother's choice to make the lead gift, "It's a humble and spiritual feeling to realize the peace these people feel having experienced such a special place," she said (DeWolf, personal communication, June 28, 2021). In addition to making their own gift to this very personal project, Suzy and Chris began to realize the power and impact of philanthropy.

Since that time, Lil' Drug Store Products has prospered. Suzy and Chris have broadened their philanthropy: they have served as campaign chairs for Four Oaks—Total Child, a child welfare program, focused on creating and implementing innovative programs for high-risk families, rebuilding neighborhoods, and providing a stable long-term investment in children's education; they have supported a new scholarship program at the University of Wisconsin, Suzy's alma mater; they invested in their church's capital campaign and created a family fund at the local community foundation so they can teach their children about making good philanthropy investments.

As they make decisions together, their philosophy and approach to giving are a bit different from others. When approached by an organization about funding something that might not be the right fit for them, instead of saying no, they ask the fundraiser to think differently and then to apply again, pushing service providers and nonprofit leaders to be more innovative and creative.

In 2021, the DeWolff's made what they describe as the most transformational gift of their lifetime. They pledged $2 million dollars to help create the Chris and Suzy DeWolf Family Innovation Center for Aging and Dementia at Mercy Hospital in Cedar Rapids, Iowa. This lead gift will build facilities for dementia patients and create a research center to help healthcare professionals learn about dementia, how to treat it and care for the entire family. When asked if the sizable gift was a difficult decision to make, Suzy replied, "No, we had been involved in the planning and visioning of this facility from the start, we trust the organization, its staff and leadership, and truly believe it can positively impact the community and families, perhaps changing the way we treat dementia patients now and in the future" (DeWolf, personal communication, June 28, 2021). While this gift is the largest the DeWolfs have given to date, Suzy believes there may be future opportunities to make transformational investments that change her community.

The Surprise of Giving

Values are created through life experiences, and no one knows that better than Dr. Tererai Trent, whose inspirational story is chronicled in her book *The Awakened Woman: Remembering and Reigniting Our Sacred Dreams.* Growing up in a small village in Zimbabwe, Trent challenged the traditional female roles of her culture and achieved phenomenal success despite a childhood filled with poverty, a teen marriage, and domestic abuse. Fortunately, she was supported and inspired by other women including her mother and a U.S. aid worker. Her goals were dreams she chose to write down: *go to America, get an undergraduate degree, a master's degree, and a Ph.D* (Trent, 2017, p. 52). Over the course of fifteen years, she accomplished all of them.

When Nicholas Kristof and Sheryl WuDunn, authors of *Half the Sky* interviewed Trent and wrote about her dreams, the story captured the attention of Oprah who invited Trent to share her journey on national TV. Oprah was truly inspired and Tererai became known as her favorite guest. But the big surprise was a $1.5 million contribution from Oprah to help build a school in Zimbabwe, a dream of Trent's. Today, Trent is an international leader, scholar, and motivational speaker. Her desire to give back to her community made Oprah's gift truly transformational for the girls in Trent's village who need an education and hope that the future can be different. Transformational gifts impact donors, recipients, and brokers, providing a sense of warmth, satisfaction, joy, peace, and, excitement some even describe it as a spiritual experience.

Understanding Wealth Capacity

Sunny Fischer, co-founder and former Executive Director of the Chicago Foundation for Women, has seen many women become empowered through philanthropy that aligns with their interests and values. She has also observed many women who don't understand their wealth, assets, or options. Years ago, when the Foundation was still relatively new, Fischer received a check and note in the mail. The $50.00 check was a small gift, but it was the note attached that caught her attention. "This is the first time I have written a check without my husband's permission." The donor went on, "He writes checks for anything he wants to without asking me" (Fischer, personal communication, 2019).

Obviously, the work of the Chicago Foundation for Women was a cause this donor wanted to support and this was her moment of empowerment, the beginning of her philanthropic journey. She took the first step of using her money to fund something that aligned with her interests and values. That $50.00 check probably felt like $50,000 when she wrote it. Choosing a cause is a beginning, but understanding the power of philanthropy includes understanding one's financial circumstances and wealth capacity.

Money is scary and exciting. It's empowering and transformative, a necessary element in life. Almost everyone needs money to survive and the amount we have, how we obtained it, how we feel about it, and what we do with it is a very personal journey. Ask anyone to describe their thoughts and feelings about money—if you are brave enough—and you'll be surprised by what you hear. Most people don't like to talk about money. It's one of those taboo subjects that's intensely personal, like sex and religion.

Here are few facts about women and their money. Sixty-six percent of women describe themselves as the decision-maker over household assets (Turner Moffit, 2015, p. 23). Seventy-five percent of wealth creators describe themselves as decision-makers as do 66% of inheritors and 43% of women whose spouse created the wealth (Hewlett et al., 2014). Women control $20 trillion in consumer spending, make the decision in the purchases of 92% of home furnishings, 92% of vacations, 91% of homes, 60% of automobiles, and 51% of consumer electronics (Silverstein & Sayre, 2009). However, many women still lack confidence in their decision-maker role. A UBS Wealth Management Report found that 85% of married women believe their husbands know more about financial matters and investments than they do and only 55% of women feel confident making long-term financial decisions versus 79% of men (UBS, 2018). The irony of this situation is that some research estimates eight out of ten women will end up solely responsible for their financial well-being due to longer life expectancy and high divorce rates. So, it is imperative that women become more knowledgeable and involved in their financial situations.

When women think about money, they envision long-term investments focused on family, college for the children and mortgage reduction, versus men who tend to be more focused on short-term immediate investment returns (Livingston, 2015, p. 11). As one investment professional told me, "Men want to compete with their friends about how well their investments are doing and are more focused on the numbers. It can be a sort of competition." On the other hand, women are more comfortable saving versus investing and proportionately save more of their income than men both in workplace retirement accounts and outside accounts like IRAs (Livingston, 2015, p. 5). Most importantly, when surveyed, 88% of women equate wealth with financial security and independence (Turner Moffit, 2015, p. 25). They want to be assured that they will have adequate funds to care for their families and their futures. But overall, men have more money saved despite these trends because their wages are usually higher than women's and they are in the workforce more consistently.

Financial guru Suze Orman, in her book *Women and Money*, explains that women have a complicated relationship with money. They have a tendency to take care of everyone: their spouse, children, friends, neighbors, but they don't take care of their money. Women tend to have a dysfunctional relationship with it (Orman, 2007, p. 12). They ignore financial matters, feel embarrassed, ashamed, or just leave it for someone else to manage. How many stories have been written about women who have been swindled out of their life savings, or didn't realize their husband was in debt until it was too late? A recent survey found that 40% of couples didn't even know how much their spouse earned and 36% disagreed on their joint investable assets (Block & Clark, 2016).

Learning about your financial situation is not easy. It takes dedication, time, and practice. One of the resources fundraisers can offer is to help connect women with financial experts who can help them understand their wealth capacity and increase their confidence about financial management. Finding an advisor who understands women and can practice good listening skills and patience is the key. One of the common complaints women have about financial advisors is that they don't listen and spend too much time trying to sell a product.

Kiplinger, a personal financial management firm, suggests that women should start asking questions and explore. In addition to the basics of knowing what is in your cash accounts and investments, they recommend reviewing your beneficiaries, saving for retirement, establishing an estate plan, and planning for the future healthcare costs of yourself and your family.

Morgan Stanley Wealth Management holds seminars designed specifically for female clients. The focus is on helping women identify the unique challenges they may face in their lifetime: caregiving, fewer years earning income, income inequality, divorce, loss of a spouse, and risk tolerance. Tailoring information for women is a smart and effective strategy. Helping women build wealth management plans that encompass their personal and family objectives makes the experience more personal. Most importantly, women want to be listened to and acknowledged, they don't want an off the shelf product. Women want to learn, consult with others, and take time to make the best decisions for themselves and their families.

Understanding their financial situation can be very empowering for women. They can begin to make choices, participate more actively in charitable decisions, and plan for their futures. But understanding is not enough. They need access, authority, and confidence. The less confident women are, the larger the gap between desire and action, between what they say they want to invest in or donate to, and what they actually do. Here are some ways fundraisers can assist women in learning more about their financial situation.

- Partner with a variety of professional financial advisors to offer workshops designed specifically for women interested in understanding their financial situations. Wealth advisors have to win over women by giving them a safe place to learn and by serving up products that align with their larger needs to deploy wealth in socially responsible ways (Turner Moffit, 2015, p. 53).
- Provide information on your website about charitable giving, with tips and updated tax laws. Design tips focused on women's issues: childcare, elder care, healthcare.
- Ask a variety of financial counselors in your community to do feature articles about charitable donations written specifically for a female audience.
- Encourage women donors to meet with a financial advisor or attorney to discuss their current asset base.
- Provide workshops on estate planning or planned giving.
- Create a women's advisory council to talk about financial situations of special interest to women: Invite guest speakers to share financial knowledge and answer questions.
- Highlight a woman donor willing to share her story about financial learning and charitable giving.

Offering these options to all interested women, even those who are not your donors, accomplishes several goals: You provide a service to current and future donors.

You can begin to match donor's wealth to interests. Your organization expands its network of possible donors. You build new partnerships.

As you help women align their philanthropic interests with their pocketbooks, they will grow in level of confidence and desire to invest. Gloria Steinem reportedly said, "We can tell our values by looking at our checkbook stubs." Although checkbooks are a tool of the past for some donors, her sentiments are still relevant. Have potential donors look where they spend their money and it will tell them what's important in their lives. Are they happy with the picture? If not, you can help them change it.

Bibliography

Block, S., & Clark, J. (2016). What women need to know about money. *Kiplinger Report*. Retrieved March 24, 2019, from https://kiplinger.com/article/retirement/t047-c000-s002-what-women-need-to-know-about-money.html

Gary, T. (2008). *Inspired philanthropy*. Jossey-Bass, Wiley, and Sons.

Hewlett, S., Moffitt, T. A., & Marshall, M. (2014). *Harnessing the power of the purse: Female investors and global opportunities for growth*. Center for Talent Innovation. Retrieved September 11, 2019, from https://cdn2.hubspot.net/hubfs/5341408/EP_Wealth_Advisors_April2019/pdf/HarnessingThePowerOfThePurse_ExecSumm-CTI-Confidential.pdf

https://www.youtube.com/watch?v=nqwaBHF45QI. Retrieved November 4, 2020. Oprah Surprises Tererai Trent.

Konrath, S. (2014/2016). The power of philanthropy and volunteering. In F. A. Huppert & C. L. Cooper (Eds.), *Wellbeing: A complete reference guide, Volume VI: Interventions and policies to enhance wellbeing* (pp. 387–426). Wiley.

Konrath, S., & Brown, S. (2012). The effects of giving on givers. In N. Roberts & M. Newman (Eds.), *Health and social relationships: The good, the bad, and the complicated* (p. 18). American Psychological Association.

Livingston, A. (2015). *Men, women and money—How the sexes differ with their finances*. Money Management. Retrieved April 16, 2019, from https://www.moneycrashers.com/men-women-money-sexes-differ-finances/

Mesch, D., Osili, U., Okten, C., Han, X., Pactor, A., & Ackerman J. (2017). *Women give 17 charitable giving and life satisfaction: Does gender matter?* Women's Philanthropy Institute.

Mesch, D., Osili. U., Pactor, A., Ackerman, J., & O'Connor, H. (2018). *Giving by and for women: Understanding high-net worth donors' support for women and girls*. Women's Philanthropy Institute.

Orman, S. (2007). *Women and money*. Spiegel and Grau.

Prasoon, R., & Chaturvedi, K. R. (2016). Life satisfaction: A literature review. *International Journal of Management Humanities and Social Sciences, 1*(2), 25–32. Retrieved May 6, 2020, from http://theresearcherjournal.org/pdfs/01021220163.pdf

Qgive. (2021). *Donor Stewardship: Create life-long donors in 6 steps*. Retrieved June 30, 2020, from https://www.qgive.com/blog/donor-stewardship-guide/

Silverstein, M., & Sayre, K. (2009). The female economy. *The Harvard Business Review*. Retrieved June 1, 2019, from https://hbr.org/2009/09/the-female-eco nomy

Trent, T. (2017). *The awakened woman*. An Imprint of Simon and Schuster, Inc.

Turner Moffitt, A. (2015). *Harness the power of the purse: Winning women investors*. Rare Bird Books.

Wallace, N. (2018). Midlevel donor programs grow in popularity- and sophistica-tion. *Chronicle of Philanthropy*. Retrieved June 15, 2020, from https://www.phi lanthropy.com/article/how-to-inspire-midlevel-donors-to-give-more/

UBS Wealth Management Report. (2018). *Top reasons married women step aside in long term financial decisions: They believe their husbands know more*. Retrieved March 8, 2019, from https://www.businesswire.com/news/home/201804130 05223/en/UBS-Reveals-Top-Reason-Married-Women-Step-Aside-in-Long-Term-Financial-Decisions-They-Believe-Their-Husbands-Know-More

8

Action: Making It Happen

Building initiatives for women donors begins with a desire to expand and enhance the impact of women in your community. The previous chapters have focused on: developing an awareness of the women's philanthropy movement, how women practice philanthropy, assessing women's wealth origins, an organization's ability to develop a women's philanthropy initiative, and aligning women's philanthropic interests and values with their wealth capacities. These elements establish a foundation for the implementation of a women's philanthropy initiative. A review of several women's philanthropy initiatives in different stages of development provides some insight into what is possible and successful.

Traditional Model of Organizational Development

Typical philanthropy programs are developed within organizations that have a defined structure and life cycle. Building an organization begins with a *vision* that is created and championed by a leader who inspires followers to join the identified cause. The implementation of the vision is realized by creating *goals and objectives*—what will be accomplished and how will it happen? *A strategy*, or overarching method of carrying out the objectives, is designed specifically for a target audience and includes different types of communication, contacts, messaging, meetings, and calls to action. Individual staff are

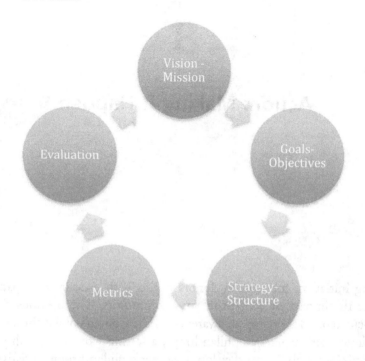

Fig. 8.1 The cycle of organizational development

assigned actions and activities intended to accomplish the objectives forming an organizational or program *structure*. To support the work of the programs and services, back office systems including technology and communications are created. Finally, before implementation, a set of *metrics* of success is outlined. *Evaluation* occurs continuously, allowing for constant adaptation. These characteristics of an organization are present in almost every nonprofit or for-profit company. How and when they are developed is directly linked to the life cycle of an organization (Fig. 8.1).

Organizational Life Stages

Most women's philanthropy initiatives develop as independent nonprofits or have an administrative home in a nonprofit. Their ability to thrive and grow is directly linked to the organization's ability to transition through its life cycle and continue to renew itself. Judy Sharken Simon, an organizational development consultant, has defined five life stages of nonprofit organizations:

Stage 1—Imagine and Inspire

Stage 2—Found and Frame

Stage 3—Ground and Grow

Stage 4—Produce and Sustain

Stage 5—Review and Renew (Simon, 2012).

Stage 1, or early-stage organizations, are small and nimble, lacking defined systems, specialization, or adequate funding. Their visionary leaders or founders inspire followers and over time, as their ideas become more defined, small programs or services evolve. Stage 2 encompasses the development of structures including a board, recruiting donors, program expansion, and a continuous pursuit for more resources. Stage 3 organizations are growing in size and complexity. They are stable, have policies, procedures, programs, structure and systems, including more staff, marketing strategies, and technology. The organizational mission has been refined and programs are securely positioned for growth, but the need for funding to sustain the organization is continually challenging. Stage 4 organizations continue to evolve and change, but with a greater degree of stability. During this life-stage, organizations become more complex, bureaucratic, larger, financially more stable with a solid donor base, established brand and produce well-recognized programs, and services. But, the possibility of complacency hovers. Organizations assume their growth will continue indefinitely, yet without attention to innovation and constant quality improvement, the organization may begin to decline, slowly or quickly. Stage 5 is the turning point in an organization's life cycle. After becoming an established institution, its practices, policies and processes need renewal. Some organizations at this phase are in decline because they haven't adapted to changing environmental conditions or are in financial distress. Ultimately, organizations have to re-emerge with new vision, vigor, ideas, and often, leadership. Stage 5 is that renewal. Without it organizations will teeter on the brink of deterioration, become ineffective, or become a candidate for acquisition by another organization that can provide stability and security.

Women's philanthropy initiatives can be found in any stage of organizational development. If they are located within a larger organization and established when the organization began, their life cycle may be dependent on their parent organization. If the initiative was added after an organization was well established, it will have its own life-stage cycle which may not coincide with the host organization.

Let's consider three case studies of women's philanthropy initiatives in different life stages. They vary in scope and size. Some are integrated into existing foundations or fund development departments while others are independent or interconnected with other community partners.

Early Stage: 5224GOOD—Grassroots and Local

Mary Westbrook, a former Senior Vice President of NCS Pearson, Inc. retired in 2008 and began to fill her time with volunteer work including acting as an interim CEO at a local United Way, serving on the board of the Community Foundation of Johnson County, Iowa and eventually becoming one of the co-founders of a women's giving circle—5224GOOD (pronounced 5-2-2-4-GOOD).

Westbrook knows her community and is well-respected as a professional and volunteer. She has been involved in numerous fundraising events in her career and is not afraid to ask for money, but it was more than money that was her interest as she developed a women's philanthropy initiative. Her path to the creation of 5224GOOD began with her involvement in a United Way women's leadership program's annual purse auction. As a volunteer primarily on the auction committee, Westbrook loved finding donations, creating opportunities for people to become engaged, and recruiting women to attend the event. She was also an astute observer of women's interactions at fundraising events, and recognized a problem with the auction approach. "The concept of big auctions where competitive bidding is used may fuel some donors, but it doesn't work for most women," she says. "Women don't want to take from other women or beat them out of a gift. They don't want to be public about everything they give, or show off. They like equality or sharing. It's better to have a lot of winners, rather than just one" (Westbrook, personal communication, February 12, 2020). Creating something that built on the ways women work with each other was at the heart of what Westbrook wanted to do.

One afternoon she and a colleague began to brainstorm about the concept of a giving circle. One of her friends had participated in a similar venture in California and wanted to bring the idea to the Iowa City, Iowa community. As Westbrook and her friend, Anne Vanderberg, talked, they identified their goals: create a women's giving initiative that would be inclusive, intimate, fun, educational and raise money for a community cause. Based in a university town, Westbrook and Vanderberg knew that they had a large pool of educated, interested women. Each invited four friends to build the core of the giving initiative. Using the Iowa City zip code 5-2-2-4-0 and substituting the final number with "good" created a catchy name.

One of their first decisions was to find a strong administrative partner, an organization that could provide the infrastructure for the program. The local community foundation had the ability to provide that support; they had a solid reputation, staff that understood philanthropy, and were interested in being a partner in the endeavor.

How to implement the concept was the devil in the details. In anticipation of the myriad questions that might arise, Westbrook and Vanderberg outlined a basic model for the start-up. Their core team included an attorney who volunteered to write by-laws, and finance experts to help establish a budget. And, they designed a meeting format before officially launching the initiative: four meetings a year: (1) Learning about the topic; (2) Inviting nonprofit agencies to tell members about their services and to possibly submit a proposal to the giving circle; (3) Selecting proposals to fund; (4) Celebrating and brainstorming the next year's issue. The core team recruited women to the giving circle, asking each to commit to giving at least $250 annually to a pooled fund that would be distributed to nonprofits which submitted proposals aligning with the topic/issue selected by the circle's members. As one member commented, "Where else can I contribute $250 and participate in the decision of granting $40,000 a year?"

They also built-in an endowment option from the start, asking for up to $1,000 from each woman, although giving at that level was not mandatory. The additional monies, up to $750 per donor, were put in an endowment fund for the legacy of the program.

While a local bank sponsors the giving circle meetings, (a good marketing strategy for promoting the bank and recruiting women customers) nonprofit agencies submit proposals for funding which are initially screened by the community foundation grants committee, minimizing work for 5224GOOD. Each year, membership dues plus a 5% draw from the endowment, fund grants distributed to nonprofit agencies. Since its inception in 2014, 5224GOOD has raised and distributed $213,500.

During COVID 5224GOOD had to pivot and adapt. Like many other organizations, the leadership resorted to virtual meetings and adjusted their granting process to prioritize COVID needs. They abandoned the focus area they had selected in the prior year and simplified their grant application. Instead of distributing funds once a year, the resources were spread out to accommodate evolving COVID needs. Members still participated by voting online and still maintained connection. Westbrook plans to have 5224GOOD meet in person as the COVID epidemic slows down and meetings can be held inside.

Her involvement in a fundraiser for another organization was an additional example of COVID adaptation. The Power of the Purse (purse auction for *Women United*) was held online and over a period of a week instead

of one afternoon, more tickets were sold because women could participate virtually and the event committee members made accommodations
for the winners of the bids, delivering their winnings. 5224GOOD and
other nonprofits have survived because of Westbrook's adaptability and perse-
verance. Now Westbrook and Vanderberg are working on increasing the
number of 5224GOOD members from 140 upwards and increasing the
number of legacy donors from 30 to 50%. Westbrook's motto is "Be bolder!"
(Westbrook, personal communication, February 12, 2020).

Adult Stage: Dartmouth College—Mature and Integrated

Many universities have established foundations, sophisticated fundraising
departments, staff with specialized skills and significant pools of potential
donors, most of them alumni. They launch annual, endowment, and capital
campaigns raising funds with a wide range of contributions and donors.
Women donors contribute, but not all universities have realized the untapped
potential of this donor segment.

In 2014, Dartmouth brought together a group of loyal alumnae and
created an initiative to recruit 100 Dartmouth women to make gifts of
$100,000 or more in honor of the 100th anniversary of the Dartmouth
College Fund (Dartmouth College, 2018) (Inside Higher Ed 2018). One
hundred fourteen women joined the Centennial Circle raising almost $15
million to support students through financial aid. This community of women
has grown to 188 with women giving larger gifts and raising more than $30
million (Valburn, 2018). The success of this initiative prompted Dartmouth
to raise the bar and boldly ask women to give even more. In 2018, it established a gender-specific campaign with a goal of asking 100 women to give
$1million each. At the launch, Dartmouth announced fifty-three alumnae
had already committed $1 million each. This women's philanthropy initiative
was part of a three-billion-dollar multi-year campaign. Other goals included
celebrating the college's 250th anniversary by increasing the membership of
the Centennial Circle to 250, and raising $25 million from alumnae and
widows of Dartmouth graduates making gifts of any size to renovate Dartmouth Hall (Valburn, 2018). This multi-level strategy offers an opportunity
for women at all income levels to participate, and significantly broadens the
base of potential donors. Seeing the impact of their gifts in the physical
changes at the college helps remind the women how they have contributed
to the evolution of the institution.

Giving financially is only part of the strategy to engage more women donors and grow the visibility of women on campus. Women make up 50% of the student body and 38% of the Board of Trustees (Valburn, 2018). Dartmouth wants to encourage more women to attend the university, hold board positions, lead committees and participate in the leadership of the university and foundation.

As a mature and well-established institution, Dartmouth used its organizational strength and stability to support a new initiative. As women donors demonstrated their commitment and capacity, the initiative evolved and continued to grow—an excellent example of a mature and integrated women's philanthropy initiative.

Beth Cogan Fastcitelli, '80, a Dartmouth Trustee said, "We want the next generation of students, male and female, to know that women and men are equally committed to the power of a Dartmouth education" (Valburn, 2018).

Renewal Stage: Iowa Women's Foundation—Adaptation and Re-Invention

From 2005 to 2013 Dawn Oliver Wiand was the Executive Director of the Women's Foundation of Greater Kansas City, Kansas, a large, successful organization located in a metropolitan area with a diverse base of women donors and a pool of HNW individuals. When Oliver Wiand relocated to Iowa City, Iowa in 2013 and was hired as the Director of the Iowa Women's Foundation (IWF) she brought her wealth of knowledge and enthusiasm for women's philanthropy across the plains. The IWF was struggling, to put it mildly; clinging to life support would be a more accurate description. The donor base had eroded. A small, but limited group of supporters performed minimal grant making, and annual luncheons for donors and prospects were modestly attended. The organization had been in existence since 1995. It had completed one life cycle and needed to adapt, modify, recreate itself or die.

IWF had made a strategic decision in previous years to focus first on grant making and secondly on fundraising. While providing grants for services is the mission of the organization, it cannot occur without funds. As Peter Brinkerhoff, a nonprofit consultant says, "No money, no mission" (Brinkerhoff, 2009, pp. 8–10). Oliver Wiand knew that the fundraising aspect of the foundation needed to be improved.

Over the course of seven years, she rebuilt the organization. In 2014, she created a higher level of awareness through *Ovation: A Tribute to Women and Girls*, an annually published book that celebrates women from all walks of life: corporate executives, secretaries, moms, and volunteers. Recognized by friends, family, or organizations, each volume features brief biographical sketches and photos and is presented to the nominees at a public event. Often the presentation is a surprise, and always it is a heartwarming recognition of a woman's impact on her family, friends, colleagues, and community.

Oliver Wiand began to use data and research to document the needs of women and children in the state. With a staff of only 1.5, she knew she couldn't gather enough information or have enough time, expertise and connections to identify the key issues and barriers of women. Partnering with other women's groups, they divided up the work. Women Lead Change and the Carrie Chapman Catt Center for Women and Politics focused on women's leadership, the American Association of University Women took on equity, and IWF focused its work on the impact of economic self-sufficiency for women. Focus groups were convened in eighteen different communities. Each group was asked the same eight questions. The goal of the study was to:

1. Learn firsthand about the most pressing challenges affecting economic self-sufficiency for women and girls in the communities.
2. Identify existing initiatives to advance their success.
3. Determine what gaps in services and resources currently exist.

Six key barriers to economic self-sufficiency were identified: employment, child care, housing, education/training, transportation, and mentors. A needs assessment study entitled SHE MATTERS: We Listen and Iowa Wins was published in 2016. This information provided a framework for grant making, creating new partnerships, and developed a credibility quotient to the IWF work. They had data to support their message about needs, to influence donors, and to support requests for funds.

Moreover, IWF's annual luncheon, a stable and historical event for the foundation, gained momentum when sponsorships and table hosts were recruited, eliminating the need to sell a large volume of individual tickets. The purpose of the luncheon was to reveal the grants that were awarded and to honor the recipients, educate donors and fundraise. In 2019, keynote speaker Dr. Angela Sadler Williamson, a cousin of Rosa Parks, shared the story of her documentary, *My Life with Rosie*. More than 800 women attended.

The women were back and excited about the foundation's work. Since its inception, IWF has distributed more than $1 million in grants to 200 organizations focused on programs for women and girls. In 2019, Oliver Wiand launched a legacy campaign with a goal of $3 million. IWF was re-created and is thriving. Then COVID hit in 2020 and IWF had to make some radical decisions. Events had been 50% of the budget. They held their annual luncheon virtually, but revenue was down 35%. "Women missed the camaraderie of getting together and it's hard to justify the cost when someone is watching it on a computer screen" (Oliver Wiand, personal communication, June 15, 2021). The pandemic did produce new opportunities though. IWF received funding from the Women's Funding Network/Gates Foundation for their work in childcare and for the first time applied for state funds through a childcare challenge grant. Their innovation plans to solicit male donors were carried out through a direct mail program. Oliver Wiand believes some of their fundraising model will change. She plans to reduce dependency on events and continue to pursue partnerships with male donors and corporations.

Women's Philanthropy versus Traditional Program Development Models

Having considered three examples of women's philanthropy initiatives in different developmental stages offers some insight into how initiatives can begin, evolve and adapt. Let's examine some differences in women's philanthropy initiatives versus the traditional organizational framework.

Vision and Mission

If women are looking for inspiration, they need to see themselves. They need to believe that they can be the champions of the cause. The more the champion is reflective of the donors being solicited, or in some cases, of the recipients of services, the more identification women will have with the initiative.

But what does it mean to be visionary? "The ability to frame current practices as inadequate, to generate new ideas for new strategies, and to communicate possibilities in inspiring ways" is one definition from a recent *Harvard Business Review* article. The title of the article, "Women and the Vision Thing" dissects the results of a 360-degree Assessment of the European Institute of Business (INSEAD) executive education program (INSEAD is an international business school with global offices and an alliance with the Wharton School of Business) (Ibarra & Obodaru, 2009).

In the study, when women were rated on their leadership skills they scored higher than men in most categories, except the leadership trait of *envisioning*

(Ibarra & Obodaru, 2009). Male respondents in the study rated women lower in their envisioning capabilities, but female respondents did not rate themselves lower than their male counterparts. These results prompted more questions. Do women really struggle with being visionary? Perhaps women are visionary in different ways? A more in-depth analysis of the findings drew some interesting conclusions.

- Women see themselves as catalysts working collaboratively to create a vision rather than doing so individually. They like input and believe they get a richer product when more people can participate (Ibarra & Obodaru, 2009).
- Women rely a lot on facts, hard data. Accustomed to executing, they don't like going out on a limb with an idea with nothing to back it up.
- Rather than engaging in grand schemes that have no basis in fact, women are more conservative and careful; they want to know how the idea will work (Ibarra & Obodaru, 2009).
- Women think about and value "vision" differently from men. Women focus on getting the work done (Ibarra & Obodaru, 2009).

As Margaret Thatcher is reported to have said, "If you want anything said, ask a man; if you want anything done, ask a woman." Women know that vision is important, but valueless if the work doesn't get completed. Thus, in building a women's philanthropy initiative, consider structuring the visioning process as a group activity versus a solo flight. Encourage women to bravely speak their ideas, even if all the details aren't worked out. The mission of the initiative needs to explain the work and purpose. What will the initiative do? Make it meaningful and easy to understand. If the women's initiative is part of a hosting organization, the mission statements will need to align.

Goals and Objectives

What is going to be accomplished? Who will do it? What are the right goals? Participants in a women's philanthropy initiative, whether staff or women donors, want to accomplish multiple goals: build awareness about an issue, raise money, create friends and supporters, and impact causes. In 2019, The Women's Philanthropy Institute Study *Change Agents: The Goals and Impact of Women's Foundation and Funds* highlighted several findings about the goals and objectives of women's foundations and funds.

- Women's funds share the broad goal of advancing women's philanthropy. Their specific objectives and the ways they pursue them vary widely (Gillespie, 2019).
- Women's funds define impact in different ways and have been most successful at achieving short-term goals through empowerment and community-based change (Gillespie, 2019).
- Women's funds pursue their organizational goals through multiple grant making approaches like gender-lens investing and community-based philanthropy (Gillespie, 2019).
- Many women's funds go beyond grant making to achieve impact through relationship-building partnerships and policy advocacy (Gillespie, 2019).
- Women's funds demonstrate intersectionality in their pursuit of goals and impact, using different lenses and voices in decision-making (Gillespie, 2019).

Although this study focused exclusively on women's funds and foundations, there are some unique aspects about the goals and objectives found in women's philanthropy that can be considered in the design of an initiative. Here are some suggestions:

In addition to promoting women's philanthropy and gender equity, many successful initiatives focus on teaching children, young women and adults about philanthropy in general. Short-term, locally focused goals are easier to measure and provide "early wins" which build momentum and donor interest. Larger long-term goals require specificity. It's very difficult to measure a broad goal like social change. Start small and grow. For example, when Mary Westbrook launched 5224GOOD, her membership goal was small. She asked three of her friends to each bring a colleague to the first meeting. The membership evolved from four to thirty over the course of a year.

Understand and define where the gender lens fits within your initiative. This includes: Who is in the population to be served? How are funds going to be distributed? What type of programs will the donors fund? How will women donors and program participants be impacted? Who will be potential partners?

Have a diverse group of women at the table when creating goals and objectives and make sure women are represented in all aspects of the initiative design. During one of my interviews, a woman executive and philanthropist (who requested anonymity) shared her experience of reminding others about a gender lens in their decision-making process. She was the only woman on the board of a large trade association planning a national sports conference.

When the board of the association received word that one of potential financial sponsors for the conference was a for-profit corporation and magazine known for its exploitation of women, the conversation centered on the financial possibilities and how great the financial support would be. She was the only voice to object, reminding the other board members that women need to be respected, not exploited. Her gender perspective was honored, the association voted against the sponsorship, and avoided a good deal of negative public controversy.

Women's philanthropy initiatives will create change intentionally or unintentionally. What systems will your women's philanthropy initiative impact and in what ways? This may include a specific goal about systems change or awareness that the women's philanthropy initiative will impact other organizational systems.

Collaboration and community building are high on the list as some of the most important activities and goals. Women's unique ability to connect to each other and network make these goals a natural part of their work in philanthropy. Stating these as goals versus outcomes emphasizes their importance in initiative development and implementation. Identify key partners who can help support and advance the goals. Oliver Wiand's delegation of foci to other community organizations is a great example of collaboration.

Intersectionality is a part of women's philanthropy. The intersections of race, culture, gender, class, sexuality, and place play a role in defining people's identity, problems, and solutions. When women participate in philanthropy, design programs or fund causes, they bring their gender and all their experiences to the table. Hearing the perspectives of many kinds of women helps us grow and learn. A great question that Melinda Gates learned from her friend, Killian Noe, founder of the Recovery Café is, "What do you know now in a deeper way than you knew it before? Wisdom isn't about accumulating more facts, it's about understanding big truths in a deeper way" (Gates, 2019, p. 27). Assessing how these factors and insights impact decisions and donor's lives provides essential insight into the type of women's philanthropy initiative that can be developed.

Strategy and Structure

When considering a strategy to implement goals and objectives, remember how and why women give. Feelings, emotions, empathy, *and facts* are primary drivers. Women have a desire to help others. They focus less on the benefits of being charitable and more on the connection, the feeling they get from giving. Strategies within women's philanthropy initiatives need to include data, structure, *and* emotion. Here is where the power of a story can inspire donors to act. We make sense of the world and fashion our identities through sharing and telling stories. Telling the story of need inspires women to get engaged. The women's philanthropy initiative will also create stories and some of them could be part of its legacy. Ask women to share their stories about how giving impacted others and themselves.

Women work in social networks and have a tapestry of relationships, some of them professional, some personal. Often, the lines are blurred. As skilled networkers, women want connections and more. Bob Little, a marketing consultant, coined the term "netweavers" which accurately describes how women connect. Rather than "networking," which is about "How can you help me? Can you give me something I need?" Netweaving is about, "How can I help you?" (Strang, 2011). Taking that question to your donors is a great foundation for a strategy: How can I help you have impact? Improve your community? Educate a child? Think of the tapestry of women that you can weave together to create a powerful network of giving. Another part of strategy is sharing data that informs women about causes and answers their questions. Take time to explain the structure of the organization and how it intersects with the donor's interests. Women's philanthropy initiatives can be structured in many different ways. Think about strategy first and then build a structure to support it.

Finally, a tip about strategy and structure comes from the principles of a concept called Human-Centered Design championed by Nobel Prize laureate Herbert Simon. It distinguishes its approach by an obsessive focus on understanding the perspective of the person who experiences the problem and involves them in creating solutions (DC Design, 2017). This process has been emphasized in many women's philanthropy programs and bears repeating.

The five steps to the process include: Empathize: Understand the problem by immersing yourself in the community affected by your design. Define: Define the problem by focusing on the key action you want to accomplish—asking constantly, why? Ideate: Come up with multiple solutions remembering that everything is a system. Prototype: Build out a model. Test and Iterate (DC Design, 2017).

The process is dynamic and cyclical. The reason this process is so powerful for women's philanthropy is that it engages the recipients of grants or end-users in the solution and engages women donors in the design of a program. It reminds you to constantly ask why, to test out ideas on a small scale, to improve, and to retest.

Metrics

What will you measure and how will you measure it? How will you define success? Often, philanthropy initiatives default to counting, trying to quantify success through numbers: how much money is raised, how many new donors? The size of donations, planned gifts, or grants distributed are all common metrics. Women's philanthropy initiatives have demonstrated that their impact is more than money and some of the markers of success aren't quantifiable: new relationships, increased awareness, policy development, and community building.

Money *is* a metric, but more importantly it is the outcome of good work in building relationships, earning trust, listening to stories, and finding a donor's passion and motivation for giving. Metrics should align with the initiative's mission and purpose. If awareness is a major goal, a metric must be assigned to it. If membership in a giving circle is a metric, "membership" must be defined. If volunteering is valued, measure how much time women volunteer. Think about metrics on two levels: the numbers which are concrete and measurable, *and* the relationships. The numbers of relationships can be counted, and the types described, but their strength, impact, and power are immeasurable.

Evaluation

Evaluation is a topic that has dominated the philanthropy and foundation literature in recent years and is under considerable debate. One of the challenges is that assessing and evaluating success is usually limited to grant making and the outcome of investments. But, on many levels, evaluations are about learning and improving. So, what should evaluation include? Who conducts and participates in the evaluation? What does the evaluation tell us about the success and impact of a philanthropic endeavor? The results of the Women's Philanthropy Institute's report, *Change Agents: The Goals and Impact of Women's Foundations and Funds* confirm that goals, objectives, and evaluation need to include grant making, but should not be limited to these exclusively (Gillespie, 2019).

Evaluation is based on the definition of success or progress. What did the initiative intend on accomplishing; what were the intended outcomes? In women's philanthropy initiatives grant making and fundraising are usually included in evaluation because these are metrics that can be quantified.

Measuring social impact is more difficult. Two possible measures in the evaluation process suggested by Omidyar Network, a philanthropic investment firm based in California, are reach and engagement. Reach is a measure of how many individuals are touched by a product or service. Engagement is the depth of the interaction (Bannick & Hallstein, 2012).

Counting the number of people "touched" by a service or philanthropic investment is possible if touch is defined. Evaluating the depth of an interaction is trickier. Is it the type or length of the interaction? To evaluate the social impact, you would need to determine the effect the interaction had on the donor or program participant. Did the donor get more involved in the cause, or increase her gift? Did the program recipient's life improve? As you can see, it is tricky and difficult to evaluate these initiatives, but necessary. Without metrics and evaluation, progress can't be described or support sustained.

One of the most productive evaluation practices women philanthropy initiatives can engage in is sharing results. Having a shared platform where all programs can post their learning helps raise all boats, as they say. The power of the Women's Funding Network or other umbrella organizations is that learning is shared through conferences, publications and conversations, understanding that all programs can benefit from the experiences of others.

Elements of High Impact Nonprofits

Building and assessing women's philanthropy initiatives is difficult. There is no one model or one-size-fits-all. Crutchfield and Grant McLeod (2009, pp. 21–23) have identified six elements of a high-impact nonprofit. As you read through these characteristics think about women's philanthropy initiatives. Do they share these elements of high impact? Does your organization model these elements?

- Advocate and Serve—Providing funding for direct services or programs is always essential, but the most impactful change occurs when funding is directed at institutional systems or legislative policies. Do both.
- Make markets work—Tapping into the power of self-interest and the laws of economics is far more effective than appealing to pure altruism. Building partnerships, influencing business or nonprofit practices, and developing earned income ventures are good strategies for long-term sustainability.
- Inspire evangelists—Create your tribe of supporters. This group does not have to be exclusively women. Having diversity helps broaden the message

and pool of advocates. (I would suggest that diversity is essential and necessary in your tribe.)

- Nurture nonprofit networks—Help your peers succeed. Women are great at helping other women. Building coalitions, sharing information, talent, and expertise can help your program and advance the larger field of philanthropy.
- Master adaptation—Programs that survive are adaptable. They may not be the biggest or fundraise the most money. They listen to feedback, modify plans, reflect and evaluate, developing a cycle of learning.
- Share leadership—Successful programs distribute authority, develop succession planning in staff, committees, and boards. They have engaged and powerful boards that invest in the program.

Bibliography

Bannick, M., & Hallstein, E. (2012, Summer). Learning from Silicon Valley Advancing Evaluation in Practices in Philanthropy. *Stanford Social Innovation Supplement*.

Brinkerhoff, P. (2009). *Mission-based management* (3rd ed., pp. 8–10). Wiley.

Crutchfield, L., & Grant McLeod, H. (2009). *Forces for good*. Jossey-Bass.

Dartmouth College. (2018). Retrieved June 12, 2021, from http://www. dartmouthcentennialcircle.com/about/

DC Design. (2017, August 14). What is human-centered design? Retrieved February 17, 2020, from http://medium.com/dc-design/what-is-human-centered-design-6711c09e2779

Gates, M. (2019). *The moment of lift*. Flatiron Books.

Gillespie, E. (2019). *Change agents: The goals and impact of women's foundations and funds* Women's Philanthropy Institute, 6(5), 5.

Ibarra, H., & Obodaru, O. (2009, January). Women and the vision thing. *Harvard Business Review*. Retrieved December 6, 2019, from https://hbr.org/2009/01/women-and-the-vision-thing

Inside Higher Ed. (2018, April 27). Alumnae establish ambitious goal: $1 million each from 100 women. *Dartmouth News*. Retrieved October 2, 2020, from https://news.dartmouth.edu/news/2018/alumnae-establish-ambitious-goal-1-million-each-100-women

Iowa Women's Foundation. (2015). *She matters: We listen and Iowa wins*.

Simon, S. J. (2012, June 23). Growing up: The five life stages of non-profit organizations. The Free Library.com. International Association of Policy Governance Conference. Retrieved May 31, 2020, from https://docplayer.et/21190196-Growing-up-the-five-life-stages-of-non-profit-organizations.html

Strang, L. (2011). Hate networking? Try netweaving. *Late Blooming Entrepreneurs*. Last modified October 10, 2011, from https://latebloomingentrepreneurs.word press.com/2011/10/10/hate-networking-try-%E2%80%9Cnetweaving%E2% 80%9D/

Valburn, M. (2018). New era for women as donors. Inside Higher Ed. Retrieved February 9, 2020, from https://www.insidehighered.com.news/2018/05/11/ colleges-are-turning-women-philanthropists-source-new-money-fund-raising-campaigns

9

Action: The ASK

When philanthropy professionals think about asking a donor for a contribution or gift, it is easy to get caught up in the process, preparation, and anxiety
of the interaction. A well-prepared plan usually ensures better results, but it's
even more important to remember that "an ask" is about creating a joyful
and memorable experience, generating happiness and ideally connecting the
donor to something self-fulfilling, meaningful, and purposeful. Perhaps you
have experienced yourself the feeling of satisfaction that accompanies an
inspirational and transformative gift, or perhaps you have seen the joy or
tears that sometimes envelop a donor when she makes a heartfelt gift. Don't
we want as many donors as possible to feel that sense of joy and fulfillment?
As fundraisers prepare "to ask" women donors, it is helpful to understand
the context of the philanthropic arena, who is giving, and what social and
economic conditions impact giving.

The Changing State of Philanthropy

In the first chapter we explored the current unprecedented wealth capacity
of women and how it will grow in the next decade. As fundraisers think
about crafting an ask, it is helpful to reflect on current shifting philanthropic
patterns and how these conditions impact the mindset of donors, specifically
women. Each year numerous national philanthropy groups analyze emerging
patterns of charitable giving. Here are a few of the latest statistics:

© The Author(s), under exclusive license to Springer Nature
Switzerland AG 2022, corrected publication 2022
L. A. Buntz, *Generosity and Gender*,
https://doi.org/10.1007/978-3-030-90380-0_9

- According to a *Chronicle of Philanthropy* analysis of Internal Revenue Service data, only 24% of taxpayers reported on their tax returns donating to charity in 2015. That's down from 2000–2006 when that figure was routinely 30 or 31%. (Lindsay, 2017).
- Target Analytics found that the median number of small donors has climbed only once in 14 years, since 2002. From 2005 to 2015, the figure sagged 25% (Lindsay, 2017).

In 2017, Congress passed the Tax Cuts and Jobs Act which altered the charitable giving landscape for individuals who give philanthropically. Several studies indicate that the number of households itemizing deductions dropped from 45 million in 2016 to approximately 16–20 million in 2018 (Frank, 2019). Meanwhile, the wealth of the Forbes 400 has increased by 2000% since 1984 (Callahan, 2017). In 2018, while giving from larger donors increased, total giving was down by 1.7% when adjusted for inflation (Giving USA, 2019). The following year (2019) total charitable giving rose 4.2% driven by an increase in giving from individuals (Giving USA, 2020). 2020 was the highest year of charitable giving on record, a 5.1% increase over 2019, boosted by the stock market, generous individuals, and foundations (Giving USA, 2021).

How the COVID-19 pandemic will impact giving over a long period of time is still an unanswered question. Currently, coronavirus giving tops $1 billion worldwide, exceeding giving during previous disasters (Parks, 2020).

So, what's happening? If there is more wealth, are people giving less, are fewer people giving, or are the givers concentrated in the High Net Worth (HNW) category? Where are the women in these changing tides? Part of the answer is that in the philanthropic world, fundraisers are spending more time working with HNW donors and minimizing their time and effort soliciting donors who give smaller amounts.

Additionally, the number of small donors has been declining for two decades. Between 2000 and 2016 the percentage of households giving to charity declined from 66 to 53% (Collins & Flannery, 2020). This trend has caught the attention of the Gates Foundation. Their belief is that large funders can help expand the quantity and quality of giving. "We want to double everyday givers. They are the closet to the needs in the community," Bill Gates commented (Hall, 2021). This includes increasing contributions from a diverse group of donors, using more digital tools that can engage a wider range of prospects, promoting events like Giving Tuesday and partnering with IDEO, an international consulting firm creating innovative ways to make giving easier for modest donors to find worthwhile causes.

Women donors are everyday donors and high net worth donors. Their interests and ability to give are growing in range and scope. Dr. Una Osili, Associate Dean for Research and International Programs and Professor of Economics and Philanthropic Studies at Indiana University's Lilly Family School of Philanthropy predicts that as more women and people of color penetrate leadership positions, they will impact not only the economy, but the future of giving (Yang & Taylor, 2019). This could help increase the number of modest donors and women donors in general.

The philanthropic community will need to adjust to these changes and it may take some time. Fundraisers need to constantly assess the changing environment considering the impact on donors. Women's philanthropy initiatives need to be inclusive of all types of donors and levels of gifts. Understanding, practicing, and implementing effective "asks" of a broad spectrum of women donors is more essential than ever.

The Goal—Purpose and Money

Making an ask of a woman donor has three primary goals: to create a memorable experience for the donor, one in which she feels supremely happy about her contribution in the short and long term; to match her gift with her life's purpose; and to obtain a contribution that aligns with her passion and purpose while helping advance your cause.

The size of the gift is not the only factor in a successful ask. One donor may give a really large gift having capacity to do that and more, while another may give a small gift, but one that represents a larger percentage of her deposable income. Both can be meaningful. Christian Smith and Hilary Davidson, sociologists at the University of Notre Dame, and authors of *The Paradox of Generosity* concluded that "people who are generous with their money or their time or generous with their relatives or neighbors on a regular basis tended to be happier and healthier" (Arent, 2014). The positive psychological returns from giving may explain one of the reasons initial modest philanthropy can snowball into something much bigger.

And it's not just giving that makes us feel good. Twenty years ago, Allan Luks, a community action lawyer and Executive Director of Big Brothers Big Sisters in New York City, introduced the first concept of the "helper's high" when he studied more than 3,000 male and female volunteers and concluded that regular helpers are 10 times more likely to be in good health than people who don't volunteer (Luks & Payne, 2001).

Yet, happiness and good health are not the same as purpose. Many people feel happy with their daily life, their jobs, family, leisure activities, and friends, but don't have a sense of purpose or answers to the abiding questions, *Who am I? What am I doing here? Where am I going?* Purpose provides the answer to these questions in an underlying sense of peace and fulfillment that transcends the everyday highs and lows, disappointments, successes, loves, and losses. Steve Taylor a senior lecturer in psychology at Leeds Beckett University in the U.K. commented, "When you're living in accordance with your life's purpose you view the challenges and opportunities of life as part of what you encounter along the road. They don't distract you from that larger vision, your ideal, which is like a magnet steadily pulling you toward it" (Taylor, 2013).

Your job as a fundraiser is to help each donor find her special purpose because it will stay with the donor forever, inspiring her to give again. And, if the donor walks away from your ask feeling good about herself and a cause, you have achieved a major step in building a relationship—not just creating a potential long-term donor—because joyfulness is contagious. Her positive experience will inspire others because she will tell others about it.

The Process—Preparation and Planning

Preparing to make a request for a charitable contribution or investment is the culmination of a process. Depending on the size and type of the request, the process can take weeks, months, or even years. It's based on a relationship that has been growing and nurtured by the fundraiser and the donor. Stories have been shared over lunches, dinners, coffees, or zoom meetings. There have been short and long exchanges through emails, notes and letters, and personal interactions. Most importantly, there has been learning and caring for each other and the cause before the eventual request. Still, even the most experienced fundraisers feel some anxiety and apprehension before making an ask.

The preparation phase is the pre-planning for an ask. It's about strategy and intent. Most visits rarely transpire exactly as we envision them, but preparation can minimize surprises and ensure a smoother, and more productive interaction.

In previous chapters we explored the process of learning about your donor's source of wealth, her giving history, and connections with the community. Before any major ask, it is imperative that you do that homework. Does she have the ability to make a gift? What is her giving history? What actions has she demonstrated that lead you to believe she will make a contribution when asked? Do you believe the donor can do more? When would be the right time to ask for a gift?

Define if the ask will be of an individual, a couple, or a family. If the audience is multiple people, having some insight into the relationship dynamics will be critical. Are all the right family members in the room? Watching interactions and assessing donors' behaviors in different circumstances is one of the reasons fundraisers have multiple meetings or interactions with donors before they make an ask.

Women are experts at relationships; they define their lives and worlds by their connections to others. Think about the connection you have to the woman donor. Is it professional, personal, built on shared experiences or acquaintances? Does it involve trust and respect? Is it casual or formal? Remember, you can be a mentor and guide in her philanthropic journey.

Cheryle Mitvalsky is the former Vice President of the Kirkwood Community College Foundation and a stellar fundraiser. She shared these thoughts about working with women donors. "You have to friend-raise before you can fundraise; it's building a genuine friendship, a genuine trust. And when it's there, when you really value them as an individual and you respect them, whether they give you a gift or not, that's the magic of relationships" (Mitvalsky, personal communication, September 28, 2017).

Recording and reviewing your experiences with a donor is helpful and insightful. Review the notes of past meetings considering what have been the most effective types of interactions with the donor. Does she like to have lots of facts, stories, or data about what other donors are doing? What do you think would be the most inspiring approach? Is there someone else—another fundraiser or donor—who should be part of the conversation? Often it can be effective to have a trusted friend or colleague of the donor join in the ask, but it is imperative that any participant in the meeting make a commitment and contribution prior to the ask. The golden rule for *volunteers* who solicit is that they have to be a donor themselves.

You have built awareness about an issue or cause, piquing the donor's interest, and she has responded with increased interactions or inquiries. Knowing her history or personal story has enabled you as the fundraiser to know how she is connected to this project. As you prepare, think about what might prevent her from responding, what might her objections or concerns be? Why wouldn't she participate? Anticipate these questions or concerns, and have your responses ready.

After assessing any objections the donor may have, think about how to present the opportunity as a positive and fulfilling experience. Think strategically about setting up the visit. If you want the donor to consider supporting a program or cause, what would be the most compelling way to reach her based on your previous encounters? How do you want to package this part of the ask? Do you want to bring documents, pictures, stories, charts, and graphs? Perhaps she needs a personal tour of a program or to meet a recipient of services.

Know what you will ask, including the amount, but remember, this is a negotiation. Do you want a one-time gift? A multi-year pledge? Is this an annual gift or part of a larger fundraising campaign? Is there an opportunity to name a building or program? You may bring a range of gift amounts, examples of other donors giving similar size gifts, or share the names of friends and colleagues who have also made a gift (with their permission.) Have several options available. As you discuss these with a donor, take her lead. What interests her, what questions does she have, and how can you create an opportunity?

Think through the options for giving. For some donors it's cash, for others, appreciated stock, a planned gift, or a charitable remainder trust. Remember that most donors giving substantial amounts have their own tax and legal representatives, so be prepared to work with their personal advisors on the mechanics of how the gift will be made. It's always helpful to determine ahead of time if there are any parameters that you need to consider as you negotiate with a donor. What is acceptable or unacceptable as a gift or contribution?

The Meeting—Setting, Story, Words

Now that the preparation phase is complete, it's time to set up a meeting. Facts and data, outcomes, results, and supportive documentation are all helpful, but the personal connection and narrative is what will sell the concept or cause to the donor. The meeting should never be a surprise. Donors who have been engaged and invested will expect a financial request at some point in time.

Whenever possible, make the ask in a face-to-face communication. Women tend to rely heavily on facial expressions, including head nodding and eye contact or "paralanguage," the pitch and speed of speaking, hesitation, and gestures, the "mhm" or "ah." All are indications that convey she is listening (Point Park University Online, 2021). Arranging a personal meeting allows the fundraiser to watch all forms of the donor's nonverbal communication including how close she sits to someone, how often and in what way she touches others, her gestures when asking questions, her posture and facial expressions of joy, sadness, confusion, or agreement. Women are very observant of others' behaviors and are better at reading nonverbal clues. Always stay attuned to the congruence of the words and expressions. If a donor says she's interested in a project, but her nonverbal expressions indicate boredom, or a desire to end the meeting, pay more attention to the body language. In the era of COVID, many donor meetings are occurring via zoom. This has proven to be a successful alternative to face-to-face. Seek out the best technology available to ensure a good visual and audio connection.

Asking women for a contribution can occur in multiple settings. Smaller gifts can certainly be accomplished in a group setting, but for a very personal or substantial ask, the donor and fundraiser need privacy. The intimacy of the setting, the quietness of the conversation, and the somber, yet hopeful tone of the ask convey the importance and seriousness of the task.

Stories engage the donor in the real work of the cause, allowing her to envision herself helping, advising, or funding the work. McCrea and Walker (2013) authors of *The Generosity Network*, describe the process "When the prospective partners see themselves as a vital part of the compelling story, they can envision a future where they are partners with your organization."

They go on to explain, citing Marshall Ganz's work on public narratives, that a story has three parts: the story of self—how the donor is involved—making it deeply personal; the story of us—the connection to the organization; and the story of now (Ganz, 2011). As a professional fundraiser, I would change now to—the story of the future. How will the world be different because of her gift?

There are multiple ways to ask for a gift, but a direct conversation usually works best. When a donor agrees to a meeting with you, she knows its purpose, and the fact that she has agreed to a meeting is a very good sign. At the very least she is interested, if not (yet) considering a contribution. Always start with the donor's name, establishing a direct connection, and reminding her that she is unique and special. If you are working with a couple, make sure to address both by name. Social conversation at the start of the meeting is a good way to break the ice. Let the donor(s) take the lead on how much time is spent catching up on life and current events.

After a brief review of the cause including some updated milestones, successes, stories and accomplishments, the fundraiser needs to ask the donor how she would like to be involved. If she responds with some set ideas, explore them, weaving them into your ask. Finally, you need to interject what you would like the donor to do.

Instead of saying "Would you consider?" say "We would like you to consider a $100k gift to fund project X." Or, "We would like you to consider a gift in the range of x to x." The drawback of offering a range option is that the donor may select the lower range so you miss the opportunity for a larger gift. But, the range option is useful when you are a bit unsure about the level of a donor's interest or ability. The question helps test out both of those factors.

Some other possible comments related to the ask are: "I hope we can work on this together," conveying a partnership and commitment on your part. Or use excitement: "I am so thrilled that we can make this happen together." "I'd be honored to work with you." "I can't wait to see the future." "You can make a difference with your gift." Using these phrases communicates a desire to build relationships, connections and equality, in the ways that women talk to others (McCrea & Walker, 2013).

Then, be silent and wait and wait and wait. Watch for nonverbal cues that the donor is interested, confused, hopeful, or excited. Try not to fill the space with your own words. Try not to anticipate what the donor may be thinking. Let her make the next move. Don't apologize, don't rush, and don't be discouraged if she says she needs to think about it. If that is the response, try to arrange a specific time to follow up. If the answer is no, ask if she is open to consider a gift in the future. Always ask for something: time, follow-up, and commitments.

If the donor makes a commitment for a gift, share your thanks and appreciation immediately! Ask how she would like to be informed about how the gift is used or about progress on a project. Ask what type of communication she would like to have in the future.

A friend and colleague, Kate, relayed this story about her response to an ask for a substantial gift. As a former United Way volunteer campaign chair, Kate knew a lot about United Way's programs. A United Way CEO and Vice President for Resource Development asked Kate and her husband for a meeting to discuss a major contribution to a new project. She and Dick are regular contributors to many nonprofit causes in education, arts, healthcare, theater, and social services. The CEO knew that Kate, a former teacher, had an interest in education for high-risk children. United Way's new project's mission was designed to work with high-risk children and their parents, providing support and education during the child's first five years of development. The discussion focused on how the program would work, the partners that would be involved, and what were the expected outcomes. The askers anticipated that Kate would want facts and outcomes. Her questions were answered. She was reassured by the documentation and thoughtfulness of the process. The positive response from her husband when he understood the project was further confirmation that they would make a gift. "I watched my husband have an "A-ha" moment and I knew then we would give a larger gift than we originally planned," she recalled. "All the boxes were checked: it was a charity we supported, a program with huge potential to reach underserved children, we were philanthropic donors in the community, and we could model giving to others" (Minette, personal communication, December 11, 2018).

Thanks and Stewardship

Following an ask, it is essential to follow up with a written note of thanks within 24–48 hours. The note is your opportunity to say thank you for taking time for the meeting and to clarify any decisions that were made. A letter is the best form of documentation and thanks. Texts and email while efficient are less personal. Perhaps there is paper work to complete or a donor needs additional information. Personalize the follow-up communication as much as possible, integrating unique events or interactions with the donor, or sharing reflections of the meeting. After one very successful luncheon meeting with a donor who had made a large six-figure contribution, my follow-up letter contained a humorous introductory sentence (suggested by a colleague.) "There's no such thing as a free lunch." Knowing your donor well enough to compliment, tease, or humor her makes the ask a personal connection. Your follow-up letter should include information about next steps, clarification about follow-up documentation, or confirmation needed to complete the commitment. Finally, invite the donor to the next event or activity connected to the cause she is supporting and begin to think about additional ways to thank and steward her.

The Debrief

What worked and didn't work during the ask? Following these intense and complicated donor meetings, it's a good idea to debrief with other fundraisers or colleagues. Perhaps you came back cheering about a great success. Reflect on what was effective and why. Perhaps you come back deflated by a rejection.

Reflect with colleagues about what could have been done differently and how to follow up with the donor.

Several years ago, I had the opportunity to ask a couple for a very large gift to our United Way endowment. I had known this couple for many years as loyal United Way supporters and leaders in our Alexis de Tocqueville Society—donors who give a minimum of $10,000 annually. I had broached the topic of giving a gift to our endowment several times in previous meetings and had shared some of the details of how their gift could allow them to endow their annual campaign pledge. They had never fully committed to make a contribution, but I knew there was interest and capacity. I needed to ask them directly if they would do it.

They spend their winters in Florida and had hosted United Way events at their home, always being generous, gracious hosts. I asked if they would have lunch with me during an upcoming visit to Florida and they agreed. Although I had other staff with me, I knew I had to take this meeting alone. The couple makes their philanthropic decisions together so it was imperative that both of them attend. On a sunny afternoon we dined on a patio shaded by palm trees and flowers. I shared with them the success that our United Way had achieved, but more importantly the need for legacy gifts to sustain our programs in the future.

This couple supports educational opportunities for children and our United Way had made a big investment in this area. Knowing them and how they make decisions, it was essential that I emphasize the successful programs that they supported, as well as the financial benefits of a new endowment. They have a multi-generational family business and take a long-term view of their investments in the community. An endowment request seemed like the right ask. I had come prepared for lots of questions or reasons they might not agree to my request.

Reminding them of our previous conversations about this topic, I finally got to the *specific* ask of a substantial six-figure gift and explained the reasons this would be a good long-term investment. I emphasized that their leadership would influence other donors, leading the way for future gifts to help children. Fortunately, they had also prepared for the meeting and clarified how the gift would be given including the timing of it. After a few moments and glances at each other, they finally said, "Yes!" The joy, excitement, and gratitude that I felt was matched by the smiles on their faces and a sincere hug of appreciation at the end of the lunch.

During the debrief with my colleagues I reviewed my history with these donors, the multiple meetings that had occurred and explained their style of giving. This couple wanted data, results, and a projected financial impact of their gift. I was very conscious to always include both husband and wife in my conversations and to come prepared with stories and information. This gift was especially attractive to them because it was a new opportunity to give to our Foundation and they would be recognized as giving one of United Way's largest gifts. It took more than a year to secure this gift, but each meeting brought us one step closer to a great outcome and a successful ask.

Bibliography

Arent, W. A. (2014). If giving makes people happy, authors ask, why not give more? University of Notre Dame, College of Arts and Science. Retrieved May 21, 2020, from https://generosityresearch.nd.edu/news/if-giving-makes-people-happy-authors-ask-why-not-give-more/

Callahan, D. (2017). *The givers* (p. 17). Alfred A. Knopf.

Collins, C., & Flannery, H. (2020). *Gilded giving 2020: How wealth inequality distorts philanthropy and imperils democracy* (p. 2). Institute for Policy Studies.

Frank, R. (2019, June 18). *Charitable giving dropped last year in the wake of the new tax law*. Retrieved July 6, 2020, from https://www.cnbc.com/2019/06/18/charitable-giving-dropped-last-year-in-the-wake-of-the-new-tax-law.html

Ganz, M. (2011). Public narrative, collective action, and power. In S. Odugdemi, T. Lee (Eds.), *Accountability through public opinion: From inertia to public action* (pp. 273–289). Washington World Bank.

Giving USA. (2019). Retrieved January 25, 2020, from https://givingusa.org/giving-usa-2019-americans-gave-427-71-billion-to-charity-in-2018-amid-complex-year-for-chartiable-giving/

Giving USA. (2020). Retrieved November 24, 2020, from https://givingusa.org/giving-usa-2020-charitable-giving-showed-solid-growth-climbing-to-449-64-billion-in-2019-one-of-the-highest-years-for-giving-on-record/

Giving USA. (2021). Retrieved December 21, 2021, from https://philanthropynetwork.org/news/giving-usa-2021-year-unprecedented-events-and-challenges-charitable-giving-reached-record-47144

Hall, H. (2021). How Bill and Melinda Gates seek to reverse declines in the ranks of small donors. *Inside Philanthropy*. Retrieved March 4, 2021, from https://www.insidephilanthropy.com/home/2021/3/4/billionaire-couple-seeks-to-reverse-declines-in-the-ranks-of-low-dollar-donors

Lindsay, D. (2017, October 3). How America gives special report: Breaking the charity habit. *Chronicle of Philanthropy*, p. 2.

Luks, A., & Payne, P. (2001). *The healing power of doing good: The health and spiritual benefits of helping others* (p. 361). iUniverse.com Inc. digital version.

McCrea, J., & Walker, J. (2013). *The generosity network* (p. 183). Deepak Chopra Books

Parks, D. (2020, March 5). Coronavirus giving tops $1 Billion. *Chronicle of Philanthropy*. Retrieved September 3, 2020, from https://philanthropy.com/article/coronavirus-giving-tops-1-billion-worldwide

Point Park University Online. (2021). Gendered communications: Differences in Communication styles. Retrieved January 7, 2021, from https://online.pointpark.edu/public-relations-and-advertising/gender-differences-communication-styles/

Taylor, S. (2013, July 21). The power of purpose. *Psychology Today*. Retrieved April 15, 2019, from https://www.psychologytoday.com/us/blog/out-of-the-darkness/201307/the-power-purpose

Yang, C., & Taylor, W. (2019). Gender and future of charitable giving. *Ms. Magazine*. Retrieved June 30, 2020, from https://msmagazine.com/2019/06/27/gender-and-the-future-of-charitable-giving/

10

Acknowledgment: Myths, Mystery and Magic

Offering gratitude for a donor's gift of wealth, wisdom, or work is one of the best parts of a fundraiser's job. As the fifth step in our six-step process to engage and work with women donors, it is imperative to think about acknowledgment as an ongoing and continuous activity, ebbing and flowing depending on the donor, gift, fundraiser, and cause. Thanking people and demonstrating gratitude is an expression of good social graces, but more importantly it connects the giver and receiver in a special bond. Yet, the type, amount, timing, frequency, choice, and enactment of a thank you or acknowledgment are still a bit of a mystery. The type of thank you that appeals to one donor may not work for another. We are learning more everyday about this process, especially as it relates to women donors.

Creating a Donor Relations and Stewardship Plan is unique to every fundraising department and organization. *Donor relations* are usually described as donor-based activities that seek to deliver the message of the organization to prospective philanthropists in order to attract and sustain their contributions; it's the overall plan that fundraisers and organizational leadership develop to guide their work (Kaufhold, 2017).

Stewardship is a process within the donor relations plan. Defined most frequently as "gift-centered activities" occurring after a donor has given a contribution, stewardship consists of communicating and nurturing the relationship with the donor including acknowledgment and appreciation, thanking donors, and ensuring compliance with the donor's intent (Kaufhold, 2017). It's about building trust between the donor and the fundraiser or the donor and the nonprofit organization. A trusted rule says that for every time you ask a donor for a gift, you should contact them two other times without asking for money (Grace, 2005, p. 146). The important point is that stewardship and donor relations are not the same. Fundraisers need to think about stewardship before they ask for the gift and have a plan for how to provide it.

The Purpose of Acknowledgment

There are countless reasons to thank donors, but most programs focus on four primary goals.

1. Gift receipt—Sending an acknowledgment documents the gift for the organization and the donor. A written acknowledgment usually includes verification of the nonprofit's tax exempt status, the amount and date of the contribution, and any conditions associated with the gift. Nonprofits are required to send tax documentation for charitable gifts. Most often nonprofits send gift receipts for donations of $250.00 or more.
2. Making the donor feel appreciated—Saying thank you is just good business. You want to make the donor feel valued and appreciated as quickly as possible. If you can surprise them, wow them, honor them, or make your thank you unique, it will be remembered long after it was received. Most nonprofits establish a guideline of thanking donors within a specific period of time, ideally 24–48 hours after receiving a contribution.
3. Improving the possibility of generating another gift, or an increased gift, next time the donor contributes. Once a donor has given a gift, the likelihood of a repeat gift increases with an acknowledgment. Considering that retention rates are not very high for first-time donors, with estimates as low as 20% and only 45.5% for overall donor retention, every acknowledgment is important (Bloomerang, 2021; Levis et al., 2018).
4. Improving the quality of the relationship. Fundraisers need to show and communicate their gratitude and appreciation for the donor's gift to build on the relationship that has been established. If donors feel positive and engaged in a relationship, the probability of creating a loyal and long-term donor increases (Shang et al., 2018).

Two barriers prevent many programs from being successful in their stewardship efforts: lack of data and continuity of staff. Investing in good data systems and having experts who can analyze and interpret the results is a substantial financial investment. Without good data, we make guesses about donors, what they want, how they give, what they care about, and what are their preferred giving methods. A lack of data makes it difficult to track the impact of a donor's investment and provide meaningful reports. As a result, we design acknowledgment programs around what professionals *think* donors want and what we *think* works.

Penelope Burke is a well-known expert in donor research and steward-ship. In her first book, *Donor Centered Fundraising*, she identifies three things donors want to know after they give a gift.

- That it was received and you were pleased with it
- That the gift was set to work
- That the project or program to which the gift was directed is having or had the desired effect (Burke, 2008, p. 31).

Burke explains that thanking donors and letting them know how their gift is going to be used can be accomplished fairly easily through a wide variety of communications. But information about the impact of the gift is more diffi-cult as it usually needs to occur over a period of time. Fundraisers will need to partner with other organizational staff to collect data and stories illustrating the importance and effect of such gifts. Take the time to identify how your donor wants to receive ongoing information—what type, how often, and in what format. If there is an opportunity to see the gift "in action," invite the donor onsite to provide a visual and more memorable experience.

The process of ongoing communication with donors leads us to the second barrier, staff continuity. Relationships take time to grow and develop. Turnover rates in the field of fundraising have always been an industry problem. According to a Harris Poll study conducted by the *Chron-icle of Philanthropy* and Association of Fundraising Professionals, 51% of fundraising professionals in Canada and the U.S. say they plan to leave their jobs within the next two years and 30% say they plan to leave the profession all together by 2021 (Joselyn, 2019). This lack of continuity of staff inhibits the possibility of good stewardship.

When K. Sujata, the former president of the Chicago Foundation for Women, arrived at the foundation, she quickly discovered that stewardship had been a challenge for the organization. Women donors were unhappy that there had been a high rate of turnover among the fundraising staff and she had to work very hard to rebuild trust. Sujata made a special effort to meet with women donors, listen to their concerns and share information about the work of the foundation. When she retired in 2019, after leading the foundation for eight years, she received a lovely note from a donor commenting on how the stewardship of donors had changed because she had been a consistent and trusted voice.

Anecdotes like this and experience observing fundraising programs for many years indicate that the most successful programs have consistency in leadership staff, continuity in their practices and long-standing relationships with donors. So how do we work with women donors to create the best and most successful stewardship programs and find the best magic and mystery of thankfulness?

Myth—Women Want What Men Want

One of the myths about donor recognition is that one-size-fits-all, or at least that is how many fundraisers operate. Driven by the need for efficiency and effectiveness, they default to standard thank you templates, mass emails, ads in the newspaper, or social media posts. While these practices might include slight modifications for the age of the donor, size of the gift or other personal factors, currently there seems to be very little difference in stewarding men and women.

Men expect to be acknowledged and thanked, but may tend to view their contributions as transactions. Often, they operate in a reciprocal relationship with other donors.

Or, as a woman donor explained, "My husband picks up the phone, calls a few of his friends, asks them to contribute to his charity and then he will return the favor." Their Return on Investment (ROI) tends to focus more on organizational results and what was accomplished rather than nurturing ongoing relationships. Women and men differ in the ways they like and want to be recognized. Acknowledging a woman donor and letting her know that you appreciate her contribution needs to be unique and special to her. Women want more than a mere "thank you." They want an *experience*, a connection, and an opportunity to use their philanthropy as an extension of their interests. Some want to grow their professional network, others want to engage their family members or friends, access career opportunities, or continue to learn about causes. This extended acknowledgment plan is another way to continue the relationship with the donor long after the gift has been received.

Connection

Beth Mann, Vice President of Institutional Advancement at the Jewish Federation of North America shares these thoughts, "Men give based on who's asking. Women give based on who's receiving" (Stiffman, 2015). Many women give to a cause because they have a personal connection with it or have experienced an emotional reaction to the proposed need and have been effectively asked for a gift. It's about touching, feeling, seeing, and experiencing impact. When a donor makes a gift, she begins to establish a relationship with the fundraiser, the organization, and the cause. She is looking for meaning and community. How that relationship is managed, maintained, and nurtured is dependent on the fundraiser. As explained in Chapter 6, making a gift that is purely transactional doesn't usually fuel a donor's mind and spirit.

One of the best ways to thank a donor is to do it through a personal interaction—a luncheon meeting, a phone call, a zoom call, or a visit to her home. These are opportunities to say thank you and explore additional ways the donor can stay engaged, including volunteering, leading a committee, participating in grant making decisions, or serving on the board. Asking a woman to increase her engagement lets her know that she is valued for all of her talents, not just her money, and expands her connections to the cause. Donors will tell you if this is an opportunity they want to pursue. Having the recipient of a donor's gift send a thank you note or letter about how it impacted their life is another way to build a personal connection.

Shared Interests

Pay attention to the hobbies and interests of your women donors. For example, a donor may like art exhibits, gardening, music, or educational research. Use that information when you communicate acknowledging her gifts. You can create and nurture a relationship with her by sharing her interests, or at the very least, being able to have enlightening and entertaining conversations with her. A donor who loves music may enjoy an invitation to a special concert. A board member, and donor to a health-related cause would feel honored to have access to a special lecture on a medical topic. Messages from recipients of the donor's gift are especially meaningful: cards from children at a camp that a donor supported or pictures from an expressive arts program, for example.

Engaging Family and Friends

Many women want to get their friends or family involved in their philanthropy. A fundraiser may not consider this a part of "thanking a donor," but remember, women love to connect with others and to share their passion. Additionally, encouraging women to bring a friend or their children to an event or program broadens the circle of potential supporters. A fundraiser can offer special praise and public recognition in the presence of family and friends, and it provides a *group thanks* to the donor. Consider for example Kathy Eno, a volunteer fundraiser, former teacher, board member, and ardent supporter of many nonprofit causes.

She and her husband, Rex, have contributed millions of dollars to universities, social service agencies, healthcare organizations, and United Way. Eno's philanthropy is a combination of volunteering and giving. Over the years she has donated countless hours to boards, committees, and capital campaigns. As her children were growing up, Eno was very engaged in volunteering and philanthropy, which sometimes caused tension. Her daughter, Lindsay, admitted feeling a bit jealous and irritated that her mother was gone so much of the time, until she was asked to accompany her mother to a nonprofit event where Kathy was going to be speaking about community causes and the need for philanthropy. As Lindsay watched her mother articulate the needs for a women's shelter and explain how women could get engaged in giving, she saw her mother in a new light. In addition to feeling proud, she was inspired. The frustration with her mother's absences dissipated. Her mom was doing something important, critical, and helpful to many women in the community who didn't have the resources Lindsay and her family had. The organization that provided the opportunity for Eno to share her story in the presence of her daughter and offer some public praise, thanked her in a unique and memorable manner.

Eno and her daughter have since talked a lot about philanthropy and today Lindsay is following in her mother's footsteps. In addition to her children's school, she has identified several healthcare causes that she supports. Eno has also inspired her son Ben to get engaged in the American Diabetes Association and Juvenile Diabetes. He and his father share the disease and giving back through volunteerism and donations is their contribution to research and treatment. Kathy's actions continue to connect her husband, children and grandchildren to philanthropy, a gift that will keep on giving for generations.

Information and Results

As discussed in previous chapters, women are information seekers. They investigate causes before they contribute, ask questions, seek advice, and want to be educated. When it comes to being thanked for their contributions, women want to know the impact of their gift, especially how it relates to their personal connection.

Several years ago, a researcher at the University of Tennessee conducted a study of the impact different types of "thanking" had on future giving by female donors to breast cancer research. The types of thanking methods were (a) computer-generated letters, (b) voice mail, (c) handwritten notes, (d) phone call or (e) personal visit. The study showed that while none of the methods lead to a financial increase in repeat gifts, thanking methods that allowed for two-way communication between the donor and fundraiser— phone conversations and personal visits—resulted in a statistically significant increase in the number of donors making repeat gifts one year later (Kleopfer, 2003).

Secondly, the study compared female breast cancer patients who received a solicitation letter for breast cancer research to a group who received the letter *and* additional information about clinical trials highlighting the impact of philanthropic dollars on breast cancer research. The clinical trial information alone did not result in the likelihood that a woman would make a gift, but it did impact the gift amount, increasing the average donation by $50.00 (Kleopfer, 2003). Women want to know their gift is working.

Opportunity

Give women an opportunity to grow, to expand their network, and to lead. When women's foundations and funds were developed in the 1990s among the organizational objectives were to teach philanthropy to younger women and to help all women grow on personal and professional levels. When designing acknowledgment programs, think about how to help your donor grow. What new opportunities may she be interested in and how can you facilitate her connections?

One question all fundraisers should ask women when they recruit them as volunteers and donors is, "What would you like to get out of this experience? What would you like to learn?" It's about giving the woman donor something back that she will treasure for the rest of her life.

Mary Lynn Myers grew up in South Dakota observing her family practicing philanthropy primarily through involvement with their church. As a college student in the 1960s and '70s she was actively involved in the women's rights movement and the National Organization for Women. She even debated Phyllis Schlafly in person during the fight to pass the Equal Rights Amendment. After completing a Bachelor of Arts in Political Science at the University of South Dakota and obtaining a Master's degree in Public Service from De Paul University, she returned to South Dakota in 1972 to accept a position in state government. In 1976, she was chosen as a White House Fellow by President Ford and appointed as a special assistant to his Secretary of Commerce. Following this fellowship, she returned to Sioux Falls, South Dakota and joined the Bank of South Dakota, now US Bank, holding numerous management positions. Over the years, Myers was encouraged to be involved in her community as a representative of the bank and served on the boards of the Sioux Falls Area Community Foundation, United Way and Girl Scouts (Myers, personal communication, March 19, 2020).

The invitation from the Executive Director of the Girl Scouts to join their board of directors and finance committee in 1978 launched a life-long passion for the organization. It aligned with Myers's belief that girls need opportunities to grow and to lead, and it allowed her to use her talents in finance to help advise the nonprofit. Her success led to additional opportunities to serve on the Girl Scouts' National Board as National Treasurer and First Vice-President and to become a delegate to six World Conferences, eventually holding the position of Deputy Chair of the World Association of Girl Guides and Girl Scouts from 2005 to 2008.

Myers traveled to 45 countries observing Girl Scouts or Girl Guides. "I visited a school in the slums of Nairobi that was run entirely by the Kenyan Girl Guides Association. Free public education did not exist for girls at that time. Without Girl Guides, the girls would not have had any access to education. It was so meaningful to me and that's why it's been my number one passion and it encouraged me to join the Olave Baden-Powell Society, an international fellowship of women and men to provide support to the World Association" (Myers, personal communication, March 19, 2020).

In addition to being inspired by the programs of Guides and Girl Scouts, Myers met amazing women and had opportunities to grow her leadership skills while advancing the cause of women and girls on a global level. Today, she and her husband have legacy and donor-advised funds at local, national and world Girl Scout organizations, several community foundations, and are active community philanthropists in Naples, Florida where they reside.

Myers's story is just one example of how thanking women can include exposure to new experiences, career and leadership opportunities, new friends, and colleagues. Her life was changed because of her initial volunteer engagement and gift to the Girl Scouts and with every thank you Myers's commitment to the organization deepens.

Mystery—Making Acknowledgment Special

Every fundraiser would be ecstatic and tremendously successful if we had *the* answer to the question, "What makes a woman donor feel special, loved, and appreciated?" What we do know is, when donors feel good about their gifts and feel thanked, they are more likely to repeat contributions, and to stay engaged with the cause. Being appreciated is good for the body, mind and soul. John Amodeo, therapist and author, outlines five ways being appreciated nourishes us.

1. We are being valued. It reinforces a positive sense of self-worth.
2. We are being seen. Someone recognizes our special qualities: goodness, wisdom, and compassion.
3. We are being liked.
4. It deepens a sense of meaning in our lives. Victor Frankl, the famous Austrian psychiatrist and Holocaust survivor, suggests that human beings are motivated by a "will to meaning." We flourish when we live with a sense of meaning or purpose.
5. It connects us. It strengthens our bond to another person. It satisfies our longing for a healthy attachment to others (Amodeo, 2016).

Reflecting on the opportunity to make a donor feel special prompted a reflection on my graduate training in psychology and counseling. Here are a few ideas about building a special acknowledgment for a donor.

Start Where Your Donor Is

In the profession of counseling therapists frequently talk about *starting where the client is*, in other words, don't make assumptions about what someone needs or wants. Don't project your ideas about a solution or outcome into the situation. Fundraisers can learn a lot from the experts in the human relationship business. Ask a woman donor about how she likes to be thanked. Before publicizing names in a newsletter or establishing a donor wall, ask permission. Most donors, but not all, like to have some public recognition. In the beginning, discover whether she prefers public or private recognition. Ask her to describe an experience where she was recognized for something she did; what made it special and why? What did she like about it or what didn't she like? The type of acknowledgment you need to provide may change over time; someone initially uncomfortable with public recognition may get more comfortable with it or she may choose to stay anonymous. But, don't assume—ask. Many women are very humble when it comes to recognition or may be reluctant to answer the question, so ask their friends or a family member for ideas.

What Makes Her Special

Secondly, therapists and fundraisers should focus on being "strength-based." Essentially this means paying attention to the positive attributes of an individual and building on them. Women donors have multiple strengths and skills; identify and recognize them. Observation is the key to building and enhancing relationships with donors. What is unique about this donor? Observe her in multiple situations if possible. How does she interact in meetings, events or social encounters? If you need more information, ask her family or friends to describe her in several words or phrases. Reflect those attributes back to her. "You are so kind." "I love your jokes." "You have great leadership skills." All of us want to feel unique and be seen and liked, so seize the opportunity to reinforce a connection to the donor through verbal and written recognition or shared experiences. Developing a personal connection to the donor in addition to a professional one is not prohibited and many times friendships and long-term relationships bloom. Just be clear about the boundaries of the relationship.

Co-Create Her Plan for the Future

Most individuals like to create their own future versus having someone else make decisions for them. Donors feel special and loved when someone listens to them and recognizes their past contribution without asking for another financial gift immediately. In fact, don't ask for another gift immediately. Let the donor bask in your admiration for a while.

If a relationship has been established between a fundraiser and donor, it can be fun and bonding to co-create a future plan. Bring ideas to her about how to stay engaged with a cause focusing on the strengths and skills she could contribute. What ideas does she have? Asking for advice is one of the most flattering overtures we can offer. People like to be asked for their input and women donors do have opinions, we just need to draw them out. Then, give her credit for the ideas that are implemented. It doesn't cost anything and will truly make her feel unique and valued. What would give her purpose and a sense of meaning?

Lydia Brown never sits still. If there is a job to be done, an opportunity to learn, or a new challenge presented, Brown is there. As an active community donor, she has been involved in many nonprofit boards and women's organizations, and eventually our paths crossed through mutual friends and United Way. Initially, I recruited her to co-chair our annual United Way campaign, moving into the chair role the following year. Campaigns had been increasing and when we met to discuss the possibility of setting a $10 million goal, the highest amount ever raised, Brown jumped at the chance. We met with previous campaign chairs and co-created a plan that would engage companies, donors, and women.

At the same time, our United Way was exploring the development of a women's philanthropy initiative. I approached Brown about the possibility of being one of its founders and again we began to hatch a plan. We hosted planning events at women's homes, held focus groups, and eventually launched a women's philanthropy and leadership group.

Brown has great ideas, tons of connections, and loves to create. She successfully raised $10 million dollars for a United Way annual campaign, beating every previous record, and continues to be one of the charter members of the United Way's *Women United* Initiative. Today, the *Women's United* Initiative has more than 300 members. The power of our co-creation was a combination of asking Lydia for her ideas, fueling her passion for philanthropy, using her connections to other donors, and offering her an opportunity to create a legacy. Thanking her publicly fueled her enthusiasm and she received accolades and recognition from others for her creativity, determination and results.

Magic—Memorable and Impactful Thanks

What is one of your most memorable philanthropy experiences? What made it memorable? During the research for this book, these questions were asked of numerous women philanthropists. The range of responses was vast, and none focused on the size of the contribution. Most of them described the intense feelings they experienced by helping individuals, making a difference or advancing a cause. They talked about the inspiration to give and feelings of accomplishment when they witnessed the results of their work. Many of the donors did not have wealth early in their life and career. As their wealth capacity changed, they felt privileged to be able to help others. For some women this was a deeply emotional interchange and reflected the power of philanthropy for both the donor and the recipient.

Salma, the co-owner of a printing company, described her decision to pay off the debt of a destitute employee. Julie chaired a successful capital campaign for her college. Fredricka funded political action activities focused on gender equality issues. Karen started a family fund at the local community foundation. Each of these women gave little thought to how they would be thanked because giving fueled their spirit. The experiences stayed with the donor because it touched her heart. The task of the fundraiser is to acknowledge the donor and multiply those tender and special feelings. Women may not want public recognition, but consider organizing a small group of grateful recipients and supporters who can provide a blanket of gratefulness—most women will bask in the warmth of knowing their gift touches other's lives.

Recognition Creates More Philanthropy

Kohler Company, a privately held 145-year-old business with more than 38,000 employees globally is best known for its bathroom design products, furniture, tile, engines, generators, as well as golf and resort destinations. Laura Kohler is the great-granddaughter of company founder John Michael Kohler, daughter of CEO David Kohler, and holds the title of Senior Vice President of Human Resources, Stewardship, and Sustainability. When you speak with her, you immediately sense her pride in the company her family founded and how seriously she takes her role as its spokesperson. She clearly loves her job and believes that she has influenced how the company engages employees, shares the story of their work, and makes new innovative philanthropic investments.

Since joining the company in 1999, Kohler has helped harness the innovation of her employees to create solutions to local and global problems in the areas of health and sanitation, community engagement and stewardship, and building new collaborations with other major foundations. She has done this by telling the Kohler story internally and externally. "I am a steward," she says. "I am here to take the company to the next level and to get millennials engaged" (Kohler, personal communication, 2018).

One of her proudest endeavors has been Kohler Foundation's work with the Gates Foundation and Caltech funding sanitation efforts in India's schools. "We know that sanitation impacts the lives of women and girls," she said in an interview. Millions of girls all over the world spend their day toting water for their families' drinking and sanitation needs. She tasked Kohler's engineers to develop a closed loop flush toilet system that recycled waste, prevented ground water pollution and could be used in homes and schools lacking existing plumbing systems. So far, the Kohler Clarity Water Filtration System has impacted more than 9,000 students in India and China. Kohler sees this kind of innovation as a way to inspire employees to use their skills and creativity philanthropically. It is an extension of the company's key brand and products while demonstrating stewardship and helping women and girls.

Listening to her employees and using their input to help create new solutions is a gift of Kohler's. She promotes volunteerism, supports the arts and social services, and taps the technical expertise of the company's engineers. Her approach to management and engagement is a bit of a departure from the company's more paternal top-down approach, and Kohler feels positive about the results. "Stewardship and sustainability can both be part of social good. And, it helps if the ideas are commercially viable. We *can* make the world a better place" (Kohler, personal communication, November 17, 2017).

Every engineer who worked on the project contributed a gift of time and talent. Laura and the Kohler Company received recognition and thanks by receiving the Mahatma Award for Social Good. The presentation of the award and an interview with Kohler created a platform for the promotion of innovative partnerships and philanthropy. While the award was memorable, the possibility of more third world projects was the best form of thanks. In this same vein, Lura McBride, a CEO of a large manufacturing company in the Midwest, says it best. "Recognition is not the driver. It is how can I be a multiplier. How can my philanthropy create more? I believe in paying it forward, – if I can inspire someone else to give, then maybe they will inspire someone else" (McBride, personal communication, January 21, 2020).

Thanking an Inspirational Woman

"The measure of one's life is not how long, how much, it is how good."
-Helen G. Nassif, philanthropist, attorney (UnityPoint-St.Lukes 2017).

Helen G. Nassif grew up in Cedar Rapids, Iowa, the youngest of nine children born to an immigrant family. While the older children worked in the family grocery store and oriental rug business, the three youngest, Michael, John and Helen were encouraged to further their educations (Unity-Point Health, 2017). She attended Coe College in Cedar Rapids, Iowa, George Washington University Law School in Washington, DC, and built a successful career in banking, government, and real estate.

Nassif and her husband began their philanthropic journey in the early 1990s. She always fondly remembered her hometown, and in 1996 made her first six-figure contribution to St. George Orthodox Church there. When she wanted to honor her brother, Dr. John Nassif, who had practiced dentistry there and died of heart disease at age 50, she made her first gift to Unity-Point Health–St. Luke's Hospital for the establishment of a new heart center. A savvy businesswoman, she asked about naming rights for that donation, which was met with great enthusiasm. Putting her name on the building let the community know that women can be bold and brave in their philan-thropy. The following year she made another donation, this time to fund the Helen G. Nassif Center for Women's and Children's Health at the same hospital. Several other large contributions followed, including funding a cancer and radiation center at UnityPoint Health-St. Lukes and additional gifts to other organizations in her community totaling more than $8 million.

When Nassif passed away at age 98, UnityPoint Health-St. Luke's wanted to recognize her legacy. A video was produced, a legacy booklet designed, and when a recognition event was planned, the Nassif family siblings, children and grandchildren, turned out in numbers. It became a multi-day event and family reunion celebrating her life and legacy bringing together and demon-strating how the power of one woman inspired her family and others to "step in and step up" their philanthropy.

Suggestions for Acknowledging Women

1. Create a Women's Gratitude Day. Have staff or board members call donors and thank them adding highlights about women who have given gifts to the organization. Thank them for joining this special group of women donors.
2. Build a gratitude scrapbook and give it to your donor. Include words and pictures of her work and how it impacted others, or make a video.
3. Create a gratitude box and include thank you notes from all the people that were touched by her gift of time or treasure. Include notes from younger women who are inspired by the donor's philanthropy.

4. Create something handmade, a dessert, a plant, a video, photo collage—and add a note of thanks.
5. At the next meeting of women donors have an appreciation circle, each woman can share an attribute about others that she admires.
6. Establish a scholarship in the donor's name.
7. Create a piece of music especially for her and play it at a recognition event.
8. Create a video interviewing other women about your donor's giving.
9. Do a "roast" of admiration and thanks, invite other women from your community who are contributors to other causes.
10. Use data to identify loyal, long-time contributors and offer them a special treat—lunch with the CEO, or front row seats at an event.
11. Post all your words of gratitude on your website or social media, creating a word cloud around her name.
12. Nominate your woman donor for special awards (with her permission).

Finally, hire the best people and keep them as long as possible to create continuity. Ask them what they do to thank donors and build positive sustaining relationships and, then, *do it*.

Bibliography

Amodeo, J. (2016). 5 ways that being appreciated nourishes us. *Psych Central*. Retrieved July 7, 2019, from https://psychcentral.com/blog/5-ways-that-being-appreciated-nourishes-us

Bloomerang. (2021). *A guide to donor retention*. Retrieved May 22, 2021, from https://bloomerang.com/retention

Burke, P. (2008). *Donor centered fundraising*, fifth printing (31). Cygnus Applied Research Inc.

Grace, K. S. (2005). *Beyond fundraising: New strategies for nonprofit innovation and investment* (146). Wiley.

Joselyn, H. (2019). Moving on: Why fundraisers leave and how to keep them. *Chronicle of Philanthropy*, pp. 8–11.

Kaufhold, G. (2017). *Fundraising: Donor relations vs. stewardship* (2). Retrieved May 3, 2020, from https://fundraisingwonks.wordpress.com/

Kleopfer, A. M. (2003). *Communicating with female philanthropic donors: How various methods of thanking women and informing them of the use of gifts impact giving* (2). University of Tennessee, Knoxville. Trace Tennessee Research and Creative Exchange. May. Retrieved July 18, 2019, from https://trace.tennessee.edu/utk_gradthes/2-35

Levis, B., Miller, B., & Williams C. (2018). *2018 fundraising effectiveness survey report: Fundraising effectiveness project.* A Project of the Growth in Giving Initiative.

Shang, J., Sargent, A., Carpenter, K., & Day, H. (2018). *Learning how to say thank you* (11). The Philanthropy Center.

Stiffman, E., (2015). What women donors want: Cultivation and steward-ship advice for fundraisers. *Chronicle of Philanthropy.* Retrieved August 20, 2020, from https://www.philanthropy.com/article/what-women-donors-want-cultivation-and-stewardship-advice-for-fundraisers/

UnityPoint Health. (2017). *Generosity, cherished—The legacy of Helen G. Nassif.* St. Luke's Health Foundation, Annual Report.

11

Achievements: Healthcare, Higher Education, Environment

Achievement is the sixth stage in the development of a women's philanthropy initiative. Often thought of as the final phase, a goal constantly hovering on the horizon, it is not the finale, but rather a milestone in the continuous evolution of an initiative. This chapter will focus on three professional sectors that have embraced women's philanthropy with unique and creative approaches, yielding successful outcomes and achievements: healthcare, education and the environment.

Healthcare

Healthcare has historically been one of the most popular charitable sectors for philanthropic support from individuals, foundations, and community-based organizations. Women participate in all of these as donors, fundraisers, and leaders. The most recent data from multiple philanthropy resources paints a picture of substantial financial investments:

- *Giving USA* reports gifts to health organizations increased 6.8% to $41.46 billion from 2018 to 2019 (Giving USA, 2020).
- The *Chronicle of Philanthropy's* 2019 America's Favorite Charities lists Mayo Clinic #2 and St. Jude's Hospital #3 (Stiffman & Haynes, 2019, p. 9).

© The Author(s), under exclusive license to Springer Nature
Switzerland AG 2022, corrected publication 2022
L. A. Buntz, *Generosity and Gender*,
https://doi.org/10.1007/978-3-030-90380-0_11

- Six of the top twenty-five U.S. individual donors in 2019 gave to health-related causes, research or healthcare institutions (Rendon & Di Mento, 2020, pp. 8–30).

Women are intimately connected to healthcare. According to the U.S. Department of Labor, women make 80% of the healthcare decisions in the U.S. (Wentz, 2017). Often labeled the "chief medical officer" in the family, they care for themselves, their families, and loved ones. Upwards of 75% of all caregivers are female and they may spend as much as 50% more time providing care than do males (Family Caregiver Alliance, 2016). Women constitute 70% of the healthcare workforce (Raphael, 2019). And, when they are done working, more than 75% of residents in assisted living communities and 70% of nursing home residents are women (American Association of Long-Term Care Insurance, 2009–2021).

Major Donors

Securing a large personal philanthropic gift from a donor is one of the highlights of a fundraiser's job. In the healthcare industry these gifts typically fund capital projects, new programs, research or innovative partnerships, and are frequently the result of a donor's personal connection to a cause. Something has happened in her own life, or in the lives of her loved ones, that inspires her to give.

Irene Pollin, for example, has donated millions of dollars to healthcare. She and her husband, Abe, earned their wealth as Washington, DC, real estate titans, eventually owning professional basketball and hockey teams, and building entertainment complexes. But wealth couldn't prevent the Pollins from experiencing two heartbreaking tragedies. Both of their children died from congenital heart defects: their son Kenneth at 15 months and their daughter Linda at age 16.

In 2009, Abe passed away and Irene began her journey of personal philanthropy. In 2013, she gave $10 million to the Johns Hopkins Ciccarone Center for the Prevention of Heart Disease in honor of Kenneth, and in honor of Linda, an additional $10 million for heart wellness to the Hadassah Medical Center in Jerusalem, and $10 million for a heart program at Los Angeles Cedars Sinai Medical Center. In addition to these philanthropic gifts, she helped establish Sister to Sister, a Women's Heart Health Foundation dedicated to educating and motivating women to make constructive lifestyle changes to prevent heart disease (Heller, 2016).

Another outstanding healthcare contributor, Lyda Hill describes herself as a "philentreprenuer," someone who combines philanthropy and entrepreneurship. A Dallas entrepreneur, her wealth was built on a career in the travel industry, investments, and a substantial inheritance from her grandfather, Dallas oil tycoon H.L. Hunt. With a total worth of $1.4 billion, she has signed the Giving Pledge indicating she intends to give it all away during her lifetime. Her personal connection to healthcare began when she experienced breast cancer in 1979. Survival prompted her to fund the Oklahoma Breast Care Center. As a firm believer in science as the answer to many of life's problems, she has made numerous investments in other institutions including $50 million to the University of Texas's MD Anderson Cancer Center's Moon Shots Program® to develop improved cancer detection tools, $25 million to establish a Department of Bioinformatics in Dallas, and in honor of her Air Force pilot nephew, $2 million to the University of Colorado to establish a Veterans Health and Trauma Clinic (Philanthropy Roundtable, 2021). In addition, she has invested in environmental projects and parks, higher education and commercial business development in Fort Worth and Oklahoma City.

The achievements associated with these women philanthropists illustrate how working with women donors over a period of time and finding their passions ignites philanthropy. These achievements can be defined from two different perspectives—the donors and the fundraisers. For the donor, it's the opportunity to invest in solutions to healthcare problems, as well, perhaps, to build a legacy. Neither of these women asked for her name on a building or sought significant public recognition, but they are leaving footprints behind, inspiring other women to give.

The fundraiser's achievement is the connection established with HNW donors resulting in a long-term relationship and eventually major gifts. As the donor's story unfolded, a fundraiser thoughtfully considered what would motivate each to give. Relationships were built over time; the fundraiser and the donor became partners. They created a future of better health for everyone. When fundraisers present opportunities to donors that match their motivations and aspirations, everyone wins, and the achievements multiply.

Women Leaders

With deep pockets and autonomy in decision-making, many foundations select illness prevention, healthcare research, treatment, and infrastructure as strategic long-term investments. Women now serve as CEOs of a number of the largest national and family foundations, bringing their gender lens to their organizations, leading countries during the pandemic, and influencing the direction of health-related philanthropic investments now and in the future. Here are a few examples.

Until 2017, Risa Lavizzo-Mourey was CEO of the largest healthcare philanthropy foundation in the U.S., the Robert Wood Johnson Foundation (RWJF). The first African American woman to hold that position, she established a Commission to Build a Healthier America, which published *Beyond Health Care: New Directions to a Healthier America*, in an effort to fight childhood obesity by studying "cross-sector interventions beyond the health care system that are likely to achieve a significant positive impact on the health of all Americans in years, not decades" (Robert Wood Johnson Foundation, 2016).

Since the onset of the COVID-19 pandemic, Robert Wood Johnson Foundation Executive Vice-President Julia Morita has advocated for adequate, sustainable, and equitable funding for public health, noting that one of the biggest public health threats is racism itself (Robert Wood Johnson Foundation, 2001–2021). As a pediatrician and parent, she has spoken about the inequalities the pandemic exposed and highlighted the urgent need for the Center for Disease Control to activate and coordinate vaccine planning to reach all populations.

Melinda Gates has brought attention and visibility to the plight of women's needs, specifically healthcare, to the Gates Foundation, and highlighted this need through her recent book, *The Moment of Lift*. A reluctant spokesperson, she had to be pushed into speaking out about the issues of gender and health. In her book, she focuses on family planning, maternal, and newborn healthcare as top priorities for the foundation. Gates has invested more than $1 billion in family planning efforts worldwide. "Access to contraception can unlock the cycle of poverty for women," Gates claims (OHSU, Center for Women's Health, 2001–2020).

But perhaps the most recent achievements in healthcare management have been the women leaders of countries across the globe as they battled the COVID-19 healthcare crisis. New Zealand's Prime Minister Jacinda Ardern, Germany's Chancellor Angela Merkel, Finland's Prime Minister Sanna Marin, Taiwan's Tsai Ing-wen, Iceland's Katrin Jokobsdottir and Barbados' Prime Minister Mia Mottley all took aggressive action, instituting quarantines, and other public health measures. As other countries left the virus unchecked and were reluctant to close businesses or quarantine residents, virus cases escalated. These women advocated for policies that protected their constituents even when those policies were unpopular. Tsai Ing-wen was among the first and fastest responders, introducing 124 measures to block the spread of the virus. Jokobsdottir offered free coronavirus testing to all citizens and Merkel bravely declared that the virus could infect up to 70% of the population as she admonished everyone to "take it seriously" (Wittenberg-Cox, 2020).

Community-Based Programs

Community-based healthcare programs offer an opportunity for women to get engaged in philanthropy on many different levels: scales of giving, networking, volunteering, learning, and leading. Usually, these programs are centered in a nonprofit organization or healthcare institution. Nonprofit charities with a specific health focus raise money to address a wide range of health issues, employing donors to give annually through an event, or to a specific person/family impacted by disease. While these fundraising drives may be small, they are useful in engaging women donors in early-phase philanthropy or in providing opportunities to step up and be more visible about their contributions. Think about the annual Alzheimer's Walk or a Juvenile Diabetes Gala as an opportunity to get women involved at multiple levels. The fundraising activities can be done in person or through social media.

Family Caregiver's Center

Kathy and Dave Good's story exemplifies the qualities inherent in their surname. Throughout their lives, they had been community volunteers and leaders, respected professionals, supportive friends, generous donors, and caring, compassionate people. Dave was a family practice attorney, bicyclist, marathon runner, and one of the kindest souls you would ever meet. In 1999, Iowa Governor Tom Vilsack appointed him a district judge. He began his new role with enthusiasm and excitement.

Four years later, at age 56, he was diagnosed with early onset Alzheimer's and Kathy began her caregiver journey. As a social worker and therapist, she was very familiar with the network of social service systems and where to look for help and support during this very difficult period of their lives. Still, it was an overwhelming responsibility. She surrounded herself with friends and helpers, managing Dave's care in their home for more than eight years. The last four years of his life were spent at the Hallmar Care Center at Mercy Medical Center in Cedar Rapids, Iowa. He passed away in 2015 and

Kathy knew that her life would forever be changed. She never dreamed her work, and Dave's life journey, would become the catalyst for a gift to the community.

In 2014, Tim Charles, president and CEO of Mercy Medical Center, was visiting Northern Westchester Hospital in New York, where he observed the Ken Hamilton Caregivers Center, a sanctuary for families whose loved ones were experiencing cancer or other chronic health conditions. Charles was intrigued and inspired by the concept of a center to support families navigating significant medical issues. Anticipating the future healthcare needs in his own community, Charles began to think about establishing a center for families coping with dementia or Alzheimer's, two of the most difficult medical and social issues for families to manage. With that, the seed had been planted for the future Family Caregivers Center of Mercy. Charles knew the right person to lead the charge, someone whose life had been personally impacted and who had passion, creativity, community connections, and organizational skills. That person was Kathy Good. Charles and Good had become acquainted when she helped select and purchase artwork for the Hallmar Care Center, where her husband had been a resident. Good also served on the local Alzheimer's Board with Charles' wife, Janice.

Together, Charles and Good co-created a plan for a community caregiver's center. Focus groups were formed and numerous interviews were conducted with community leaders, as well as families that had been touched by dementia. Based on overwhelmingly positive responses, the Mercy Hospital Foundation contracted for a feasibility study to determine support for an endowment campaign. In early 2015, a $2.5 million-dollar campaign was launched. Just months later, in December 2015, Good helped cut the ribbon for the Family Caregivers Center of Mercy, one of the first of its kind in the nation. More than 700 donors, including a woman who changed her estate plans to direct a six-figure gift to the center, contributed to its unique programs.

The center has grown and evolved over the last five years. More than 1,050 educational sessions have been provided and 1,157 caregivers have received information and support as they deal with a wide range of issues including respite care, financial plans, emotional, physical and medical care, and the loss of a loved one. Seventy-eight percent of the caregivers seeking services are women.

This critical community health center would not have been possible without the dedication and passion of Good, the support of the hospital and its foundation, and the generosity of the community.

United Way's Healthcare Initiative for Uninsured Women

Developing a women's philanthropy healthcare initiative in small or mid-sized nonprofits is possible with a dedicated focus and defined strategy. One of the *Women United* groups in Iowa selected healthcare for uninsured women as their focus for giving. As a member of *Women United*, each woman gave $500–$1,000 annually. These membership dues were pooled and a committee of women donors reviewed grant proposals from local nonprofit agencies that provided healthcare to women. One of the primary partnerships that helped promote the women's philanthropy initiative was the local Community Free Health Care Clinic. The clinic's CEO was a nurse whose insight into women's health needs helped the committee learn about the particular needs of uninsured women and make informed decisions about grants. The clinic staff had expertise and insights that were matched with United Way's ability to raise funds from annual donors. The partnerships also provided opportunities for donors to see the work of the clinic through tours or volunteering.

Each year a different woman chaired the *Women United* Committee and co-hosted fundraising and social events. Dr. Johanna Abernathy, an obstetrician and healthcare advocate, became involved and provided her expertise and insights about women's healthcare. Her involvement added a new level of credibility to the decisions the committee made regarding grants and investments. Grants were distributed to more than ten different health agencies for women's annual health exams, breast exams, diabetes testing and education, medications, mental health services, and prescriptions.

The achievements of *Women United* were celebrated at its 10th anniversary in 2015: the group had grown from 30 women to more than 350; more than $1 million dollars had been raised and distributed; hundreds of uninsured women in the community had received healthcare. Fundraisers within this program were extremely successful in promoting *Women United* within local companies as part of the annual campaign, networking women through social events, and providing metrics about community needs. Harnessing the power of the founders' group, each woman donor helped recruit new members. United Way committed staff to this affinity group so fundraisers could build the capacity to steward these women, increase their gifts, and sustain them as members for many years.

Mental Health

One of the most difficult areas of healthcare to attract donors to is mental health, because stigmas attached to these diseases make it difficult for nonprofits to raise philanthropic funds. The Centre for Addiction and Mental Health (CAMH) in Toronto, Ontario has recently launched a new initiative, *womenmind*. Supported by two gifts totaling $6.5 million, its goal is fueling philanthropy focused on "tackling the unique gender issues that underrepresented people face when it comes to their mental health and supporting female researchers to become leaders in the sciences." Sandi and Jim Treliving and family contributed $5 million describing it as "a gift from our family to women everywhere" (CAMH, 2020). The Hudson Bay Foundation added to the Treliving gift providing another $1.5 million to launch the project.

Dr. Catherine Zahn, President and CEO of CAMH says, "Health care research has overlooked the biological and socially determined issues unique to women. At CAMH we have worked hard toward gender parity in recruiting, retaining and supporting our women scientists, and research that addresses mental illness and its manifestations in women. We are leading important projects focused on women's mental health and today, 40% of our researchers are women" (CAMH, 2020).

In the first five years (2020–2025), *womenmind* plans to recruit female scientists, hold research grant competitions, offer mentoring for women in science, and host an annual global research symposium. These financial contributions will help more girls and women as they experience needs for treatment related to mental health issues and encourage women to become involved in the mental health sciences, addressing severely underfunded health issues. *Womenmind* is an example of a private philanthropist and foundation partnership funding innovative strategies and addressing current needs. Fundraisers leverage these types of personal gifts and match them with other public or private funding sources to multiply the gift and outcomes.

Suggestions for Fundraisers Working in Healthcare

There are numerous opportunities to pursue a women's philanthropy initiative in the healthcare arena. Here are a few opportunities to explore.

1. Select donors who have a personal connection to a specific cause and ask them to help co-create, support, and lead the development of a new program or service within an existing healthcare institution.
2. Incorporate women donors into wellness programs at your company and local charity events. As they model healthy living, they will inspire others to follow.
3. Ask local sports celebrities to promote giving to healthcare causes.
4. Nonprofits with a recreational focus can align with women donors to sponsor events and encourage healthy lifestyles for girls and young women.
5. It is important to advocate for mental and emotional health. Look for a brave spokesperson and donor who can share stories and encourage others to step up their giving for nonprofits that provide such services. Ask these donors for a challenge grant to match gifts.
6. Use digital giving options. Women give more online than do men. Friends give when friends ask; develop a social media giving campaign for a specific cause. Focus on national heart month or breast cancer awareness, for example.
7. Tier your giving programs to provide opportunities for all levels of donors: Small annual or one-time gifts can be used to support ongoing programs within a healthcare facility or be pooled to help launch new ones. Larger gifts can be directed to capital projects or endowments.
8. Offer opportunities to get involved through learning and volunteering about healthcare-related diseases, treatments, and interventions. Visit clinic sites, hospitals, and research facilities so donors can hear firsthand the stories of patients and families.
9. Have women doctors, nurses, researchers, or administrators become the spokesperson for a specific health issue encouraging giving. Kathy Krusie, Community Physician Network Chief Administrative Officer in Indianapolis, Indiana, shared her story of volunteering for a Heart Association fundraiser. Krusie had promised to raise a certain amount of money for the fundraising campaign and if she achieved her goal, the Heart Association would feature her picture on a community billboard. As she solicited gifts, she explained the promise of a billboard picture. Her friends wanted to see her picture posted around town and gave generously. They knew that Krusie, a rather humble person, would never really like seeing her picture big and bold on street signs; their gifts were a form of affectionate teasing. The other more important incentive was that Krusie was the only woman healthcare executive in

their community. They wanted her to be seen and recognized. (Krusie, personal communication, June, 22, 2020)

10. Create support groups for your health professionals and ask others to support them as essential workers.
11. Partner with public health officials to promote education and address critical and emerging healthcare needs, especially during times of community health crises.
12. Ask women donors to sponsor the cost of healthcare assessments and studies. Research and knowledge are important to women and help inform the development of programs or initiatives.
13. Ask women donors to support healthcare through memorials, endowment gifts, and other activities that can honor loved ones who have passed away.
14. Ask women donors to support prevention-related services: annual physicals, breast exams, and immunizations through giving circles or other women's organizations.

Higher Education

Education is another sector with a long history of engaging philanthropic donors. With a built-in constituency base of alumnae, university foundations spend countless hours and resources courting HNW prospects, students, faculty, and graduates. Many elite universities have alumnae who have amassed considerable wealth through their professional lives, entrepreneurial activity or inheritance. These donors invest in programs they have personal connections to or in honor of the influential role the university played in their personal and professional development.

As state and federal financial support for universities has dwindled and more schools are investing resources in securing private dollars to replace public funding, the search for donors and major gifts has intensified. The following are a few examples illustrating the current state of philanthropy in education and scale of donor's gifts.

• Between 2005 and 2014, a period in which the combined net worth of the Forbes 400 nearly doubled, over 14,000 gifts of $1 million or more were made to colleges and universities. At least 100 of these were worth over $100 million (Callahan, 2017, p. 239).
• In 2016, nearly half of all donations from the 50 largest donors in the U.S. went to colleges and universities (DeBoskey, 2017).

- Allen and Patricia Herbert gave $89 million to the University of Miami where they met as students in 1954 and earned their business degrees. This brings their total lifetime giving to the University of Miami to more than $100 million (Jones, 2019).
- Lorraine Casey Stengl, a physician and real estate investor, donated $38.6 million to her alma mater, the University of Texas at Austin, before her death in 2018 (Rendon & Di Mento, 2020, p. 8).
- MacKenzie Scott recently gave $30 million to the Borough of Manhattan Community College, $50 million to Prairie View A&M University, a historically black college in Texas, and significant donations to women's universities and technical colleges—a rare move that demonstrates support for smaller institutions serving women and minority populations (Redden, 2021).

More than thirty years ago, Martha Taylor at the University of Wisconsin helped launch a women and philanthropy initiative in higher education. A leader in this field, author of several books on women and philanthropy, Taylor is frequently referred to as the "mother of the women's philanthropy movement in education." She began the conversation about how women give differently from men, documented that belief with qualitative and quantitative research, and helped establish the Women's Philanthropy Council in 1998.

In 2009, the Women's Philanthropy Institute published *Women's Philanthropy on Campus: A Handbook for Working with Women Donors*. A survey of twenty-seven different women's philanthropy programs at universities and colleges yielded some interesting results, as well as recognition that higher education could play a larger role in engaging women donors. When the study was published fewer than 10% of higher education institutions had a women's philanthropy initiative. The handbook offers advice and guidance on how to develop one in an educational setting.

Working with woman donors would seem like a natural fit for colleges and universities, especially with the rising number of female students and graduates. In 2017, women comprised 56% of the students on college campuses, and overall there were some 2.2 million fewer men than women enrolled in college that year (Marcus, 2017). In 2019, 36.6% of women in the U.S. completed four or more years of college compared to 35.4% of men (Duffin, 2020). Despite these statistics not all higher education institutions have embraced the fact that there are more women on campus and graduating from their institutions. How many universities currently have women's philanthropy initiatives has been impossible to track.

One factor in the apparent lack of women's philanthropic initiatives in education is the belief that women lack the financial resources to be mega donors. It is true that although women outpace men in terms of earning college degrees, they still lag in earning power. In addition, the number of women faculty lags behind men. While the situation has improved from 31% in 2003 to 45% in 2019, a closer look reveals that women are filling instructor and lecturer roles, not tenured positions (Turner, 2019). And, the American Council on Education 2017 study found that only 30% of college and university presidents were women. Yet, despite these statistics, some programs have achieved stellar results in their efforts to engage women donors.

Arizona State University

Through the leadership of Foundation Chief Executive Officer, Gretchen Buhlig, Arizona State University (ASU) has built a very successful women's philanthropy program. When Michael Crowe became President of ASU in 2002, his wife Sybil Francis became an advocate and leader in the development of the initiative. Alumnae, business sector representatives, and current philanthropists were invited to the table and asked for their ideas about the creation of a program for women donors. The suggestions offered were abundant.

Three core goals were identified: education, philanthropy, and networking. Educating women on what philanthropy can do and what the university offers was essential. Networking current and future women philanthropists with students proved to be an exciting and inspiring interchange. As students provided zest and ideas for the future, shared their stories of struggle and accomplishments, professional women mentored them. The connections established help to build a pipeline of new philanthropists.

ASU's women's philanthropy initiative has never been viewed as competition with other foundation fundraising. Women giving $1,000 each raise $300,000–$400,000 annually. The university asks internal programs or departments to submit requests for funds which are screened and prioritized. The women's philanthropy committee votes on the grant distributions. Since its inception, many women have contributed and now are engaging their daughters and younger donors in the work.

The achievements of this program are the result of careful planning and strategizing. By successfully integrating the women's philanthropy initiative into the foundation's fundraising strategy, the foundation staff and initiatives members have created solid partnerships and support for many of the university's programs. Faculty and alumni from many different disciplines support the women's philanthropy initiative because it brings money back to their programs. It also builds a pipeline for other women in the university to become members of the women's philanthropy initiative (Buhlig, personal communication, March 11, 2020).

Arizona State University's model helps us understand how a women's philanthropy initiative can be successful. Here are a few of the lessons learned:

1. Secure a leader to support the program. Select someone who is respected, well-known, and will stay in the position for longer than a year.
2. Develop a strategy that does not compete with other fundraising within the college or university, but rather complements and integrates with it.
3. Involve multiple generations of women including alumnae, students and community members.
4. Handpick your initial team of committed volunteers, selecting people who are highly connected and networked and will bring friends to the work. (Currently women philanthropy members at ASU are 30% alumnae and 70% friends.)
5. Develop joint ownership with university administrators and women's philanthropy members for the selection of grants.
6. Engage the women to participate in site visits and learning opportunities.
7. Create partnerships with community companies and nonprofits that have women leaders. The university can support their work and engage potential women donors into the philanthropy initiative.

The 4W Initiative—Working Within an Institutional Setting

Another example of developing women's philanthropy within higher education is 4W, Women and Well-Being in Wisconsin and the World, a program created by Martha Taylor, former vice-president at the University of Wisconsin-Madison Foundation, and five leaders from the university. When asked about the need for such an organization Taylor explained, "Fund development departments within universities are organized primarily by school or college affiliation and development officers are rewarded for securing money for their unit, not for advancing women's causes or diversity issues. Activist women interested in creating social change don't view higher education as cutting edge enough to impact women, even though seeding research, teaching, policy work, and leadership development can help advance women and society as a whole. This creates a double bind" (Taylor, personal communication, March 24, 2020).

4W seeks to reconcile these competing forces, working with faculty, staff, and students across campus to bring innovative research to practice and good practice to scale. The programs range from ending human trafficking to promoting women in science, technology, engineering, mathematics, medicine (STEMM) to supporting rural women artisans. 4W has helped UW-Madison become a leading voice on gender and well-being. This model could be replicated at other educational institutions especially during and after the challenging times of COVID-19. 4W has attracted new donors to both its program and the university, demonstrating the meaningful role that women's initiatives can play in supporting women while advancing the university's mission of contributing to the greater good. Taylor concludes, "Higher education and other major institutions in society can be women's most powerful social change partners to make meaningful advancements for women and gender equality in society. Development officers must partner with their institutions to create programs to both attract women donors and make real social change" (Taylor, personal communication, March 24, 2020).

Suggestions for Fundraisers Working in Higher Education

1. When recruiting women donors who are alumnae, highlight what the institution is doing to help advance women.
2. Create a partnership with faculty to create new programs that address social issues impacting women.
3. Fund a scholarship program for women who want advanced degrees in nontraditional fields or where women are underrepresented.
4. Raise money and recruit donors to endow a faculty position for women scholars or an adminstrative position.
5. Organize a group of donors who are "like minded" and pool gifts to create a larger impact, organize a women's giving circle, or women's learning about philanthropy.

Environment

In most of the countries of the world today women remain intimately tied to their environments doing the majority of farming and domestic food production. Efforts to improve these women's lives by improving the conditions of their labors and the environmental issues with which they interact have been in progress for hundreds of years. Yet in the U.S., women's involvement with environmental issues didn't begin until the early twentieth century, and interestingly, were then focused on urban issues related to sanitation, coal smoke, noise reduction, and other problems related to living in cities.

The first American women involved in environmental activism were upper and middle-class women like social worker and philanthropist Jane Addams (1860–1935), and physician, research scientist, expert in the field of occupational health and pioneer in the field of industrial toxicology, Alice Hamilton (1869–1970) for whom the American Society for Environmental History has named its annual award for the best article published outside their *Environmental History* journal. Perhaps the most famous of all-American environmentalists is Rachel Carson (1907–1964) whose book *Silent Spring* spurred a reversal in national pesticide policy which led to a nationwide ban on DDT and other pesticides and "inspired a grassroots environmental movement that led to the creation of the U.S. Environmental Protection Agency" (Paull, 2013, p. 3).

Increased awareness and media attention on a plethora of environmental issues suggests that the environment is a sector of women's philanthropy that will continue to grow for a number of reasons. First, very limited philanthropy is occurring; less than 1% of international philanthropy goes to women's environmental initiatives (Odendahl, 2019). And only 4–6% of Western philanthropy goes to the environment (Campden Wealth Limited & Rockefeller Philanthropy Advisors, 2020). Secondly, women's land ownership and connection to environment will increase; an estimated 70% of U.S. farmland will change hands over the next two decades and 75% of that land will go to women (Heggen, 2018, p. 14). As women gain more access to property, income and inheritance, they will become influential decision-makers. Thirdly, organizations like Rachel's Network, named in honor of Rachel Carson, have successfully promoted women's giving and distributed $2 million since 2000 toward strategic partnerships investing in women leaders and solutions. Their members occupy 100 director positions on boards of major environmental organizations (Rachel's Network, 2015). And Women for the Land, a nonprofit affiliated with the American Farmland Trust, is launching women landowners' learning circles with great success increasing the number of women who are learning about conservation and environmental issues (American Farmland Trust, 2021). Finally, Millennial donors rate the environment their third-highest interest area for giving.

Giving to environmental issues has lagged behind other types of philanthropy partly because these issues have become so politicized. But now individual donors are starting to step in and step up. In the past forty years, world-renowned primatologist and anthropologist Jane Goodall has been one of the most ardent advocates of wildlife, plants, environment, and a generous philanthropist supporting nearly twenty charities, including Heifer International, Live Earth, Amazon Conservation Team, and Best Friends Animal Society. As a scientist, explorer and writer, she has demonstrated that raising awareness and advocating for environmentally friendly legislation is important.

Liz Simon with her husband, Mark Heising, have used her father's hedge fund winnings to bankroll advocacy on climate change. They teamed up with Bloomberg Philanthropies to give $48 million to the Obama administration's efforts to regulate greenhouse gases (Callahan, 2017, p. 174).

Roxanne Quimby, co-founder of Burt's Bees, donated 87,500 acres of land and millions of dollars to reforest and return to wilderness land in Maine's North Woods that used to feed paper mills. It is now permanently protected as Katahdin Woods and Waters National Monument (Wang, 2017).

The Gordon and Betty Moore Foundation has been another large donor to environmental causes. Gordon is a scientist and co-founder of Intel. Betty has had a life-long interest in patient care and helped establish the Betty Irene Moore Nursing Initiative in California. Their Foundation has distributed more than a thousand grants totaling more than $4.5 billion (Gordon and Betty Moore Foundation, 2020). Their environmental projects include helping conserve 170 million hectares in the Amazon and protecting marine ecosystems in the North American Artic. The Moores clearly articulate their desire to invest in conservation and believe that global climate change may be one of the most important challenges of our times. "The Foundation's ability to take risks and make long-term and relatively large commitments should allow it to undertake challenges not accessible to many other organizations. We seek durable change, not simply delaying consequences for a short time," said Gordon and Betty (Gordon and Betty Moore Foundation, 2020).

Another example of women donors and environmental advocacy is the story of *Women of the Storm* chronicled by author Emmanuel David, assistant professor of women and gender studies at University of Colorado, Boulder. David captures the history of how a few privileged white women in New

Orleans used their power to create an interracial alliance that effectively pressured members of Congress to invest in the city and coastal regions revival. The book captures the power of women's activism and demonstrates how political coalitions can be developed across gender, racial, social, and economic class.

Following Hurricanes Katrina and Rita, Women of the Storm was created by women whose families, businesses, and lives had been affected. Led by twelve women and supported by 130 diverse individuals this nonpolitical alliance met weekly to promote legislation, advocacy, and programs. After months of limited activity and support from the state and federal government, they invited state and national legislators to see the destruction. The women successfully advocated for the Coastal Protection and Restoration Fund and won approval from the Louisiana legislature. Years later they advocated again and were successful in getting the Obama administration to sign the RESTORE, Resources and Ecosystems Sustainability Tourist Opportunities and Revived Economies of the Gulf Coast State Act. As a result, 80% of the civil penalties paid in connection with the Deepwater Horizon oil spill were deposited into a trust fund for programs and projects that protect the environment of the Gulf Coast. Women leaders and activists proved that collaborations, partnerships, and determination can result in public and private support for the environment.

Small agencies and small donors also participate in environmental giving. Trees Forever, an environmental nonprofit, was founded thirty-one years ago by Shannon Ramsey. Over the course of three decades, this organization has helped plant three million trees and shrubs throughout Iowa and Illinois. Now, Ramsey wants to expand her donor base and include more women. After a devastating derecho in Cedar Rapids, Iowa on August 10, 2020, that destroyed 75% of the city's tree canopy, Ramsey established a campaign goal of $10–15 million to fund the replanting of trees in the community.

Winona LaDuke

Winona LaDuke is a force in the field of environmental advocacy and philanthropy. A Harvard graduate and member of the Ojibwe Mississippi Band Anishinaabeg, she moved to the White Earth Ojibwe reservation in Minnesota after graduation in 1982 and became principal of the reservation high school. Although she did not grow up on the reservation, she quickly became interested in a variety of issues impacting the Native population and in 1985 established the Indigenous Women's Network focused on increasing the visibility of Native women and encouraging them to get involved in the political process (Brandman, 2021).

Her advocacy continued when she began to read about the Nelson Act of 1887, a treaty that limited how much communal land was given to each Ojibwe household and allowed the surplus land to be purchased by non-Native people. By 1920, 99% of the original White Earth Reservation land was in non-Indian hands (Walljasper, 2012). LaDuke began advocating for returning the lands promised to her people by joining a lawsuit that unfortunately was dismissed after four years of litigation. As a result of that defeat, she established the White Earth Land Recovery Project (WELRP), one of the largest reservation-based nonprofits in the country. Leveraging her own philanthropic power, she used the proceeds from a human rights award ($20,000) she had received from Reebok to fund WELRP's mission to buy back land that had been purchased by non-Natives. By 2000, the foundation had bought 1,200 acres which are held in a conservation trust (Walljasper, 2012).

In 2000, LaDuke ran on the Green Party ticket as vice-president and in 2007 she was inducted into the National Women's Hall of Fame. Today she is the program director of Honor the Earth Fund, a national advocacy group seeking to create support and funding for Native environmental groups. LaDuke has been very successful at establishing partnerships with other foundations and community groups as well as using her celebrity status to create interest and money from other donors.

Women donors are not alone in their quest for environmental advocacy; major foundations have pledged support and resources to study the climate, disasters, health, and science. Most recently the Adrienne Arsht-Rockefeller Foundation Resilience Center announced a commitment to reach one billion people with resilience solutions to climate change, migration, and human security challenges by 2030 (Atlantic Council Annual Report, 2020). And, numerous civic organizations and nonprofits, many of them led by women, advocate, donate and influence policy: Rachel's Network, The Garden Club of America, Women's Environment and Development Organization, Women's Environmental Action, Women's Earth Alliance, Women for the Land-American Farmland Trust, Global Greengrants Fund, and *ecowomen*, an organization that promotes and supports women to become leaders across environmental careers, are just a few of them.

Suggestions for Fundraisers Working in Environment

Advocates for women's philanthropy and the environment can invest in a wide range of programs and initiatives on a local, regional, national, and global level. There are a number of ways fundraisers can help guide women who have an interest in this sector to practice philanthropy and to find resources for their own organizations:

1. More than 125 different foundations are listed on the Inside Philanthropy website as supporters of conservation. Women's initiatives can apply for funding from these foundations, influence their decision-making by connecting to their leaders, and providing valuable information to them about environmental causes. Fundraisers in environmental nonprofits need to find allies among these HNW funders and capture their attention. On a local level, it may be a connection to the community foundation for grants to pursue land preservation, tree planting, clean water, environment restorations, or disaster recoveries.

2. One of the advantages of gifts to environmental causes is that many times there is something tangible to view and touch. It's easier to engage a donor if she can see the results of her gift. For example, Bette Midler founded the New York Restoration Project in 1995 to beautify New York City through transforming open spaces, renovating parks and gardens (New York Restoration, 2021). In 2001, Betty Brown Casey pledged $35 million to restore the tree canopy in the District of Columbia and helped establish Casey Trees, a foundation that carries on the work of planting and caring for trees (DCGov, 2015). While connecting with high-powered celebrities isn't highly probable, you can find philanthropists in your community invested in the environment and encourage them to donate land, connect with state legislators, write articles, or make financial contributions. For example, a local philanthropist and millionaire has invested considerable resources in restoring the Monarch butterfly population in Iowa using his farm as an incubation site, hosting fundraising campaigns, engaging school classes, Master Gardener programs, and numerous other civic groups in the work.

3. Connect with women who work in the agricultural industry, forestry, public gardens, parks, green spaces, or water quality, and with female teachers in these fields at community colleges and Land Grant institutions and invite them to learn about philanthropy.

4. Create giving circles for cause-specific environmental issues or disaster relief.
5. Some activists work primarily on systems change. On a local level, there are issues unique to each community—find yours. For example, in New Orleans, a social innovation and entrepreneurial nonprofit, *Propeller*, collaborated with educational institutions, government agencies, and local neighborhoods to develop water management initiatives post-Katrina (Flandez, 2020).

Fundraisers and community organizers can collectively find new ways for philanthropists to use their financial and political power to create change. Look at the issues facing your community, and ask yourself, "How could environmental advocates and donors help?" Although environmental causes may not be the first choice for many women philanthropists, it is an area that will continue to grow in popularity and need. If our environment is going to sustain us, our families, children and communities, the time is now for fundraisers to help women to consider environmental causes as another philanthropic opportunity.

Bibliography

American Association of Long-Term Care Insurance. (2009–2021). *Long-Term care-important information for women*. Retrieved August 10, 2020, from https://www.aaltci.org/long-term-care-insurance/learning-center/for-women.php

American Farmland Trust. (2021). Women for the Land. Retrieved July 6, 2021, from https://farmland.org/project/women-for-the-land/

Atlantic Council Annual Report. (2020, July 21). Retrieved December 2, 2020, from https://www.atlanticcouncil.org/in-depth-research-reports/report/2019annual-report-adrienne-arsht-rockefeller-foundation-resilience-center/

Brandman, M. (2021). *National Women's History Museum*. Winona LaDuke. Retrieved May 28, 2021, from https://www.womenshistory.org/education resources/biographies/winona-laduke

Callahan, D. (2017). *The givers*. New York, p. 174.

CAMH celebrates the launch of womenmind. (2020, March). Retrieved April 1, 2020, from https://www.camh.ca/en/camh-news-and-stories/camh-celebrates-the-launch-of-womenmind

Campden Wealth Limited & Rockefeller Philanthropy Advisors. (2020). *Global trends and strategic time horizons in family philanthropy*. p. 24.

DCGov, Department of Energy and Environment Case Study. (2015). *Casey trees*. Retrieved January 3, 2021, from https://doee.dc.gov/service/case-study-casey-trees

DeBoskey, B. (2017). *Higher education philanthropy*. Wealth Management. Retrieved February 2, 2020, from https://www.wealthmanagement.com/philanthropy/higher-education-philanthropy

Duffin, E. (2020, March 31). Percentage of the U.S. population who have completed four years of college or more from 1940–2019 by gender. *Statista*.

Family Caregiver Alliance. (2016). *Caregiver Statistics: Demographics*. Retrieved June 11, 2021, from https://www.caregiver.org/resource/caregiver-statistics-demographics

Flandez, R. (2020, August 17). Voice from the Gulf. *Chronicle of Philanthropy*.

Giving USA. (2020). *Charitable giving showed solid growth, climbing to 449.64 billion in 2019, one of the highest years on record*. Retrieved June 11, 2021, from https://givingusa.org/giving-usa-2020-charitable-giving-showed-solid-growth-climbing-to-449-64-billion-in-2019-one-of-the-highest-years-for-giving-on-record

Gordon and Betty Moore Foundation. (2020). Retrived July 30, 2020 from https://www.moore.org/

Heggen, K. (2018). A woman's place. *Iowa Natural Heritage Magazine*. Summer, p. 14.

Heller, K. (2016, July 4). At 92, Irene Pollin tells her story spares no details. *The Washington Post*. Retrieved April 16, 2020, from https://www.washingtonpost.com/lifestyle/style/at-92-irene-pollin-tells-her-story-and-spares-no-details/2016/07/04/5c2cc4aa-3ca78-11e6-a66f-aa6c1883b6b1_story.html

Jones, R. (2019). Miami business school receives a new name to honor philanthropist. *News at the U, Miami Magazine*, 10–15–19. Retrieved March 3, 2021, from https://news.miami.edu/stories/2019/10/miami-business-school-receives-a-new-name-to-honor-philanthropists.html

Marcus, J. (2017, August 8). Why men are the new college minority. U.S. Department of Education. *The Atlantic*.

New York Restoration Project. (2021). Retrieved February 21, 2021, from https://www.nyrp.org/

Odendahl, T. (2019, October). *How funders are stepping up: Women and environment*. National Committee for Responsive Philanthropy. Retrieved December 4, 2020, from https://www.ncrp/201/how-funders-are-stepping-up-women-and-the-environment

OHSU. (2001–2020). *Center for Women's Health. Women who inspire us: Melinda Gates*. Retrieved June 2, 2021, from https://www.ohsu/womens-health/women-who-inspire-us-melinda-gates

Paull, J. (2013, July). The Rachel Carson letters and the making of Silent Spring. *Sage Open, 3*, 1–2. https://doi.org/10.1177/215824401349461

Philanthropy Roundtable. (2021). *Women's history month spotlight: The scientist: Lyda Hill*. Retrieved April 20, 2021, from https://www.philanthropyroundtable.org/10-exceptional-women

Rachel's Network. (2015). *Opening doors*. 2013 Annual Report. https://rachelsnetwork.org/wp/wpcontent/uploads/2015/01/AR2013.small_pdf

Raphael, R. (2019, January 14). Here's why we need more women in health care leadership. *Fast Company*. Retrieved June 11, 2021, from https://www.fastcompany.com/90291711/heres-why-we-need-more-women-in-healthcare-leadership

Rendon, J., & Di Mento, M., (2020, February). Billion-dollar giving streak. *Chronicle of Philanthropy*, 8–30.

Redden E. (2021). *A fairy godmother for once overlooked colleges.* Inside Higher Ed. Retrieved June 11, 2021, from https://www.inside-higher-education.com/news/2021/01/04/mackenzie-scott-surprises-hbcus-tribal-colleges-and-community-colleges-multimillion

Robert Wood Johnson Foundation. (2016, September 13). *Risa Lavizzo-Mourney stepping down as President and CEO of the Robert Wood Johnson Foundation.* Retrieved April 1, 2020, from https://www.rwjf.org/en/library/articles-and-news/2016/09/rlm-stepping-down.html

Robert Wood Johnson Foundation. (2001–2021). Retrieved June 13, 2021, from https://www.rwjf.org

Stiffman, E., & Haynes, E. (2019, November 9). America's favorite charities 2019: Can the boom times last? *Chronicle of Philanthropy.*

Turner, B. K. (2019, March 29). *Though more women are on college campuses, climbing the professor ladder remains a challenge.* Brown Center Chalkboard.

Walljasper, J. (2012, May 16). Our home is on earth. *On the Commons*. Retrieved February 1, 2021, from https://www.onthecommons.prg/magazine/our-home-earth

Wang, J. (2017, October 24). Burt's Bees Co-founder on why she gave away 87,000 acres in Main. *Forbes.*

Wentz, K.G. (2017). Women responsible for most health decisions in the home. *Oregon Health and Science University News.* Retrieved May 25, 2020, from https://news.ohsu.edu/2017/05/11/women-responsible-for-most-health-decisions-in-the-home

Wittenberg-Cox, A. (2020, April 13). What do countries with the best coronavirus responses have in common? Women leaders. *Forbes.* 2020. Retrieved June 13, 2021, from https://www.forbes.com/sites/avivahwittenbergcox/2020/04/13/what-do-countries-with-the-best-coronavirus-responses-have-in-common-women-leaders/

12

Achievements: Women Investing in Business and Leadership

Investing in Women-Owned Businesses

In addition to healthcare, higher education, and the environment, supporting the development of women-owned businesses and leadership programs designed for women are rich fields of endeavor for professional fundraisers. Let's consider some inspirational examples.

Nancy Hayes spent almost twenty years as a senior executive at IBM and had the promise of a long-term career. She remembers distinctly when her superiors offered her a job managing the Southeast Asia operations. Although flattered, she said to herself, "Maybe it's time to leave. I enjoyed my career at IBM, but I had a sense of wanting to feel that my work had more direct impact on people's lives" (Hayes, personal communication, December 17, 2018).

She pursued nonprofit work, accepting a position to lead the STAR-BRIGHT Foundation, an innovative nonprofit charity serving children with serious physical and mental health issues, chaired by film director Steven Spielberg and General H. Norman Schwarzkopf. This introduction to nonprofit work was followed by an opportunity to serve as the CEO and President of WISE Senior Services in Los Angeles. Her experience in nonprofit and for-profit work caught the attention of San Francisco State University and in 2005 she was recruited to be the Dean of the College of Business. Eventually she became Chief Administrative Officer of the university.

How to put all those great experiences to work as she thought about the third phase of her life was a new challenge. "I knew that many

L. A. Buntz, *Generosity and Gender*, https://doi.org/10.1007/978-3-030-90380-0_12

women who owned small businesses were underfunded and couldn't pay me for consulting, so a former IBM colleague and I developed a rewards-based crowdfunding site called Moola Hoop and eventually I drifted into angel investing in women-led start-ups" (Hayes, personal communication, December 17, 2018). Numerous studies support Hayes's observation that women entrepreneurs have a very difficult time getting investment revenue.

- In a study conducted in 2017 at the Tech Crunch Disrupt New York funding competition, male-led start-ups raised five times more funding than female-led ones (Kanze et al., 2017).
- Only 8% of venture capital firms in the U.S. have female partners (DuBow & Pruitt, 2017).
- In 2018 only 3% of venture capital in the U.S. went to companies with a female CEO (Hassan et al., 2020).
- The International Women's Entrepreneurial Challenge Foundation (IWEC) found that women entrepreneurs get only 2% of all venture funding despite owning 39% of all businesses in the U.S. (Kanze, 2019).
- According to *All In: Women in the VX Ecosystem 2019* by Pitchbook and All Raise, only 12% of venture capital decision-makers in the U.S. are women (Stengl, 2020).

Why is it so difficult to get financial support for women-owned businesses? One reason may be that women don't promise the moon to investors or expound on aspirational possibilities. While men are willing to make big statements by painting visionary pictures, women come off as less exciting or confident. Numerous studies have proven that women are asked different questions by investors and are treated differently. This is particularly evident in an analysis of how investors view entrepreneurs making their "pitch" for investment funding.

Pitch events are opportunities for entrepreneurs to give short, informative talks about their companies, or products, and to present their business cases and needs for funds. Dana Kanze, a Ph.D. from Columbia University, and Assistant Professor of Organizational Behavior at the London Business School analyzed pitch presentations and the questions asked by both male and female investors. She found that women were asked more "prevention questions," those focused on safety, responsibility, and security. Male entrepreneurs were asked more "promotion questions," those focused on gains, hopes, accomplishments and advancements. Male entrepreneurs were asked promotion questions 67% of the time while women were asked prevention questions 66% of the time (Kanze, 2019).

So, one piece of advice for women business owners seeking venture capital is, "ditch the pitch," don't participate in these pitch events until the panel of judges is better educated, less biased, and more informed about women-led businesses.

Since her transition to angel investing, Hayes has invested in twenty-three women-led companies. Her philanthropy is the pro bono work she does consulting with women-owned businesses and women entrepreneurs in pitching their companies, working with organizations that support women entrepreneurs and founders of color, as well as executive coaching of women leaders in for-profit companies, and career coaching for women in nonprofit organizations. Additionally, she works to bring other women into angel investing. "Women enjoy being part of an investing community. They are more comfortable when they can join a group, get educated together, talk with each other, compare notes and maybe invest together" (Hayes, personal communication, December 17, 2018).

The importance of female investment decision-makers cannot be over-stated; women are twice as likely to invest in female founders as are their male counterparts, and the number of venture investment firms aimed at women has been growing steadily. Their achievements are teaching us how to engage women as investors, and how to grow women-led businesses. In 2014, for example, entrepreneur Anu Duggal founded The Female Founders Fund, a venture capital firm dedicated to funding new tech-related companies created by women. Through previous experience launching two businesses in India, Duggal discovered the challenges of creating a fund that would offer access to capital for female-owned businesses and create a base of operators who could advise and help women starting companies, particularly those in the technology industry. It took 700 meetings over a two-year period to raise $6 million. One key strategy was asking for introductions to other interested parties when an investor turned her down. Doing so helped her build a large, effective network of funders. Her first major achievement was the company Eloquii, retail clothing for plus-size women, which was acquired by Walmart for a reported $100 million (Chafkin, 2019). With her partner, Sutian Dong, a second phase of funding scored $27 million from well-known investors Melinda Gates, Stitch Fix CEO Katrina Lake, and Girls Who Code Founder, Reshma Saujani.

Another venture capital firm, Golden Seeds Venture, was one of the first angel groups to invest exclusively in women-led businesses. Golden Seeds helps early-stage founders with diverse management teams, expecting that at least one woman is in executive management "the C suite." Nancy Hayes served as the Managing Director of the Silicon Valley/San Francisco chapter of the Golden Seeds angel group for three years. Now, running four venture funds with six U.S. locations, it has 275 members, 170 companies, and has invested more than $120 million since 2005.

In addition to raising capital and launching businesses that help women succeed, the achievements of these venture fund firms changes the narrative about women's ability to develop and grow companies. HNW women donors who are focused on growing women-led businesses may find this type of investment aligning with their interests. They can offer advice, mentor, serve on committees, help vet new businesses, or start an investment group. Many successful women with backgrounds in finance, marketing, investments, or business management are great candidates for these types of contributions.

Suggestions for Fundraisers—Creating Partnerships with Women Investors

1. Survey and list the number and types of women-owned businesses and women start-ups in your area.
2. Partner with your local entrepreneurial center offering to match up women donors with women who are starting businesses. Consider it a mentoring program.
3. Partner with local business schools, specifically MBA programs that have women students and faculty and have them share skills with women entrepreneurs.
4. Gather women donors who have an interest in economic development and consider starting an investment group, including investment advisors.
5. Host a start-up contest with all the winners receiving grants or in-kind support.
6. Work with your local chamber of commerce or state economic development program to get their financial support for women-owned businesses.
7. Feature women-owned businesses in your newsletter, web page and news outlets.

Women in Leadership—Corporate Boards—How Women Lead

Another way women donors can be involved in philanthropy is through volunteer engagement and participation on corporate boards. The following statistics reflect the sobering story of the disproportionate participation of women in the top echelon of the economic sector.

- In 2016, Fortune 500 companies reported that only 6% of women held board chair roles (Whitler & Henretta, 2018).
- The number of women on boards of directors in the Russell 3000 index increased from 15% in 2016 to only 20.2% by 2019 (Stych, 2019).
- Every company in the S&P 500 has a woman on its board of directors, but they make up only 27% of all board seats (Stych, 2019).

Recruiting more women to serve on corporate boards has been a passion of Julie Castro Abrams, the founder and CEO of How Women Lead. Recently described as one of San Francisco's QueenMakers, women power brokers who are making it happen in the community and world, Abrams has developed an *ecosystem* approach to her work with women philanthropists and leaders (Poblete, 2019). Organized under three flagship programs, How Women Lead, How Women Invest and How Women Give, the organization's goals include: influence legislation that impacts women's representation on corporate boards, train and place more women on corporate boards, recruit women venture capitalists to invest in women-owned businesses, and provide grants to programs for women and girls through philanthropic endeavors including a giving circle. "There is a hunger for women to be connected to each other," says Abrams, and all this great work takes money.

Abrams' achievements include a successful legislative campaign in California to get asset management firms to require companies they invest in to have at least two women on their board (Castro Abrams, personal communication, December 3, 2019).

Abrams works diligently to broker requests from corporate boards for women members. She says that there is still a lot of unconscious bias about women's qualifications and abilities to serve on boards recalling the board chair of a large insurance company saying, "I'd love to talk to you about putting a woman on our board, but she has to be qualified."

"The fact that he thinks there aren't any qualified women in insurance who could serve, just makes me crazy!" exclaimed Abrams. "He thinks he has good intentions, he thinks he's on the right side of the issue, but he has a bias and isn't even aware of it."

Another director of a publicly held company called Abrams asking for some women board candidates. She found twelve women in two weeks and when he saw the list he replied, "I could replace everyone on my board with these women; they would all be more qualified than my current board members."

Getting women on corporate boards is a multi-layer process: getting the first woman on boards, getting more than one woman on a board, and moving those women into roles of influence or leadership as committee and board chairs (Whitler & Henretta, 2018). To support and prepare women for board leadership, How Women Lead offers training and education. Charging for such training helps fund some of the work, but Abrams admits they need more strong supporters and philanthropists. "Women need to help other women. At our organization we have a credo - we need to connect each other, move the needle for the good for all women, and be unabashedly visible." She suggests the following five tips for women who want to get on boards.

1. Define your value proposition and practice telling it with a memorable story so people remember you.
2. Be specific about what board role you can play (search firms are typically tasked with finding someone for one of the key committees).
3. Identify 5–10 company boards you would like to serve on and tell people the specific board you would like to support.
4. Reach out and build connections with leaders on the board and C-Suite in the companies you would like to serve.
5. Be of value to recruiters and others with recommendations (Castro Abrams, personal communication, December 3, 2019).

How Women Lead pairs philanthropists with nonprofits who serve women and girls. In the past several years, it has funded multiple programs for women and children in the Bay Area including Prospera, a Latina economic empowerment program, Women's Recovery Services for alcohol and drug treatment and Love Never Fails, a program for the homeless and prevention of domestic violence. In addition to all this, Abrams trains women to be angel investors in women-owned businesses. Currently, she is working on putting together a $10 million-dollar fund.

Developing Women's Leadership Through Training—Women Lead Change

Increasing women's leadership skills and abilities is a part of women's philanthropy. Building women's confidence and encouraging them to take on leadership positions in economic, social and political sectors and to mentor younger women as donors and leaders in their communities builds a pipeline for the future. One women's leadership training program that has had a number of notable achievements is Women Lead Change.

Launched in 2006 by Donna Katen-Bahensky, the CEO of the University of Iowa Hospitals and Clinics and a small, dedicated group of volunteers, it began as a conference for women offering education, training, and support. The concept was to create a venue that would be high quality, exciting, and informative by bringing well-known women leaders to the community to share their knowledge, stories, advice, and to help develop women in their professional careers.

After the initial launch, the conferences that followed included a vast array of famous and accomplished national speakers including: Maya Angelou, Diana Nyad, Marian Wright Edelman, Arianna Huffington, Suze Orman, Betsy Myers, Tina Brown, Gloria Steinem and Barbara Corcoran, to name a few. To fund a conference of this magnitude, the all-women-led planning committee created a successful strategy to sell cost-efficient corporate sponsorships, promoted company brands, and helped build leadership training for female employees. Annual conferences grew to more than 1,000 attendees. Company CEOs realized that at a fraction of the cost of more traditional training, their female employees could learn from women who were leaders in journalism, sports, politics, universities, corporations, art, and film. Obtaining hundreds of thousands of dollars in sponsorships was a major accomplishment that funded the conferences and made money for the nonprofit.

After several years of being managed by volunteers, Women Lead Change hired Diane Ramsey in 2010 as executive director. A woman Chief Financial Officer at Rockwell Collins, a large aerospace company, convinced the company to underwrite Ramsey's position for three years to help launch the nonprofit. Within six years Ramsey took the organization to a new level including the following achievements: expanding conferences across the state, bringing men on the board of directors, establishing a CEO forum for men and women to talk about the value of advancing women at all levels of their organizations, especially senior management; recruiting women to corporate boards, developing a student track to encourage young women in their career paths, funding conference scholarships for students and general attendees, launching pitch events for women start-ups and partnering with the Iowa Governor Kim Reynolds to establish the EPIC challenge to get more women on corporate boards and into leadership positions.

Today, Tiffany O'Donnell runs the organization that has grown to eight staff with a budget of more than $2.7 million. More than 19,000 women and men have attended the conferences. The organization now funds critical research on topics ranging from workplace equity to imposter syndrome, facilitates the Women Connect networking and development program, and offers the 12-month virtual Ascent leadership program, designed to support mid-level, high potential, "pipeline" leaders.

Bibliography

Chafkin, L. C. (2019, January 15). Anu Duggal's female founders fund scored a multi-million dollar exit: Male investors are finally paying attention. *Inc Magazine*. Retrieved June 10, 2020, from https://www.inc.com/christine-lagorio/anu-duggal-female-founders-fund-founders-project.html

DuBow, W., & Pruitt, A. S. (2017, September 18). The comprehensive case for investing more VC money in women-led start-ups. *Harvard Business Review*. Retrieved April 5, 2020, from https://hbr.org/2017/09/the-comprehensive-case-for-investing-more-vc-money-in-women-led-startups

Hassan, K., Varadan, M., & Zeisberger, C. (2020, January 13). How the VC pitch process is failing female entrepreneurs. *Harvard Business Review*. Retrieved June 28, 2020, from https://hbr.org/2020/01/how-the-pitch-process-is-failing-female-entrepreneurs

Kanze, D. (2019, January 24). *TED talk*. IWEC Foundation.

Kanze, D., Conley, M. A., Higgins, T. E., & Huang, L. (2017, June 27). Male and female entrepreneurs get asked different questions by VC's and it affects how much funding they get. *Harvard Business Review*. Retrieved March 29, 2020, from https://hbr.org/2017/06/male-and-female-entrepreneurs-get-asked-different-questions-by-vcs-and-it-affects-how-much-funding-they-get

Pobleto, P. N. (2019, November 17). Meet the bay area's pivotal power brokers: The queenmakers. *The San Francisco Magazine*. Retrieved January 13, 2021, from https://sanfran.com/queenmakers-reshaping-politics-and-the-boardroom

Stengl, G. (2020, January 1). The next decade will bring more venture capital to female founders. *Forbes*. Retrieved April 6, 2020, from https://www.forbes.com/sites/geristengel/2020/01/01/the-next-decade-will-bring-more-venture-capital-to-female-founder/

Stych, A. (2019, September 12). Women's representation on boards reaches a milestone. *Biz Women's Business Journal*. Retrieved September 12, 2019, from https://www.bizjournals.com/bizwomen/news/latest-news/2019/09/womens-representation-on-boards-reaches-a.html?Page=all

Whitler, K., & Henretta, D. (2018). Why the influence of women on boards still lags. *MIT Sloan Management Review*. Retrieved November 4, 2019, from https://sloanreview.mit.edu/article/why-the-influence-of-women-on-boards-still-lags/

13

New Trends in Women's Philanthropy

As fundraisers and organizations across the globe continue to work in the field of women's philanthropic initiatives, new trends, innovations, and exciting connections happen every day. Some of these are emerging in existing nonprofits, others are collaborations with for-profit-partners, HNW philanthropists, and women's foundations. Several areas of emerging trends will be explored in this chapter, including impact and gender lens investing, LLCs as an alternative to family foundations, and global initiatives that attract and engage women donors.

Impact Investing

The Rockefeller Foundation introduced the term "impact investing" in 2007 when it convened leaders in the field of finance, philanthropy, and development with the aim of building the investing for impact industry (Kanani, 2012). Impact investments have a dual purpose: deliver financial returns while creating social and environmental benefits. Scholars Paul Brest and Kelly Born call it "actively placing capital in enterprises that generate social and environmental goods, services or ancillary benefits such as creating good jobs, with expected financial returns ranging from the highly concessionary to above market" (Brest & Born, 2013). In other words, a middle ground between philanthropy and traditional financial investments. Philanthropists

L. A. Buntz, *Generosity and Gender*,
https://doi.org/10.1007/978-3-030-90380-0_13

can be impact investors, but their contributions are not considered *philan-thropy* because a financial return is expected. Examples of impact investing include micro-finance loans, healthcare research, investing in women-owned businesses, environmental projects, or social impact bonds. Defining "social impact" and "returns" varies considerably. Some investment organizations focus more heavily on impact while others emphasize returns.

Today, there are several emerging groups of impact investors. One of the largest is the Global Impact Investing Network (GIIN), a membership orga-nization of more than 20,000 individuals and organizations that promotes impact investing through metrics, data, a global directory, and media events. GIIN manages $239 billion in assets (Mudaliar et al., 2019). The impact investing market is diverse including foundations, fund managers, financial institutions, and family offices. More than 50% of the participants in the GIIN 2019 Survey target social and environmental impact objectives.

One well-known impact investor is Muhammad Yunus, Nobel Prize winner and founder of the famous Grameen Bank, which in 1976 was designed as a credit delivery system to provide banking services to the rural poor of Bangladesh. As of January 2011, borrowers totaled 8.4 million, 97% of whom were women. The repayment rate was nearly 98% compared to that of the U.S. banking sector's 96% (Kowalik & Miera-Martinex, 2010). The difference in repayment rates may seem small, but consider the vast differ-ences in the population of borrowers for Grameen and the U.S. banking sector. Grameen Bank continued to expand its services by establishing a U.S. presence, Grameen America, in 2008. Previously, it relied strictly on philan-thropic donations, but in 2018, on its ten-year anniversary, Grameen America announced its foray into impact investing by establishing an $11 million Social Business Fund providing additional money to nearly 100,000 women entrepreneurs (Field, 2018). Large-scale investment funds like these offer opportunities for women to act as investors, recipients, and philanthropists.

As the field of impact investing continues to grow, philanthropy profes-sionals are studying who is interested in these concepts and why; most importantly, are women interested and engaged in opportunities to invest in social good? Morgan Stanley, the well-known wealth management firm, has conducted two surveys of 1,000 investors gauging their interest in *sustainable investing,* that is investments in companies or funds that target social and environmental outcomes. In 2015, the first survey found that 76% of women compared to 62% of men show an overwhelming interest in socially respon-sible and impact investing (Morgan Stanley, 2015). When the survey was repeated in 2017, women's receptivity to sustainable investing had grown to 84% versus men at 67%. Fifty-six percent of women focus at least partially on making a positive impact with their investments versus 45% of men. Millennials have even higher levels of interest, ranging from 84 to 86% (Morgan Stanley, 2017). And 40% of women versus 36% of men were integrating sustainability into their investment decisions (Morgan Stanley, 2017).

Women Impact Investors

If women's philanthropy initiatives are going to capitalize on this emerging trend, it is essential that we understand what motivates women to become impact investors. What is the profile of an investor? A report analyzing the results of the *Bank of America/U.S. Trust Study* of *High Net Worth Philanthropy* series found that three factors influence impact investing action for HNW philanthropists (households with annual income of at least $200,000 or net worth of at least $1 million, excluding the value of their primary home): education, level of income, and age (Osili et al., 2018).

Men and women had nearly the same levels of awareness of impact investing: but women are more likely to want to learn more. Those with at least a bachelor's degree were statistically significantly more likely to impact invest and two out of five women with college degrees participated in impact investing, a statistically significantly higher percentage than similarly educated men (Osili et al., 2018, p. 15). Thus, identifying college-educated women as prospects could be a primary strategy for fundraisers and investors.

Income level is the second factor influencing investments. As women's incomes grow, they are more willing to take financial risks and having disposable income allows them to explore a wider range of investments (Osili et al., 2018, p. 14). Women participate in impact more often than men at all three levels of HNW (<$200,000 annually, $200,000–$500,000 and > $500,000), but the biggest difference is for those with annual incomes between $200,000 and $500,000 a year (Osili et al., 2018).

Age is the third factor influencing action in impact investments. Individuals surveyed were the Silent Generation (1925–1945), the Baby Boomers (1946–1964), Generation X (1965–1979), and Millennials (1980–2000). Baby Boomer women have participated in impact investing at a higher rate than Boomer men. Gen X and millennials men were more likely to participate in impact investing than women, but not at a statistically significant level (men 45.1%, women 40.1%) (Osili et al., 2018). Gen X and millennial women donors participated at a higher rate than Baby Boomer women (40.1% compared to 37.7%).

Although the sweet spot for fund development/investment professionals who want to attract women investors is college-educated, older women with HNW, women's philanthropy and investment initiatives must proactively engage women of all ages and income levels. Impact investing is a door to younger donors, especially those who are not yet HNW individuals.

There are impact investment opportunities for women who are not high net worth donors. The Colorado Women's Foundation has started an impact investing giving circle, the first in the country. Focused on cultivating women entrepreneurs, women of color and women in rural areas, each woman gives $2,000 annually. This encourages learning and participation from a broad spectrum of donors. Another example of a unique and successful impact investment organization designed for the *household investor* is Capital Sisters.

Capital Sisters International is a nonprofit organization whose mission is to connect impoverished women in developing countries who need tiny business loans with investors willing to provide them. Capital Sisters offers zero-interest *Sisters Bonds;* working through partnerships with nonprofit micro-finance institutions, women with businesses are given micro-finance loans. When the loans are repaid, the nonprofit partners keep the interest while investors get their principal back and receive a Social Dividend Report—usually a case study of the women who were helped and the impact their businesses had on their families and communities. Each $1,000 investment helps finance ten women's businesses at $100 each. Targeting developing countries and small-scale women-owned businesses is an opportunity for women who are not big donors to help solve global poverty (Capital Sisters International, 2021).

As fundraisers think about increasing a woman donor's financial and philanthropic knowledge through seminars and education, impact investing should become part of the conversation. Identifying impact champions can help create a network of women who want to participate and connect through their love of investing in social causes.

The good news is several large foundations as well as individual investors are making the choice to explore and practice impact investing. The Ford Foundation recently shifted $1 billion of its endowment to impact strategies and the National Geographic Society, where Jean Case, CEO of the Case Foundation and a strong advocate of impact investment is board chair, has also shifted a small portion of its $1 billion endowment to impact.

Gender Lens Investing

Gender lens investing, often a subset of impact investing, is the practice of integrating gender factors into investment analysis and decisions with the goal of earning financial return while addressing gender disparities.

Applying a gender lens is analogous to putting on a new pair of glasses. You may still see a sunset, but it is clearer, revealing details you'd missed previously. Or, think about using binoculars to magnify your view. Suddenly the picture is more vivid and close to you. As we apply this concept to investing, think about examining the culture, governance, projects, and programs of a company through a gender lens. Gender lens investors research how companies treat employees, produce products and services, and manage their profits with an eye on sexism before making investments with them. If women donors and investors truly want to improve the economic and social conditions for women domestically and globally, then the companies that they invest in need to adopt a gender lens.

Gender lens investing tends to focus on three primary areas: access to capital, workplace equity, and products and services. Some financial investment firms have identified five dimensions of gender equity to be considered in gender lens investing: women in leadership (women on the corporate board and in senior management roles), access to benefits, diverse supply chains, pay equity, and talent and culture. There are so many great examples of how this concept has grown in the past several years:

- Gender Lens Investing (GLI) investments in public markets strategies have grown from $100 million to $2.4 billion in four years (Business Wire, 2018).
- In 2018, Project Sage 2.0 (a global scan of gender lens investors published as a collaboration between Wharton Social Impact Initiative and the University of Pennsylvania) identified 87 total funds deploying capital with a gender lens via private equity, debt, and venture capital. Total capital raised cleared $2.2 billion (Hunt & Kuhlman, 2018).
- The World Bank's Women Entrepreneurs Finance Initiative (IFC We-Fi) allocated $129 million to grow 70,000 women-owned businesses (World Bank, 2019). IFC-We-Fi tests innovations and scales models within a three-pillar framework: supporting women entrepreneurs through mentoring, training, and peer networks, expanding financial services to reach more women-owned businesses, and improving market access integrating women-owned enterprises into the domestic and international value chains.

While women philanthropists still have a long way to go to engage more actively in impact and gender lens investing, they are embracing learning about and practicing it as evidenced by the recent announcement from the Texas Women's Foundation, that 100% of its $36 million in financial assets are now invested in a gender impact portfolio. Roselyn Dawson Thompson, former CEO of the Texas Women's Foundation, spoke at a 2019 Women's Funding Network conference explaining how it has taken time and promotion on her part to get her board and Investment Advisory Committee to agree to becoming the first, and to date the only, women's fund or foundation to move its entire assets into gendered impact portfolios. "We hope that we can inspire others to become part of what is now a global movement around impact investing. Specifically, for women's funds and foundations, we can demonstrate how, by mission-aligning 100% percent of our assets with our philanthropy, we can powerfully accelerate the change we seek in the world" (Dawson Thompson, personal communication, April 18, 2019). Other woman's foundations are working on similar strategies:

- The Women's Foundation of Colorado (WFCO) formalized a commitment to Gender Lens Investing (GLI) of 51% of its endowment assets to be attained by 2021 (WFN, 2019). In 2020 they had 100% gender lens investing pool in their donor-advised funds.
- The Women's Funding Network (WFN) offers its donor-advised funds a 100% GLI option and has established a Programmatic Investment committee to establish policies and procedures for impact investing considerations.
- Canada's Vicki Saunders, the founder of Radical Generosity and SheEO, aspired to have a million investors and a billion dollars for 10,000 women entrepreneurs by 2020 (McIntyre, 2016). The COVID pandemic interrupted some of the progress of this goal. Following the news of the lockdown, Saunders held an emergency meeting with 68 of the ventures they support and triaged their needs. All 68 were able to keep their doors open with help from SheEO and loans from other ventures.

One of the most common questions investors ask is, "Does gender lens investing have comparable financial returns to other investments?" There are many different financial and investment companies currently tracking data to answer the question. The field of gender lens investing is new, so getting longitudinal data is just beginning. However, there is evidence that Fortune 500 companies with female board members did better than those without them when it came to *return on equity* (ROE), return on sales and return on invested capital, according to a 2007 study by Catalyst (Joy et al., 2007). Morgan Stanley Research reports higher ROE, lower accruals, and lower ROE volatility for companies with high gender diversity, relative to sector peers, making it appear that applying a gender lens is a good financial investment and an opportunity for all women to expand their financial and philanthropic influence (Morgan Stanley Research, 2016).

Here are a few questions for women donors or foundations/nonprofits to consider as they think about making gender lens investments.

1. What is the purpose of your capital, assets or investments?
2. Why would you consider using a gender lens for your investments?
3. Do you want to be engaged in the investment process as a leader, learner or mentor?
4. What principles or values guide your investment decisions?
5. What would be the advantages or disadvantages of using a gender lens for your investments?
6. What type of impact do you want your investments to achieve?

Non-traditional Models of Philanthropy: Emerson Collective

In 2014, Laurene Powell Jobs founded the Emerson Collective, a social change organization focused on education, environment, immigration, media, journalism, and health. Named after Ralph Waldo Emerson and based on the theme of self-reliance, the Emerson Collective is a new type of philanthropy, one unencumbered by some of the traditional rules and regulations guiding the work of major foundations. Choosing to establish an LLC rather than a traditional family foundation was a conscious decision. Jobs described her vision for the Collective, "I'd like us to be a place where great leaders want to come and try to do difficult things. I think we bring a lot more to the table than money... If you want to just be a check writer, you'd run out of money and not solve anything" (Levine, 2019).

By establishing an LLC, Jobs avoids the federal restrictions on *how much* she can invest and the *types of investments* she can make. The LLC can hire the best people unrestricted by compensation laws or disclosure rules. Although the company sacrifices some of the benefits of reduced taxes, this new group of entrepreneurs and philanthropists are willing to forego that perk. They want flexibility and power. Seeking to change old systems, Jobs looks for answers to wicked and vexing social issues from the outside. With money to back up her ideas, she says, "Failure is seen as a badge of courage not a death knell. Embracing ambiguity is a key value."

Laura Arrillaga-Andreessen, a lecturer at Stanford Business School, philanthropist and author, describes the attributes of the Collective, "When philanthropists are engaged in the type of system change that Laurene is, you have to be as nimble as possible because ecosystems are constantly shifting, stakeholders are developing new positions on particular issues, political contexts change, economic forces evolve" (Levine, 2019).

Since its inception the Emerson Collective has taken a systems approach, blending the work of nonprofit and investments in for-profit companies. While addressing specific social issues like curbing gun violence in Chicago through funding and grants, the Collective has also bought the majority stakes in magazines like *The Atlantic* and invested in journalism and media to help craft the story and message about these social issues, believing that creating a narrative about social problems is critical to engaging funders, activists, and politicians. Without the restrictions typically placed on nonprofits regarding investing in political advocacy, Emerson can also influence legislation on these same issues.

At about the same time Jobs created the Collective, Pierre and Pam Omidyar, founders of eBay, established the Omidyar Network, an umbrella organization for a nonprofit foundation and a for-profit LLC. Many of Omidyar's investments focus on financial inclusion, such as Flutterware, a finance technology company providing payment infrastructure for banks and businesses to make and accept digital payments in Africa, and Propel, which builds software to improve low-income Americans' experience with the food stamp program (Resier, 2019).

In 2015, to mark the occasion of the birth of their first child, Mark Zuckerberg and Priscilla Chan formed an LLC, the Chan Zuckerberg Initiative, announcing their intention to give 99% of their Facebook shares to "advance human potential and promote equality for all children" (Reiser, 2019). Since its inception, the Chan Zuckerberg Initiative has invested in medical research, technology, immigration, and criminal justice reform projects. They see policy and advocacy work as key to their objectives.

These new legal institutions may lead the way for large-scale philanthropists to maximize their privacy and control, avoid the regulatory requirements that accompany tax-exempt status, and influence social, economic, and political systems.

Maverick Collective

Kate Roberts, Director of Population Services International (PSI) and co-creator of the Maverick Collective believes that money can't create change—but people can. In 2007, Roberts was named a Young Global Leader at the World Economic Forum and began developing a friendship with Her Royal Highness the Crown Princess Mette-Marit of Norway. In 2012, Roberts and the Princess visited India as part of their work advocating for girls and women. It was there that the concept for the Maverick Collective was hatched. PSI's previous work with the Gates Foundation had established a partnership and shared vision to end extreme poverty through the investment and support of women and girls worldwide. As the idea for the Collective began to take shape, Melinda Gates became an enthusiastic advocate and signed on as a co-chair.

In 2015, the United Nations agreed to a set of Sustainable Development Goals and in response to their call for action, Roberts, HRH Mette-Marit and Melinda Gates launched the Maverick Collective in 2016 in Copenhagen. PSI is a global health Nongovernmental Organization (NGO) with operations in 65 countries. The Maverick Collective is an initiative of this organization. The Collective developed an all-female initiative focused on raising money, training members, and advocating for change by investing in girls and women. Members were strategically selected and asked to commit three years of their time, $1 million, and to do the actual work to solve a social problem. The selection criteria for the initial members were women who had skills, interest, money, and abilities to move the agenda forward. Fourteen women stepped up, creating a seven-figure fund that in three short years built partnerships, raised $60 million, launched 25 programs in twenty countries, and served more than one million women. The programs range from reducing teenage pregnancy in Tanzania to establishing health centers in India for women with cervical cancer.

Roberts describes the Maverick Collective as disruptive—in a good way. Women have been marginalized in the world of philanthropy and this initiative is an opportunity to engage at a bold level. So, what is this initiative doing differently? Each member is matched with a partner "liaison" to identify impact areas that align with a donor's interest and to zero in on a geographic location to target. "This is an executive management course in saving the world" (Hullinger, 2016).

This model of engagement challenges the members to learn about the issues in the country they are assigned. Through an intensive technical training program, they get an in-depth view of the challenges to women and girls in third-world countries. They also partner with recipients to design the programs that will be implemented. Members of the Maverick Collective feel engaged in the process of philanthropy at a completely different level, learn about social issues, become ambassadors for women's issues, and through the experience feel a sense of pride and unity with women around the world. And the Maverick Collective is investing in the next generation of women philanthropists through their program Maverick NEXT, a specific initiative to train and engage young advocates, entrepreneurs, and philanthropists.

Two other innovative and creative programs include Blue Meridian and the Audacious Project.

Blue Meridian

Led by a visionary woman named Nancy Roob, Blue Meridian is a conglomeration of partners including nationally known foundations: Bill and Melinda Gates, Edna McConnell Clark, Eugene and Marilyn Steiner, George Kaiser, and William and Flora Hewlett to name a few, plus HNW individuals including MacKenzie Scott. Using a performance-based model, Blue Meridian makes strategic and large-scale investments in organizations that address poverty and economic mobility for young people and families in the U.S. By connecting people and families who need assistance to organizations that can deliver services and philanthropists who want to see impact, Blue Meridian uses a multi-step process to vet their grantees. After assessing an organization's ability and capacity to work on critical social issues, Blue Meridian invests in funding a planning grant. Following a two-year planning process, successful organizations may receive up to $200 million over the course of 10–12 years to invest in services, programs and infrastructure. This model helps pool philanthropists who have common goals and emphasizes the need to listen intently to the providers of services so solutions can be co-created. By making long-term investments in the social sector, it is possible to see social change happen and create a plan for sustainability.

The Audacious Project

Social entrepreneurs are the agents of social impact philanthropy. They create solutions to tricky social problems and in some cases produce investment results for their investors. The Audacious Project (AP) supported by the Bridgespan Group (a nationally known nonprofit and research organization) addresses one of the most common problems social entrepreneurs face—finding venture capital one donor at a time. The Audacious Project brings creatives together to imagine solutions to global problems and provides a venue for social change agents to pitch their ideas to investors. Collaboration is one of the key tenants of this approach. AP gathers nonprofit experts, philanthropists, creators, and researchers to dream big and bold. Since 2006 AP has supported the *One Acre Fund*, a project that funds Sub-Saharan African farmers through micro-loans, seeds, fertilizer and agronomic training, enabling the farm families to increase their income. In the next five years, One Acre Fund will serve 1.98 million farm families per year (https://audacious project.org/grantees/one-acre-fund, 2021). Currently, many of their projects are focused on COVID-19 solutions targeting recovery and response. This includes speeding up contact tracing, better access for minority communities, and assistance to health workers. Some of the projects in the idea stage include a global surveillance network to stop the next pandemic or mental health support via text messages.

New models of women's philanthropy are developing everyday enticing donors to learn, analyze, and act using a creative and innovative lens. Fundraisers will need to learn with them and bring a wider variety of options to donors. Traditional fundraising techniques cannot be the primary and or only source of engaging women, it will not continue to work. And as more women become leaders in the field of philanthropy, they will explore and find new types of investments to offer to their constituents. Now is the time to partner with women board members, volunteers and donors to create initiatives that will increase the resource pool and create systemic and social change.

Bibliography

Audacious Project. Retrieved July 2, 2021, from https://audaciousproject.org/gra ntees/one-acre-fund

Brest, P., & Born, K. (2013). When can impact investing create real impact? *Stanford Social Innovation Review, 11*(4), 22–31.

Business Wire, A Berkshire Hathaway Company, Veris Wealth Partners. (2018, October 30). Retrieved September 10, 2020, from https://www.businesswire. com/news/home/20181030005112/en/Gender-lens-Investing-Assets-Rise-85-in-Past-Year-and-Now-Exceed-2.4-Billion

Capital Sisters International. (2021). Retrieved December 20, 2020, from https:// ww.capitalsisters.org

Case, J. (2017). *Bringing the last decade of impact investing to life: An interactive timeline.* The Case Foundation. Retrieved April 27, 2020, from https://casefound ation.org/blog/bringing-last-decade-impact-investing-life-interactive-timeline/

Field, A. (2018, January 31). Grameen American expands into impact investing. *Forbes.* Retrieved October 10, 2019, from https://www.forbes.com/sites/annefi eld/2018/01/31/grameen-america-expands-into-impact-investing/

Hullinger, J. (2016, May 16). How a princess and CEO are applying the VC Model to philanthropy. *Fast Company.* Retrieved February 18, 2020, from https://www.fastcompany.com/3058981/how-a-princess-and-a-ceo-are-app lying-the-vc-model-to-philanthropy

Hunt, S., & Kuhlman, S. (2018, October 29). *7 Takeaways from Project Sage 2.0—The global scan of gender lens private equity, VC and private debt funds.* The Wharton School, University of Pennsylvania. Retrieved May 30, 2019, from https://www.wharton.upenn.edu/story/7-takeaways-from-project-sage-2-0-the-global-scan-of-gender-lens-private-equity-vs-and-private-debt-funds

Joy, L., Wagner H. M., Narayanan, S., & Carter, N. (2007). *The bottom line: Corporate performance and women's representation on boards* (Report). Retrieved April 8, 2020, from https://www.blogs.cfainstitute.org/investor/2019/06/24/how-are-gen der-lens-fund-performing

Kanani, R. (2012, February 23). The state and future of impact investing. *Forbes.* Retrieved January 22, 2019, from https://www.forbes.com/sites/rahimkanani/ 2012/02/23/the-state-and-future-of-impact-investing/#5ea682eded48

Kowalik, M., & Martinez-Miera, D.(2010, April). *The creditworthiness of the poor: A model of the Grameen Bank.* The Federal Reserve Bank of Kansas City Economic Research Department. Retrieved August 14, 2019, from www.fdic.com

Levine, M. (2019, June). Does the Emerson Collective square with philan- thropic accountability? *The Nonprofit Quarterly.* Retrieved November 30, 2020, from https://nonprofitquarterly.org/does-the-emerson-collective-square-with-phi lanthropic-accountability

McIntyre, C. (2016, December 13). How Vicki Saunders plans to get a million women involved in venture capital. *Canadian Business.* Retrieved September 18, 2020, from https://www.canadianbusiness.com/innovation/sheeo-radical-genero sity-vicki-saunders/

Morgan Stanley Research. (2015, February 27). *Morgan Stanley Survey finds sustainable investing poised for growth.* Retrieved March 24, 2019, from https:// www.morganstanley.com/press-releases/morgan-stanley-survey-finds-sustainable- investing-poised-for-growth_06490efO-a8b2-4a68-8864-64261a4decO

Morgan Stanley Research. (2016). *The gender advantage: integrating gender diversity into investment decisions.* Retrieved September 30, 2020, from https://www.mor ganstanley.com.pub/content//dam/msdotcom/ideas/genderdiversity-toolkit/Gen der-Diversity-Investing-Primer-pdf

Morgan Stanley Research. (2017, August 9). *Sustainable socially responsible investing millennial drive growth*. Retrieved August 30, 2020, from https://www.mor ganstanley.com/ideas/sustainable-socially-responsible-investing-millennials-drive- growth

Mudaliar, A., Bass, R., Dithrich, H., & Noshin, N. (2019). *Annual Impact Investor Survey*. GINN. Retrieved January 20, 2021, from https://thegiin.org/research/ publication/impinv-survey-2019

Osili, U., Mesch D., Ackerman, J., Bergdoll, J., Preston, L., & Pactor, A. (2018). *How men and women approach impact investing*. Lilly Family School of Philanthropy, Women's Philanthropy Institute (4). Retrieved November 8, 2020, from https://scholarwork.iupui.edu/bitstream/handle/1805/16229/Imp act%20Investing%20%Report%20FINAL.pdf

Reiser, B. D. (2019, Summer). Is the Chan Zuckerberg initiative the future of philanthropy? *Stanford Social Innovation.*

World Bank. (2019, May 13). *Women entrepreneurs finance initiative allocates second round of funding: Expected to grow 70,000 women's businesses*. Retrieved October 25, 2020, from https://www.worldbank.org/en/news/press-release/2019/05/ 13/women-entrepreneurs-finance-initiative-allocates-second-round-funding-exp ected-to-grow-70000womens-businesses

14

Diversity and Philanthropy—Engaging Women of Color and the Next Generation of Donors

Women's philanthropy advocates have frequently addressed the concept of *intersectionality*, the ways multiple factors such as race, ethnicity, gender, class, economics, and social status *intersect* creating unique issues and identities, in their efforts to build new initiatives. For decades fundraisers have struggled with successfully engaging a broader range of philanthropists, particularly women of color, and understanding the issues, concerns, motivations, and interests that may be unique to these populations. Unfortunately, there has been limited progress on the landscape of diversity among philanthropic professionals and donors. Though numbers change depending upon the source one gleans them from, it's safe to say that 60 to 70 percent of people in the U.S. identify themselves as white or Caucasian (U.S Census Bureau, 2021) yet:

- In 2017, Board Source, the nonprofit expert in board leadership and governance surveyed 1800 foundations and public charities and found that 90% of CEOs and board chairs were white as were 84% of board members (Board Source, 2017).
- According to the 2018 Demographic Report of the Association of Fundraising Professionals, of its more than 31,000 members, fewer than 10 percent were people of color (Burton, 2020).
- In 2020, fundraising software company, Blackbaud, found that 75% of donors were white (Hayes & Stiffman, 2020).

© The Author(s), under exclusive license to Springer Nature Switzerland AG 2022, corrected publication 2022
L. A. Buntz, *Generosity and Gender*,
https://doi.org/10.1007/978-3-030-90380-0_14

In the past several years, there has been more research about race and charitable giving, but very limited information about *gender, race, and charitable giving*. In 2019, The Women's Philanthropy Institute conducted a research study: *WomenGive19: Gender and Giving Across Communities of Color*. The results confirm the generosity of women and that gender differences in giving pointed out in earlier chapters hold across racial lines: in communities of color, single women are more likely to give than single men, and married couples are more likely than single men or women to give (Mesch et al., 2019). The good news is, women of color are moving into leadership roles, developing programs and affinity groups, hosting conferences, trainings, and giving.

Identify Specific Affinity Groups

Women often engage in philanthropy along personal affiliations sometimes referred to as *identity specific affinity groups* such as: Asian Women in Science, Technology, Engineering and Math (STEM), *Women United* for Young Professionals, Hispanics in Philanthropy, #BlackHer, (a website for black women philanthropists and activists), and the Asian Women's Giving Circle (AWGC). Black sororities are powerful identity networks. Alpha Kappa Alpha (AKA) is a 110-year-old international sorority of Black college graduates primarily dedicated to giving money for college access. Sixty percent of the giving circles identified in the *Landscape of Giving Circles/Collective Giving Groups in the U.S.* were formed around a particular identity (Bearman et al., 2017).

Such identity-specific groups engage in what is referred to as *social capital*. Defined as early as 1916 by L.J. Hanifan, a state supervisor of rural schools in West Virginia, social capital refers to "those tangible substances that count for most in [the]daily lives of people, namely: good will, fellowship, sympathy, and social intercourse among the individuals and families who make up a social unit" (Hanifan, 1916, p. 130). *Bonding* and *bridging* are two primary types of social capital (Gittell & Vidal, 1998, p. 8). Bonding creates connections between the donor and consumer *within* a group or community. Examples are: ethnic fraternal organizations, church-based study groups, or specific ethnic-based giving circles supporting women of the same ethnicity. Bonding helps build solidarity and social support within groups. Robert Putnam, the well-known Harvard social scientist, describes it as superglue (Putnam, 2000, p. 23) and (Mesch et al., 2019) notes that when donor and recipient share the same identity, donors tend to give more.

The Latino Community Foundation (LCF) in California is a good example of social capital bonding. In 2012, they launched the Latino Giving Circles Network, a collection of 22 giving circles including more than 500 members which have distributed nearly $1.7 million to 100 Latina-led nonprofits. Since the recent pandemic, the circles have pledged $150,000 for COVID-19 relief to the foundation's Love Not Fear fund. In addition to supporting nonprofits, the LCF's work includes building economic and political power for Latinos through voter registration efforts and census participation (Di Mento, 2020).

Another pertinent example is the Asian Women's Giving Circle (AWGC) of New York founded by Hali Lee, a strong advocate for women donors of color. Born in South Korea, Lee graduated from Princeton, earned a Master's in Social Work from New York University, and led philanthropic services at J.P. Morgan. Since its inception, AWGC has donated nearly $1 million to support Asian artists, filmmakers, writers, and advocates (https://asianwomengivingcircle.org/).

Bridging social capital occurs *between* different groups of people (Mesch et al., 2019) generating broader identities and creating linkage across social and economic lines. The Ms. Foundation, one of the nation's oldest women's foundations, is an example of bridging and bonding social capital. Teresa Younger, CEO, recently announced the foundation will launch a five-year strategic plan to invest $25 million in resources and support for organizations led by and for women of color (PND Candid, 2018). The Ms. Foundation has a long history of supporting women and girls, but its grantmaking and advocacy had been broad-based, not ethnic-specific. It has been a bridge linking many different ethnic groups. This new plan helps bond donors of color to a specific groups and causes. The foundation will also increase its investments in support of political action to help elect representatives who advocate for policies that benefit women and girls of color through its new 501(c) 4 fund.

Donors of Color—Black Women

Data on donors of color, specifically HNW donors, is scarce, most of it gleaned from banks, wealth management firms, and consulting businesses. Attorney Urvashi Vaid, President of the Vaid Group and co-founder with the aforementioned Hali Lee of the Donors of Color Network, was curious about HNW people of color who are philanthropists. With support from the Marguerite Casey Foundation, Vaid and Ashindi Maxton interviewed this donor population. Their study *The Apparitional Donor: Understanding and Engaging High Net Worth Donors of Color*, and the *Chronicle of Philanthropy's* article "How to Connect with Donors of Color" offer some insights (Haynes & Stiffman, 2020, pp. 9–17; Vaid & Maxton, 2017).

- 1.3 million African American, Asian American and Hispanic American individuals have a net worth of over $1 million.
- Donors of color have more often built their wealth versus inheriting it.
- Donors of color feel uncomfortable participating in philanthropy networks which are predominately white.
- Donors of color are not connected to other donors of color.
- Donors of color say that they would give more if asked.

Donors of color have resources. Their names may not be recognized as community leaders, show up on the lists of boards of directors, or donor lists for sponsorships and contributions. Rather than funneling contributions through traditional nonprofit organizations or foundations, their giving may be more informal. How can fundraisers use this information? We need to look deeper and in different places to truly understand where donors of color are giving, and why.

Marion Brown, the first Black Vice President of Development in the Big Ten, began her long development career at the University of Wisconsin-Madison by securing funds for an innovative new scholarship program for students of color. She continued overseeing this work after she assumed broader responsibilities at the University of Wisconsin Foundation. "Blacks have always been philanthropic, however not always in the traditional model," she said. "Many Blacks have given first to family members and neighbors needing help. We have given most generously to churches and organizations such as the NAACP, Urban League, and traditionally Black colleges - all activities of great interest and commitment. Philanthropy among Blacks has always existed but, it is becoming more visible with the increasing number of publicly announced major gifts. One of the common misperceptions is that Blacks lack resources and interest to warrant the attention of development officers. During my entire career, I encouraged colleagues and staff to visit Blacks who superficially didn't appear wealthy. Women are similar in that their names don't appear at the top of research reports because their assets may not be so readily apparent. To gain the interest of both Blacks and women potential donors, just as with anyone else, you have to demonstrate that their gifts will have a personally meaningful impact. In order to gain their support, you must explain how the institution is supportive of them and their priorities" (Brown, personal communication, June 1, 2021).

Eddie and Sylvia Brown are examples of African American philanthropists who want to encourage more giving from people of color. Brown is the owner of Brown Capital Management, an $8 billion investment company he founded in 1983. Thanks to a wealthy woman donor in Allentown, Pennsylvania he was able to obtain a university education as an engineer. Unfortunately, he never knew the donor's name and was never able to thank her. His debt to her is what prompts him and his wife Sylvia to give generously and to encourage other African Americans to become donors. As HNW people they were initially reluctant to be public about their giving. Finally, after some encouragement from fundraisers, they agreed to be recognized and to speak about their philanthropy. "We're very concerned about giving from the African American community" says Eddie. "People with capacity aren't stepping up commensurate with their capacity to give. Matches encourage them. Some are wealthier than we are and they don't want to give, or lead or be out front, but they don't mind giving quietly." Thus, one of their strategies as donors of color is to spur other philanthropists to step up. Almost all of Brown's giving comes in a "match" format, grants with the stipulation that the organizations receiving their philanthropy raise donations from other wealthy African Americans (Di Mento, 2019). Realizing that donors of color need role models and leaders, the Browns have chosen to fill that gap by expanding their philanthropic strategy to help fundraising professionals connect with more donors of color (Di Mento, 2019). When Susan Taylor, former editor in chief of Essence magazine, honored the Browns at a gala several years ago, they attracted a big crowd, helping her raise $1.1 million.

While the Black Lives Matter movement cries out for institutions to diversify programs for Black citizens and to advance social justice, it also notes that development offices need to be more focused on securing funds *from* Black Americans. After all the race sensitivity training, for example, some colleges still fall short in even simple development and marketing efforts such as diverse faces or the voices of Black students in campus videos. Yet, more highly educated than their brothers and with prominent roles in their families and communities, Black women are particularly strong donor prospects. Are we treating them as such?

Within the women's philanthropy movement, fundraisers are still learning about what motivates and inspires women of color. Melanie Brown is a senior consultant at the Gates Foundation and a Black woman. Her interest in women's philanthropy was sparked when she was selected as an Atlantic Fellow by the International Inequalities Institute based at the London School of Economics and Political Science. Fellows work on research, learning, connection, and reflection in the areas of social change and economic inequalities. During her capstone project, she interviewed women of color who were philanthropists and leaders. One of the themes Brown discovered in those interviews is that women of color bring two identities to their philanthropy— being a woman and being black. "They want to bring those lenses to all of their decision-making. It's philanthropy and movement building. Their gender *and* race guide them as they think about their philanthropy" (Melanie Brown, personal communication, February 17, 2019).

This dual identity is an important insight for fundraisers and a reflection of the intersectionality theme. Using this information for women donors can help fundraisers expand their knowledge and skills to engage more women of color. Jocelyn Harmon, co-founder of #BlackHer, an online platform educating and inspiring Black women to act for change, has developed a Black Woman's Guide to Philanthropy. She confirms some of the earlier themes. Black women have a spirit of service and inclusiveness; they hold families and communities together. Family is often their first thought for philanthropy. This devotion to family includes a sense of legacy—how to honor their parents or others who have helped them along the way.

One of the newest and brightest women leading the effort to diversify the professional philanthropy community and to connect with donors of color is Yolanda F. Johnson. As the first African American President of Women in Development, New York City's premier organization for women and fundraising, she has always been a game changer. In 2020, Johnson launched Women of Color in Fundraising and Philanthropy to help advance women of color within the profession, offer training, and education and build a network of women who can support each other. Using her background as a performer, she blends artistry with knowledge and experience helping nonprofit organizations strategize about how to fundraise and reach women of color. A frequent consultant on inclusion, equity, and diversity issues, Johnson believed the timing was right for Women of Color in Fundraising and Philanthropy; the fund development world was hungry for information, ideas and experts. Although only a year old, the organization has a thousand members from four countries. "Donors and fundraisers now have a space to be together," said Johnson.

When she is not serving on a panel or bringing diverse women and funders together, Johnson is advocating for social change and encouraging women to give bigger and bolder. As she said, "There's a lot of money left on the table because fundraisers don't ask women. We have to change who's sitting at the table" (Johnson, personal communication, March 9, 2021).

Hispanics in Philanthropy (HIP)

Today, there are more than 60 million Latinxs in the U.S. and by 2060 it is projected that Latinx will make up 28% of the U.S. population. It is the largest ethnic or racial minority in the U.S. (U.S. Census Bureau, 2021). The term "Latinx" is a gender-neutral, non-binary alternative to the traditional Spanish language construction of Latino (male) or Latina (female). The Latinx population has continued to grow in size and influence, yet historically it has been disproportionately impacted by wage and income inequities. According to Amalia Brindis Delgado, Associate Vice President of Strategy at Hispanics in Philanthropy, Latina women make only 0.55 cents to every $1 earned by a white male (Delgado, personal communication, April 22, 2020). Latinx median household wealth is $6,600 compared to $147,000 for white families, and their median household income is $50,486 compared to $68,145 for whites (PowerUp Fund.org, 2019). 45% of households report income below $50,000 per year (Rovner, 2015). Latinx hold only 2% of the U.S. wealth.

Despite these glaring disparities and lack of financial resources, philanthropic giving within Latinx communities tells a different story. Sixty-three percent of Latinx households gave to charity and in 2015, they sent $68 million to their home countries in Latin America and the Caribbean (Goodwin, 2018). Latinx donors are among the youngest in the philanthropic space and most households are likely to have children. They give a larger percentage of income to church than other donors and have a strong commitment to children's causes. The percent of men who are donors still exceeds the number of women (Rovner, 2015).

Economic investments in the Latinx community are also woefully lacking. Less than 2% of venture capital investments went to Latino and Black entrepreneurs in 2016 and only 0.66% of all philanthropic funding was earmarked for Latinx communities (PowerUp Fund.org, 2019).

One organization that is addressing the needs of Latinx families and women donors is Hispanics in Philanthropy (HIP) a transnational organization strengthening Latinx leadership, voice, and equity by leveraging philanthropic resources with a focus on social justice and the goal of prosperity across the Americas. HIP makes impactful investments in Latinx communities and develops leaders in the social and philanthropic sector to effectively address issues impacting communities in the U.S., Latin America and the Caribbean.

The development and evolution of HIP has been heavily influenced by women. In 1981, HIP was founded when Luz Vega-Marqui, former President/CEO of the Marguerite Casey Foundation, Elisa Arévalo, Vice President of Wells Fargo Bank and Herman Gallegos, Trustee of the SBC Foundation organized an informal meeting at the Council on Foundations. By the time HIP was incorporated two years later, its leadership included Wilma Espinoza from Levi Strauss & Co., and Christina Cuevas of The San Francisco Foundation. In the late 1990s, Diana Campoamor was hired as president of HIP, serving for nearly three decades before passing the baton to the current HIP President and CEO Ana Marie Argilagos in 2018.

Brindis Delgado explains that HIP has continually expanded its services across the Americas, and in 2006 established an office in Mexico. "Having our feet on the ground and our ears open brings us closer to the communities we serve" (Brindis Delgado, personal communication, April 22, 2020). Since 2000, it has partnered with more than 270 funders to invest roughly $60 million in grants to more than 800 nonprofits working to increase resources for Latinx communities, businesses and nonprofits, enhancing philanthropic participation, and advocating for equitable policy change. Since January 2018, HIP has made over $6.2 million in investments to hundreds of organizations and created the first and only Spanish–English bilingual digital crowdfunding platform, HIPGIVE.org.

Latinx lead as philanthropists in their families and communities in the U.S. and in their home countries. Born in Venezuela, Brindis Delgado, like many other Latinas in the U.S., feels a far-reaching responsibility to take care of her family at home—here, and in her native country.

In recent years, HIP's work has actively responded to public policies impacting vulnerable communities. When the Family Separation policy was implemented in 2018, HIP brought together a 50-member delegation of the country's most important philanthropic organizations to better understand and witness first-hand the inequities and challenges faced by migrant families. Brindis Delgado believes this has had a tremendous impact on potential partners and philanthropists, motivating them to get engaged.

While addressing the immediate needs of children and families is critical, getting funding to work on the root causes of issues and intersectional long-term strategies is equally important. As an organization that focuses on the needs of women of color, HIP has been involved in examining and publishing information about the social determinants of health and how these adversely impact Latinas.

One of HIP's programs supports midwifery initiatives in Mexico. By strengthening the midwifery models, HIP contributes to improving women's reproductive health addressing precarious conditions and challenges to accessing quality sexual and reproductive health, while promoting women's leadership and workplace rights. Additionally, in 2018, HIP's report "*Maquilando el Cambio*" presented the case for national corporations to create sustainable and equitable labor practices with a gender perspective in Mexico in both the traditional and fast fashion industry.

"*We* need more women in decision-making roles. HIP's *Líderes* fellowship program emboldens a new generation of Latinx to move into decision making positions in philanthropy and to promote increased investments in their communities" (Brindis Delgado, personal communication, April 22, 2020). HIP centers its Fellowship curriculum as well as its grants on addressing systemic issues of race equity and implicit bias within philanthropy. Institutional racism in mainstream philanthropic institutions continues to create a gap in seeing and creating a pipeline for women of color to advance to leadership and decision-making roles in the sector. Without this representation, philanthropy will fall short in addressing inequities internal to the sector, especially impacting Black, Latinx, indigenous, and other people of color.

Finally, rather than relying on traditional foundation funding through grants, HIP has established its own social finance fund. The *PowerUp Fund* launched in 2020 has a goal of investing $60 million into Latinx-owned small businesses—$1 for every Latino who calls the U.S. home. Faced with the threat of losing 50% of Latinx-owned small businesses due to COVID-19, HIP responded by activating its PowerUP Fund to provide emergency small business relief. Originally conceived to address the dearth of capital flowing to promising Latinx entrepreneurs, PowerUP's strategy pivoted to support immediate-term economic resilience for Latinx communities. In summer 2020, PowerUP began to deploy grant capital as cash assistance to small Latinx-owned businesses—a continuation of its model in post-Hurricane Maria Puerto Rico. Through its PowerUP Fund, HIP aims to raise $60 million in 2020–2025 to transform the business and investment climate for Latinx enterprises.

Asian American and Pacific Islander Women

Asian American and Pacific Islanders (AAPI) comprise approximately 7% of the U.S. population and are among the fastest growing racial and ethnic groups (AAPIP, 2020, p. 3). From 2000 to 2019 this population experienced a 95% increase from 11.9 million to 23.2 million. Chinese Americans are the largest Asian-origin group in the U.S., making up 23% of the Asian population (Budiman & Ruiz, 2021).

Philanthropic support from foundations and individual donors for AAPI populations has been among the lowest of many minority groups. A recent analysis by the Philanthropic Initiative for Racial Equity (2018) found that between 2005 and 2014 the proportion of foundation dollars focused on communities of color never exceeded 8.5%. In 2014, only 0.26 percent of philanthropy was targeted to AAPI, less than to the Native American, Latinx and Black communities (https://racialequity.org). Providing research and donor management for nonprofits, Blackbaud surveyed 1,096 U.S. adults and reported that only 5% of Asians are donors and that percentage is projected to grow only 1% by 2030 (Rovner, 2015).

Violence, bullying, and physical attacks on Asian Americans during the pandemic have brought attention to the discrimination they experience and prompted a surge of philanthropic support. The California Endowment recently pledged $100 million to AAPI communities in California (PND Candid, 2018). The Asian American Foundation Board committed $125 million over five years to support AAPI causes (Ax, 2021). Numerous national news stations reported that nearly 30 donors pledged more than $25.8 million for this population following the March 16, 2021 shooting in Atlanta that killed six Asian women (Ax, 2021; Hadero, 2021).

Prior to these tragic incidents, the philanthropic support for AAPI had been minimal. Asian philanthropy has not been studied extensively and is not very well understood. Ruth Shapiro, Chief Executive of the Centre for Asian Philanthropy and Society (CAPS), a research and advisory organization based in Hong Kong, suggests several reasons for this (Shapiro, 2018, pp. 1–12). Many individuals living in Asia were not able to give to others, as they struggled with survival. It is only in the past thirty years that China has moved a significant amount of people out of poverty. Naturally, the country focused on economic development first. There was neither history nor interest in creating social programs and nonprofit organizations.

The question of whose responsibility is it to help others has influenced philanthropy within Asia and may still impact immigrants in the U.S. Is it the government's or an individual's role to help others? Who is responsible for the social sector? In Asia, service delivery organizations and NGOs are viewed with some skepticism due to their advocacy roles and perceived misalignment with governmental policies. How much history and culture continue to impact U.S. Asian American and Pacific Islander attitudes about philanthropy is still uncertain and will most likely change over generations. The good news is that Asian Americans are increasing their wealth capacity and engaging in philanthropic endeavors. The annual median household income of Asian Americans is \$94,903 compared to Caucasians at \$74,912 and overall U.S. households at \$67,521 (https://www.statista). BNP Paribus a wealth management firm in the U.S., Asia and Europe highlighted several women who have risen to prominence through their wealth capacity and philanthropy, let's have a look at some of them:

Zhonghui You, founder of Shenzhen Seaskyland Technologies, an educational software company became the first women from mainland China to sign the Gates Giving Pledge. Listed as one of 169 billionaires worldwide, You wants to encourage other wealthy Asian women to get engaged in philanthropy.

Yoshiko Shinohara, Japan's first self-made billionaire, made her fortune by creating part-time jobs for women through her publicly listed company Temp Holdings. She established the Yoshiko Shinohara Memorial Foundation in 2014 which grants scholarships to students in nursing and social work programs.

What to do with newfound wealth is a question for many newly wealthy AAPI women. How do they blend their cultural beliefs and norms with the current philanthropy models practiced in the U.S and the world? Do they give directly to nonprofit organizations, establish foundations or give directly to communities and individuals? Only 30% of Asian women billionaires have established foundations compared to 80% of American women on the list of global billionaires (BNP Paribus, 2018).

Diversity in Giving: The Changing Landscape of American Philanthropy provides a few additional insights about women in the AAPI community and philanthropy. Asian women are more likely than Asian men to be donors, 60% versus 40% (Rovner, 2015). Fifty-four percent of Asian donors are Millennials and Generation Xers. Overall, they have a higher education level, with 40% having college degrees compared with the overall U.S population of 32.1% (Rovner, 2015). AAPI women want what many other women donors want: financial security, career advancement, and access. Although there are differences depending on the country of origin, age and wealth, many AAPI are more financially literate and confident in their decisions and investments than the average American woman (Turner Moffit, 2015, p. 84).

In selecting priorities for philanthropy, AAPI donors choose education and emergency relief efforts while placing little emphasis on giving to faith-based organizations (Rovner, 2015). Some AAPI women donors interviewed for this book emphasized the need to support arts and culture organizations as ways to promote awareness and understanding of other ethnic groups. In a review of the grant selection from Asian Women's Giving Circles, many of the organizations supported were arts and culture oriented.

Nearly half of Asian Americans surveyed will support a friend or family member's request for a donation to a cause, and similar to other ethnic populations, they give to their families and children first using informal networks. When they do access more formal philanthropic networks, Asian donors who are ardent users of technology and social media are likely to visit a nonprofit's website and to further investigate an organization before making a charitable contribution. When they do, they're twice as likely as the non-Asian community to give via crowdfunding (Rovner, 2015). One Vietnamese woman is using this tech-savviness to her advantage.

Hong Hoang

Hong Hoang was born in 1972 in the midst of the Viet Nam war. As a precocious, intelligent child, she was fortunate to join a performance group, the Hanoi's Children's Palace, and to travel the country performing. At 13 she traveled to Russia to attend the International Youth and Student Festival and International Children's Camp. Perhaps these experiences seeded her interest in cultures, connections, and entrepreneurship.

At the age of 23, participating in a UNESCO expedition team including 35 youth from 25 countries, she was the first Vietnamese person to go to the Arctic Circle. Prior to the trip, Hoang had not thought much about environmental issues, but the expedition opened her eyes to the climate crisis facing the world. She has never looked back. Developing awareness of environmental issues and advocating for policy change became her passion and life's work. CHANGE, the nonprofit she launched to address the climate crisis in her country has been growing ever since. Through marketing, performance, and education Hoang is trying to increase interest and action, engage volunteers and use her limited resources to shift the mindset of her country's people.

Hoang admits that progress is slow. In a country that had been devastated by war, people have been more focused on critical needs like food, shelter, and poverty. Despite ongoing issues of plastic and air pollution, illegal wildlife trading, and the threats of climate change, the environment seems to most a low priority. Engaging volunteers and interested funders is difficult, especially in a country that does not support nonprofits. To date, like most of Viet Nam's NGOs which are run and worked by women, eighty to ninety percent of Hoang's workforce and volunteers are women who care about their environment and the impact on their families (Hoang, personal communication, May 19, 2021).

While culturally, philanthropy is not widely used or practiced in Viet Nam, Hoang believes she is making small inroads with some sensitive and environmentally aware corporations. Fundraising through grants, corporate support, and funding from foundations and individuals is still a struggle. Her hope is that as economic conditions in her country improve more people will begin to care about the environment. In the meantime, her work has been recognized by numerous organizations. She has been named one of 50 most influential Vietnamese women by Forbes Vietnam, a Top 5 Ambassador of Inspiration at the WeChoice Awards, featured on the Climate Heroes website, and in 2018, was chosen to join the inaugural class of Obama Scholars. In 2019, she received the Green Warrior of the Year Award at the Elle Style Awards (LinkedIn Hong Hoang, 2021).

Hoang believes that reaching the younger generation is one of her best bets to create change. She uses her talents in social media and performance to get their attention (Hoang, personal communication, May 19, 2021). Perhaps all of us should heed her advice.

The New Generation of Women Donors

Every fundraiser and nonprofit organization would like to find a way to "crack the code" of what makes younger donors tick. We want to know how to define them. What do they care about? How will they practice philanthropy? How can we engage them? The Matures/Silent Generation (people born before 1946) and Baby Boomers (1946–1964) have higher participation rates for philanthropic donations, 78 and 75%, respectively, and give higher amounts annually than the "new generations," but their place at the top the donor ladder is time-limited (Blackbaud, 2018, p. 8).

Generation X (1965–1980), Generation Y, better known as the Millennials (1981–2000), and Generation Z (2001–2021) are labeled and defined by a confusing alphabet soup of terms. Fifty-one percent of them are women who will achieve increasing amounts of economic and philanthropic power. What do women in these age categories want from their giving experiences? What is the best way to reach them and to tap their philanthropic interests and capacities?

- By 2025 Gen Y-Millennials (1981–2000) will earn 46% of the total income in the U.S. (Kasasa, 2021).
- Millennials are expected to be 75% of the U.S. labor force by 2030 and to inherit $30 trillion in wealth from Baby Boomers (Asset, 2019).
- Generation Z and Generation Y have buying power expected to exceed $500 billion (Salisbury, 2019).

These generations of women donors will have more education, employment opportunities, inheritance, and access to technology than previous generations, resulting in the ability to chart new courses of philanthropy. And, the philanthropy arena they have available to them is much larger, more complex, and diverse than the arenas of previous generations. International disasters are known the same day they occur, social movements spread like wildfire over social media, and pandemics touch everyone's lives. These women live in a world that military planners call "VUCA"—volatile, uncertain, complex and ambiguous (Rovner, 2018, p. 4). Fortunately, they possess a zest for revolutionizing philanthropy through social innovation, entrepreneurship, impact investing, and new strategies. And, they are willing to give more if asked. In one survey, 53% of donors under age 35 said they could have given more in the previous year compared with 36% of donors overall (Joselyn, 2019, p. 39). Let's examine each generation in more detail.

Generation X

Comprised of roughly 65.6 million people, or one-fifth of the U.S. population, Generation X (1965–1980) is considered the "sandwich" generation, lodged between Boomers and Millennials. Approximately 55% of them give, totaling $32.9 billion each year (Rovner, 2018, p. 8). As latchkey kids, they witnessed their parents giving their souls to their jobs and have concluded that time is more valuable than money. Gen X women are active volunteers because they are connected to their communities through their children, home ownership and stable employment. In fact, Gen Xers are the second largest age group for volunteering (AmeriCorps, 2018).

Middle-class Gen X women have grown up in an era of changing women's roles; more are working and contributing to the household income than did their mothers. A few years ago, a Pew Research Study found women the primary breadwinners in four out of ten households with children (Wang et al., 2013). Many balance multiple jobs: raising their children, managing careers and homes while tending to their Baby Boomer/aging parents. Their contribution to household income influences their role in philanthropic decisions giving them more confidence and power.

More women in this generation than any other postponed marriage or children until later in life. This means that as well as seeking out married philanthropic prospects, philanthropy professionals need to pay attention to single female Gen Xers. The number of single-person households in the 2000s nearly doubled compared with the 1970s.

GenXers don't write big checks like their parents, but do give smaller amounts regularly. They tend to align with causes based on family tradition. Similar to all other giving generations they prioritize health, religion, and local social services. As they enter their prime giving years, philanthropic observers are calling the Generation X and Millennials the leaders of a "Golden Age of Giving" (Crutchfield et al., 2011; Lenkowski, 2007). Increased financial resources, including inheritance and earned income, will propel their giving power and make them a force in philanthropy.

The Millennials

Why does this group get so much attention? Well, recently surpassing the number of Baby Boomers, they are now our largest population at 67.1 million. Fifty-one percent of them are donors giving $20.1 billion per year (Rovner, 2018, p. 8). This group will not reach their peak giving for another 20–25 years, and when they do—watch out. The shift to more independent thinking and giving becomes evident with the Millennials. They are less influenced by their parents, more willing to explore their own interests, and different from other givers in three additional ways:

- They are active. Forty-two percent say they want to help companies develop future products and services.
- They are more peer driven. They trust the messages they get from their peers.
- They are more trust sensitive than other donors. They expect and want transparency from the organizations they interact with and will give if they have a trusting relationship with staff (Josephson, 2019).

Millennial women are taking a more active role than any previous generation in marital- decision-making-for-charitable-giving, perhaps due to the higher number of them working outside the home. They view philanthropic decision-making with their spouse as a way to deepen their relationship.

In Chapter 5 we discussed the patterns of decision-making among couples emphasizing that many couples do this jointly. Younger women are more willing than Baby Boomers to take a stand on what they want, demonstrating independence while seeking to engage with their partner in meaningful discussions. *Womengive 16—Giving in Young Adulthood: Gender Differences and Changing Patterns Across Generations* found that among young married couples who give large amounts ($100 or more for pre-Boomers and $600 or more for Gen X/Millennials), Millennial women had some influence over marital decision-making for charitable gifts 83.7% of the time in the 2000s versus 73.4% for preBoomer women (women who were in a marital relationship in the 1970s) (Mesch et al., 2016).

- Millennials are more likely than older donors to support new causes (Joslyn, 2019).
- In 2017, 48% of Millennials increased the number of charities they supported (Joslyn, 2019).
- 71% of Millennial women said they give in the moment (Fidelity, 2016, p. 3).
- 75% are motivated by their hearts versus their heads (Fidelity, 2016, p. 3).
- The causes that Millennials prioritize will certainly change over time, but hunger and access to food has been a top priority, access to healthcare #2 and protecting and preserving the environment #3 (Fidelity, 2016, p. 7).

Generation X, Millennials, and Gen Z all value volunteering and spreading the word of need and causes through their peer-to-peer networks. Here are two examples of Millennials in action.

Philanthropy Women

Kiersten Marek is a social worker and founder of *Philanthropy Women*, a website and information portal for women interested in women's philanthropy with an emphasis on feminist funders. As a GenXer interested in philanthropy, she wanted to shine a light on the need for more gender equality. She didn't have the resources to become a substantial financial donor to all the causes that were near and dear to her. Her solution was the development of a mobile platform that helps recruit donors and spread the women's philanthropy message by making the latest information about it easily sharable. Her audience is HNW donors who have focused their giving on women and girls and the women who work within organizations funded by these donors.

"I see many Millennial women donors shifting back toward racial and gender lens investing in their giving and advocacy," she says. "Donors like Priscilla Chan and Padma Lakshmi are calling attention to the very different health and social needs of women and finding ways to fund work that will improve women's access to health, education, and job opportunities. Millennials have a much keener awareness of what racism and sexism look like and how to respond to it" (Marek, personal communication, May 4, 2021). *Philanthropy Women* is one such response from the first generation to have had their teenage years enhanced by the Internet.

A Time for Art

If younger donors have limited resources, try engaging them through volunteering. Several years ago, United Way launched a "Time for Art" event for their young donor group. The purpose was to engage younger donors in giving time, not money. Local artists were recruited to donate art to United Way for an auction event where all the art was displayed. Artists were present to talk about their work, promote their art, and share their stories of investments in the community. Through a silent auction donors bid for the art with commitments of volunteer hours to local nonprofits. Naturally, the donor committing the most volunteer hours won the artwork—but she didn't collect it until completing the community volunteer commitment, recording hours and reporting them to United Way, which released the object of art. This inventive program enabled donors to become familiar with local causes and organizations they may not have known about, to learn more about art and local artists, and, to collect some nice pieces for their homes or offices while feeling good about their contributions. Over time many of these young donors became financial supporters of United Way and other nonprofits.

Generation Z

Generation Z has been labeled the "philanthro-kids" for their extensive involvement in fundraising, donating, and volunteering (Jarvis, 2021). The oldest of them are just hitting their mid-twenties and yet 44% of them give, totaling $3.2 billion annually (Rovner, 2015). One-third view giving as part of their legacy. One in ten want to start a charity or become an activist for a cause versus developing an estate plan (Jarvis, 2021).

Growing up with the internet, these digital natives can't imagine a world without technology. Eighty-two percent of Generation Z versus 38% of Boomers are willing to donate via a mobile device (Rovner, 2018). More than 57% had done research on an organization before making a gift (Jarvis, 2021) and are highly engaged with news outlets and media as sources of information. These donors are going to rely on technology to give them answers.

Gen Z may expect a different level of personal contact with organizational staff. They tend to blur the lines between their work and personal life and are motivated by having relationships with fundraisers. They will want access to as much information as possible, emphasizing the transparency of giving and the impact of their gifts. Show them results and give updates regularly. Finally, remember this generation identifies with causes not organizations, so don't expect long-term donor loyalty.

Suggestions for Fundraisers Working with the New Generations of Women Donors

1. Think about your work with them as a long-term investment. If you begin a relationship with a donor when she is 30, you, or your organization, could connect with her over the next 50 years—if you're lucky enough to stay in contact.
2. Recognize that they change their priorities often.
3. Recognize that they are cause driven, not organization driven.
4. Their access to data and information will be instantaneous and media outlets will constantly be drawing them into new national and global needs. Their menu of options to give will be vast.
5. Technology is their friend, embrace and use it. Think of it as a complement to your personal connection to a donor. Become a social media expert.
6. Poor social media presence is the #1 reason Gen Z will stop giving to your cause.
7. Report on your progress and how you are "changing the world." They want to be inspired.
8. Create peer-to-peer giving contests.
9. Encourage them to tell their friends about their philanthropy.
10. Create projects they can do as a group.

11. Communicate in pictures, video, sound bites and facts.
12. Track their professional and wealth capacity growth. Congratulate them when they achieve and give them positive feedback on their progress.
13. Engage them in decision-making. Give them a seat at the table even if they don't have the same capacity to give large-scale gifts as some other donors. They don't want to be on the "junior board." They want to be on THE board of directors.
14. Offer a wide set of giving options. This group will use nontraditional methods, crowdfunding, workplace fundraisers, purchasing products, Giving Circles, point of sale (donating at a store when checking out).
15. This group will be more diverse in ethnicity, interests and activities, politically and financially than previous generations. Diversify your staff so you can engage the broadest range of donors.
16. Build in some FUN.

Co-create the Future

This brief overview of diversity in giving and the future generations of donors provides a glimpse into the possibility to engage a broader array of advocates, volunteers, and donors.

Increasing the diversity of organizational staff and leadership will help engage more women of color and the next generation of donors. There are pools of passionate, committed women in your community who are waiting to be asked. There are significant opportunities to learn about diverse communities, if everyone begins to listen with open ears and minds. And, there are new institutional models developing every year, initiated by philanthropists who have grown tired of waiting for fundraising teams or philanthropic foundations to bring them new options. Convene thought leaders to help you and your organization think differently about how to solve the complex and systemic problems of the present and the future. Join or lead these discussions and do some research. Stay ahead of the curve and most importantly, ask women for their thoughts and ideas!

Bibliography

AAPI Data, CSIUCR. (2020, September). *State of philanthropy among Asian Americans and Pacific Islanders*. Retrieved September 30, 2020, from https://aapidata.com/wp-content/uploads/2020/09/aapi-state-of-philanthropy-2020-report.pdf

AmeriCorps. (2018). *Volunteering in U.S. hits record high.* Retrieved August 10, 2021, from https://content.govdelivery.com/accounts/USCNBCS/bulletins/21b2aa

Asia's women billionaries in philanthropy: working from within. Retrieved December 23, 2021, from https://wealthmanagement.bnpparibus/asia/en/expert-voices/asias-women-billionaires-in-philanthropy-working-from-within.html

Asset, M. (2019). *Millennial consumers primed to reshape the US economy.* Retrieved October 25, 2020, from https://www.globalxetfs.com/millennial-consumers-primed-to-reshape-the-economy

Ax, J. (2021). *Asian American business leaders launch $250 million effort to fight hate.* Retrieved December 23, 2021, from https://www.reuters.com/world/us/us-foundation-launches-with-125-min-business-leaders-combat-anti-asian-hate-2021-05-03/

Bearman, J., Carboni, J., Eikenberry, A., & Franklin, J. (2017). *The landscape of giving circles/collective giving groups in the U.S.* The Women's Philanthropy Institute.

Blackbaud. (2018). *The next generation of America giving: The charitable habits of generation Z, millennials, generation X, baby boomers, and matures.*

Board Source. (2017). *2017, In the News.* Retrieved August 13, 2020, from https://boardsource.org/news/2017/09/nonprofit-boards-still-not-diverse-report-finds/

Budiman, A., & Ruiz, N. (2021). *Key facts about Asian origin groups in the U.S. Pew Research Center.* Retrieved April 30, 2020, from https://www.pewresearch.org/facts-tank/2012/04/29/key-facts-about-asian-origin-groups-in-the-us/

Burton, B. S. (2020, February 3). *The issue of racism in the fundraising profession, AFP.* Retrieved July 15, 2020, from https://afpglobal.org/issue-racism-fundraising-profession

Crutchfield, L., Kanna L., & Kramer, K. (2011). *Do more than give.* Jossey Bass.

Di Mento, M. (2019, August 6). How quiet donors became champions for black giving. *Chronicle of Philanthropy.* Retrieved July 10, 2020, from https://www.philanthropy.com/article/how-quiet-donors-became-champions-for-black-giving/

Di Mento, M. (2020). Latino community foundation builds a new generation of donors. *Chronicle of Philanthropy.* Retrieved March 15, 2021, from https://www.philanthropy.com/newsletter/philanthropy-today/2020-10-20

Fidelity Charitable. (2016). *Women and giving: The impact of generation and gender on philanthropy.*

Gittell, R., & Vidal, A. (1998). *Community organizing: Building social capital as a development strategy.* Sage Publications.

Goodwin, A. (2018). *Hispanic philanthropy and the moral imagination.* Retrieved June 23, 2020, from https://blog.philanthropy.iupui.edu/2018/09/19/hispanic-philanthropy-and-the-moral-imagination/

Hadero, H. (2021). *Donations for Asian American groups surge after killings.* Retrieved December 26, 2021, from https://apnews.com/article/race-and-ethnicity-shootings-coronavirus-pandemic-philanthropy-atlanta-96ad457055441cbc4eab4c48389fa85

Hanifan, L. J. (1916). The rural school community center. *The Annals of the American Academy of Political and Social Science, 67*(1), 130–138.

Haynes, E., & Stiffman, E. (2020). How to connect with donors of color. *Chronicle of Philanthropy.*

Hong Hoang. (2021). Retrieved August 4, 2021, from https://vn.linkedin.com/in/hong-hoang-7b44bb3

https://asianwomensgivingcircle.org/. Retrieved July 30, 2020.

https://racialequity.org/. Retrieved July 10, 2020.

https://www.statista.com/statistics/233324/median-household-income-in-the-united-states-by-race-rethnic-group/. Retrieved April 10, 2020.

https://www.Kasasa.com/exchange/community-rising/generations-explained. Retrieved October 10, 2020.

Jarvis, A. (2021). *Generational giving: Generation Z—Giving trends, preferences and patterns.* Retrieved June 3, 2021, from https://www.qgiv.com/blog/generational-giving-generation-z-giving-trends-preferences-patterns

Josephson, B. (2019). *How are millennials different from other donors?* National Center on Family Philanthropy. Retrieved April 2, 2020, from https://www.ncfp.org/2017/12/26/how-are-millennials-different-than-other-donors/

Joselyn, H. (2019, February). A youth movement. *Chronicle of Philanthropy.*

Kasasa. (2021). *Boomers, Gen X, Gen Y and Gen Z Explained.* Retrieved December 29, 2021, from https://www.kasasa.com/articles/generations/gen-x-gen-y-gen-z

Lenkowski, L. (2007). Big philanthropy. *The Wilson Quarterly, 31*(1), 47–51.

Lindsay, D. (2017). Diversity among nonprofit leaders still a long way off. *Chronicle of Philanthropy.* Retrieved August 14, 2019, from https://boardsource.org/news/2017/09/diversity-among-nonprofit-leaders-still-long-way-off-report-says/

Mesch, D., Osili, U., Ackerman, J., Bergdoll, J., Williams K., Pactor A., & Thayer A. (2019). *Womengive 19: Gender and giving across communities of color.* Women's Philanthropy Institute.

Mesch, D., Ottoni-Wilhelm, M., Osili, U., Han, X., Pactor, A., Ackerman, J., & Tolley, K. (2016). *Womengive 16: Giving in young adulthood: Gender differences and changing patterns across the generations.* Women Philanthropy Institute.

Philanthropic Initiative for Racial Equity, Race Forward and Foundation Center. (2018). *Infographic.* Retrieved February 15, 2020, from https://racialequity.org/pre-graphics/

PND by Candid. (2018). *Ms. Foundation announces new strategy focused on women, girls of color.* Retrieved June 11, 2020, from https://philanthropynewsdigest.org/news/ms-foundation-announces-new-strategy-foucsed-on-women-girls-of-color

PowerUp Fund.org. (2019). Retrieved January 6, 2021, from https://powerupfund.org/

Putnam, R. (2000). *Bowling alone.* Simon and Schuster.

Rovner, M. (2015). *Diversity in giving: The changing landscape of American philanthropy.* Blackbaud Institute.

Rovner, M. (2018). *The next generation of American giving: The charitable habits of generation Z, millennials, generation X, baby boomers and matures.* Blackbaud Institute.

Salisbury, D. (2019, March 29). Will gen Z and Gen Y save the economic day? *California Review Management.* Retrieved October 4, 2021, from https://cmr.ber keley.edu/2019/03/gen-z

Shapiro, R. A. (2018). *Pragmatic philanthropy.* Palgrave Macmillian.

Turner Moffit, A. (2015). *Harness the power of the purse: Winning women investors.* Rare Bird Books.

U.S. Census Bureau. (2021). Retrieved August 10, 2021, from https://www.census.gov/library/stories/2021/08/improved-race-ethnicity-measures-reveal-united-sta tes-population-much-more-multiracial.html

Vaid, U., & Maxton, A. (2017). *The apparitional donor: Understanding and engaging high net worth donors of color.* The Vaid Group.

Wang, W., Parker, K., & Taylor, P. (2013). *Breadwinner moms.* Pew Research Center. Retrieved September 28, 2019, from https://pewsocialtrends.org/2013/05/29

15

A Call to Action

As we have journeyed through the history of women's philanthropy, identified the milestones in its development, outlined the steps in creating a women's philanthropy initiative, shared the stories of women who have given to causes, and learned from women who have led organizations engaging women philanthropists, we have come to a place of choice and action. Can a fourth wave of women's philanthropy happen? What will it take to make women's philanthropy an integrated and essential part of our work as fundraisers? When will it be the norm, not the exception?

The history of women's philanthropy spans more than one hundred years. During these decades fund development professionals have grown and learned about how women give. Systems and organizations that support and engage women as leaders, donors, volunteers, and clients have been created. Women donors have grown in number and risen to the challenge of giving more. The impact of women's presence and growing influence in our society cannot be denied. Yes, there has been progress, but there is more to do. We need to keep moving forward.

What Can Fundraisers Do?

As fundraisers and professionals who work in philanthropy daily, we see the needs and the opportunities, but too few of us have asked women to be our

L. A. Buntz, *Generosity and Gender*, https://doi.org/10.1007/978-3-030-90380-0_15

partners. We haven't engaged their knowledge, talents, connections, testimonials, or bank accounts. Until we start asking, we only reinforce the old beliefs that women can't contribute or help us achieve the change we desire.

The six-step model outlined in the book is a process that is linear and circular. Each step can build on the previous one, enriching and deepening your connection with a woman donor until you reach a pinnacle of alignment. But relationships are rarely linear. They are a continuous loop of interactions, fluid, active, and ever-changing. Assessments can occur many times, a donor's interests and passion may change with life experiences, and asks, stewardship, and celebrations can and hopefully will happen frequently.

Talk with your professional colleagues and ask them what they know about women's philanthropy and share the tools, suggestions, and questionnaires from this book. Ask a group of fundraising professionals to host seminars or learning opportunities about women's philanthropy, incorporating how to work with a diverse group of donors. Reassess your own prior interactions with women donors and make a commitment to learn more. Most importantly start talking to your women donors and ask them what works? How do they want to be engaged with your organization and you?

What Can Organizations Do?

Every organization that is dependent on fundraising to achieve its mission needs to thoroughly assess its connection to women donors? The process outlined in previous chapters is a guide to help leaders determine if and how a women's philanthropy initiative fits with their organization. Examine the organization's strategic and fund development plan and ask why your organization would want to pursue a women's philanthropy initiative. Perhaps professional development is a place to start, teaching staff about how women give, or integrating new practices into a traditional fundraising program. If your organization has already been actively recruiting women donors, you may be ready to build an entirely new initiative.

Integrating and fully engaging more women in your fundraising process will most likely increase the total donor base and perhaps increase the total dollars raised. Think about women's philanthropy as a value added to your fundraising strategies. Most importantly, remember the full support of organizational leadership will be necessary to achieve success.

What Can the Philanthropic Community Do?

If the face of a philanthropist is truly changing, then the face of the philanthropic community needs to reflect this new reality. The leadership within the fundraising community is growing more diverse daily, but not fast enough. Listen to the voices of those who have not been an integral part of the conversation, invite them in, and fully invest in their ideas about change. Make room at the table for new partners. Implement diversity, equity, and inclusion policies and practices, including gender lens and impact investing. Provide women fundraisers opportunities for career advancements and protect them from harassment.

Make a commitment to continue learning about women's philanthropy and promote opportunities for content experts to share their knowledge and research. The literature on the topic is still scarce and very few conferences have had women's philanthropy as an educational session. Professional organizations have the power to change the agenda and conversation. Finally, recognize women philanthropists who have made significant contributions and women in leadership roles.

What Can Women Donors Do?

Begin by asking yourself what you are interested in and what fuels your passions in life? What do you want to see changed in your community or country? How could you get involved? Call the nonprofit or organization that focuses on the cause you care about and set up an appointment. If you don't know where to start, call your local United Way or Community Foundation. They can direct you and answer your questions. If you are uncertain about doing this, ask a friend to go along with you. Attend community events where nonprofits talk about their work and listen, read, and learn. Reach out to a recognized and trusted fund development professional in your community and have a conversation. Fundraisers can be guides and mentors.

Learn and study your financial situation and capacity. What and where are your assets, how are they invested, and how could you use them to accomplish your goals? Then list and prioritize your values and interests. Write a mission statement about what you hope to accomplish with your philanthropy. Volunteer, if you aren't ready to start giving. If you are giving, start to imagine how to do more and engage your friends and family. You can take control of your own philanthropy and create a legacy.

Create Your Own Story

When I began this project, I believed that when women philanthropists shared *their stories* it would encourage others to act.

As I continued to explore women's philanthropy I realized it is also about *our stories*. Every woman who has helped a person in need or supported a cause, volunteered at school or on a campaign, served on a board, given a million dollars or ten dollars, has been a woman philanthropist. Women are masters at collaboration and cooperation. Working together we have accomplished so much and created exciting and innovative networks for change. Share your stories or create new ones with a group of friends, or fellow givers. Encourage women to talk about their philanthropy.

Now I am asking you to think about *your story*. Who has inspired you? What models of giving have you observed? What have you done or what could you do? You don't have to be a professional fundraiser or an organizational executive to get engaged. You just have to care enough to take the first step.

Dorothy Day, the Catholic social activist said the greatest challenge is "how to bring about a revolution of the heart." How can we in the field of fundraising help women to use their hearts and heads to begin to act?

So, as we end this journey, here are some questions to consider. "When will you step into the work? When will you step up your giving of time, talent, testimony, ties, and treasure? When will you start engaging women and helping them blossom into generous givers? What kind of crisis will it take to prompt you to act? What kind of opportunities do you want to create? When will you become a part of the women's philanthropy movement and build a women's initiative? There's an old African proverb that says, "If you want to go fast, go alone; if you want to go far, go together." Let's not wait another moment; come join me. Together, we can create change for women and the world.

Correction to: Generosity and Gender

Correction to:
L. A. Buntz, *Generosity and Gender*,
https://doi.org/10.1007/978-3-030-90380-0

The original version of this book was inadvertently missed to amend the author's revised corrections, which have been now corrected. The corrections to the book have been updated with the changes.

The updated version of the book can be found at https://doi.org/10.1007/978-3-030-90380-0

© The Author(s), under exclusive license to Springer Nature
Switzerland AG 2022
L. A. Buntz, *Generosity and Gender*,
https://doi.org/10.1007/978-3-030-90380-0_16

Index

© The Editor(s) (if applicable) and The Author(s), under exclusive
license to Springer Nature Switzerland AG 2022
L. A. Buntz, *Generosity and Gender*,
https://doi.org/10.1007/978-3-030-90380-0

CPSIA information can be obtained
at www.ICGtesting.com
Printed in the USA
LVHW042231220822
726560LV00002B/11